MW00900055

THE HOURGLASS:
Life as an Aging Mortal

Pamela Cuming

Copyright © 2016 Pamela Cuming
All rights reserved.

ISBN: 153084021X
Library of Congress Control Number: 2016906295
CreateSpace Independent Publishing Platform
North Charleston, South Carolina
ISBN 13: 9781530840212

For my daughters, Monica and Melissa

…with love and hope that *The Hourglass* will help you better understand the burdens and joys of growing old

THE HOURGLASS:
Life as an Aging Mortal

-Table of Contents-

FOREWORD

In youth we are invincible. The world is forever: we are forever. But, sentient creatures that we are, time inevitably plays its part. Aging and illness shadow those early sensibilities until one day we feel the lurking presence of death itself. Fearful of our own dark thoughts, too often we keep such anxieties to ourselves.

To deny our own mortality is a parlor game of sorts, played within our own heads and frequently played alone. Pamela Cuming will have none of it. In her latest book, *The Hourglass*, she throws back the parlor curtains and lets the light stream in. This is a powerful, objective, unflinching, and yet profoundly empathic work that explores the rewards of honest caring—the privilege and the pain—not only for one's friends and family but also for one's self.

Drawing upon an uncanny intuitive understanding of human foible plus a broad knowledge of character development, honed from decades of consulting in the business world, this is a book filled with personal stories both engaging and instructive. In short, *The Hourglass* is a must read for all those who seek to live life to the full, from start to finish.

Peter C. Whybrow MD, Director of the Semel Institute for Neuroscience and Human Behavior at UCLA and award-winning author of *The Well-Tuned Brain: Neuroscience and the Life Well Lived*.

1: THE HOURGLASS: Birth, Death and The In-Between

"You could drop dead at any moment," Dr. Hertz said as I followed him down the hall to his office after my annual stress echo. His pronouncement stunned me. I couldn't respond. I could scarcely breathe. I feared I might fall down and die right there in the narrow corridor. I imagined he would keep walking, not even noticing that I no longer followed on his heels like a scared puppy.

I treated my body like a sack of fragile eggs as I lowered myself into the chair on the other side of his cluttered desk. I listened without hearing as he recited the statistics that proved I was at risk of Sudden Death Syndrome. Stunned, I heard him decree that I must have a portable defibrillator implanted in my chest that would shock my damaged heart back into rhythm when it went haywire. The procedure needed to happen immediately.

Death. It should not have seemed like such a stranger. I had been surrounded by its dark presence for months. Less than twelve weeks before Dr. Hertz read my death sentence, I had watched as a piece of my mother's calcified aortic valve broke off and made its way into her brain, turning her into a demon possessed and bringing her one step closer to the final seizure that would claim her life. Then, on the eve of my mother's funeral service in Perth, Western Australia, her sister, my beloved Aunt Jill, dropped dead on the other side of world.

It took me over a month to help my brother deal with our mother's Australian estate and then to travel half way around the world to deal with my aunt's affairs. When I finally returned to my mountaintop home in the Pacific Northwest, I learned that my dearest friend, Katherine, had only months to live. A virus was devouring her brain.

Sitting next to her hospital bed, I had been aware that death hovered nearby, and yet I had not been afraid. After all, death was there for her, not for me. Weeks later, a single sentence spoken by a man in a white coat changed everything. I was not immune. Death was stalking me, too. At the age of sixty-two, I had finally come face-to-face with an adversary I could not defeat. I was genuinely frightened for perhaps the first time in my life.

Like Caesar when he led his troops across the river into Rome, I had crossed the Rubicon, and could never return. I was now somewhere between here and nowhere; between existence and non-existence; between ego-driven and Nirvana; between consciousness and oblivion; between lightness and darkness.

Getting closer to the grave is serious business. It's gravitas, and it's gravity. As we get older, we get tethered to one thing or another. Sometimes it's to the cannula on an oxygen tank. Sometimes it's to an EKG lead. Sometimes it's to a tube that infuses poisons into our bodies. Sometimes it's to a cane, or a walker. Sometimes it's to each other! The last phase of our lives is like the first phase: we become dependent; we rage; we whine; we get impatient; and, we have little time for delayed gratification.

As I sat contemplating how the end of our lives resembles the beginning, I thought about the hourglass as a symbol of life. The beginning is like the ending. If we turn the glass over, the ending becomes the beginning of another cycle. The only problem is, in life, we can't turn the hourglass over. When the sand runs out, life ends.

The Hourglass.

The hourglass is made up of two glass bulbs connected at the neck. Grains of sand or their equivalent pass from the upper bulb to the lower at a precise and measurable rate. The amount of sand remaining at the top and resting on the bottom indicates how much time we have spent, and how much we have left.

The device was invented in medieval Europe. It represented an improvement over its predecessor, the water clock, in which the seepage of water from one chamber to the next was used to measure time. Water clocks were of little use on ships since they had to be stable to be precise. The hourglass was widely adopted in the fourteenth century as the clock of choice by ship captains and, therefore, by the public at large.

Though now relegated to the shelves of antique shops, and kitchens where they are used as egg timers, the hourglass remains a powerful symbol of *Life as Time*. Unlike a clock, which tracks seconds, minutes, hours and even days ad infinitum (as long as the battery keeps running), the hourglass has a definite beginning (representing the moment of birth) and end (the moment of death).

As a symbol of the end of mortal time, the hourglass was often placed in coffins, or embossed on gravestones. Pirates used the hourglass on the flags of their ships instead of the skull and crossbones. The symbol of the hourglass was often engraved on clock faces accompanied by the Latin slogan *Vulnerant omnes, ultima necat*—"Every [hour] wounds, and the last one kills."

Fear of Dying.

Thanatophobia is the fear of being dead, or of the process of dying, or both. When afflicted with thanatophobia, there are only four choices: to escape into a drug-induced fantasy world; to embrace a life that is so busy and so driven that there is no time for contemplating one's demise; to commit suicide; or, to confront death.

My heart problems made it difficult to escape into drugs. That would have been tantamount to suicide. I frankly didn't have the energy to continue being so driven that I could avoid thinking about the end of life. And suicide? I admit that I have contemplated ending my own life. As I did so, I thought about David's aunt and his father. Both had chosen to end their own lives.

David's aunt was a very independent lady. She prized her space so much that when she came to visit her son, daughter-in-law and granddaughter for the holidays, she always rented a room in a nearby motel. She had done this for so many years that the motel began holding the same room for her. They even stored many of her possessions—small paintings she liked to hang on the walls, and knick-knacks she liked to place around the room to make it feel like home.

Because we lived across town, she always spent several nights with us. One night, she confided that she'd been saving up sleeping pills. She said if she had a stroke or believed one was imminent, she would take those pills, thereby ending her life. That is exactly what transpired a few years later.

David's father, a surgeon, committed suicide when he realized that a third stroke was likely and would probably paralyze him. He visited his lawyer to make certain that his affairs were in perfect order. On New Year's Day, he surrounded himself with television sets (one for every major ball game), got a big bottle of single malt scotch, filled a china bowl with barbiturates, and sat down. As the games progressed, he sipped his scotch and snacked on barbiturates. Before half time, he passed out, and soon after died.

Yes, I thought about suicide, and I believe that was a constructive thing to do. When I was in my early twenties, I worked with Dr. Fredric Flach, a physician and psychiatrist who was world-renowned for the management of depression and author of the widely read book, *The Secret Strength of Depression*. Under his supervision, I scripted a series of audiotapes for general practitioners to enable them to recognize suicide risks among their patients. A central message of the tapes was Dr. Flach's belief, "No one really chooses to live until they have chosen not to die."

I chose to live. I had things I wanted to do. I did not want to leave my children, or my grandchildren. Nor did I want to leave David. He and I have a deal. When one of us dies, he or she will wait on what we have dubbed "the red couch." Since I have a hopeless sense of direction, it would be better for both us if he died first. That could happen. Although his heart and lungs are stronger than mine, at seventy-eight, he is seven years my senior.

Although we know the red couch is a fantasy, we engage in it to take the edge off. It helps us forget for a moment or two that that there is one universal and inescapable condition of humanity: **Every man and every woman is a mortal being who will die, and die alone.** Although the timing is uncertain, the outcome—a solitary death—is a given.

Confronting Death.

Michel de Montaigne, one of the most influential writers of the French Renaissance, once said, "To begin depriving death of its greatest advantage over us, let us deprive death of its strangeness. Let us get used to it. To practice death is to practice freedom. A man who has learned how to die has unlearned how to be a slave."

As part of confronting death, I try to visualize my own demise. When I lie in bed, I imagine myself lying on a white raft that is slowly floating out to sea. That calms me. It's as though oblivion overcomes me so slowly that I am unaware that it is happening.

Maybe I got the idea from Burt Lancaster in the film *Rocket Gibraltar*, made only six years before his own death. In the film, he plays a patrician who brings his four children, their spouses and eight grandchildren to his Long Island estate to celebrate his seventy-seventh birthday. While they are there, busy squabbling, his health begins to fail. Lying in bed, surrounded by his devoted grandchildren, the old man uses his treasured model boat as a prop as he regales them with stories of the Vikings. Among these stories is a tale of a Viking funeral. That tale inspires the children.

Unbeknown to the parents, the grandchildren retrofit an old rowboat and equip it with a Viking sail as a gift to their grandfather. One day they overhear hear him talking with his doctor and learn that he has only weeks to live. Realizing it is up to them to give their grandfather his Viking funeral, they go into high gear.

They take turns keeping a close watch on the old man, and realize he has died hours before the parents are aware. The eldest of the grandchildren steals the keys to a catering van that they use to get their grandfather's blanketed body to the beach and onto the boat. By the time the hysterical parents catch up with them, they have launched the boat, and are poised to shoot an arrow and set it on fire. The parents can do nothing to intervene. They watch with their children as their father's remains become ash and part of the sea.

I found this story soothing; perhaps that's a reflection of my Celtic heritage. I also found it comforting to talk to friends who had lost loved ones, or had themselves been diagnosed with a life-threatening disease. As my friend Katherine lay dying, I often sat beside her bed, willing myself to observe her steady physical deterioration and to watch her internal flame grow dimmer. When she told me she only had two months to live, I forced myself to maintain eye contact. Instead of trying to give her false hope, I simply nodded and squeezed her hand.

I visited the home of another friend who had her ninety-four-year-old dying mother living with her. As I sat with the mother in the family room,

I studied her and tried to imagine what it was like to be her, and to know that death was imminent.

I sat cross-legged on the floor of my home office with my friend, Luna, who had just lost her husband. We sipped white wine and ate cold shrimp and read each other passages from the multitude of books I had accumulated about aging and dying. She wept quietly and talked openly. She told me she felt comfortable doing so because she had read *Widow's Walk*, the memoir I had published after the sudden death of my husband when I was thirty-four years old. [1] I was no stranger to death, and yet I still felt a need to immerse myself in others' stories and in the philosophers'perspectives in order to equip myself to accept my own mortality.

I read books written by experts on death and dying. Elisabeth Kubler-Ross's *On Death and Dying* was on my bedside table for weeks. When I moved it, it was to make room for Sogyal Rinpoche's *The Tibetan Book of Living and Dying*. I consumed Sandra Gilbert's *Death's Door* as though it was a five-course meal and I was a starving street person. I read several accounts of people who had died of the worst disease I can imagine—ALS, or Lou Gehrig's disease. Dying of this disease is like being trapped inside a body that is already dead with a mind that is fully alert. Somehow envisioning death's worst possible scenario helped me believe I was ready to confront it.

Finally, convinced that I finally understood enough about aging and dying, I chose to write this book. *The Hourglass* is about coming to grips with both aging and death. To confront one without the other is pointless. The two are entwined. As the famous Swiss psychiatrist, Carl Jung, once said, "Shrinking away from death is something unhealthy and abnormal which robs the second half of life of its purpose."

---

[1]Pamela Cuming, *Widow's Walk*, (New York, Crown Publishers, Inc., 1981)

[2]Phillip Roth, *Everyman*. (Boston, New York, Houghton Mifflin Company, 2006), 156.

Many of us, even when our bodies have begun to betray us, attempt to turn a blind eye to death. My husband, David, is different. An anthropologist by training, he is an avid reader who has long contemplated the question, "In the face of death, can life have meaning?" His quest began very early. His mother died from a brain tumor when he was only eight years old.

He keeps two skulls in his office to remind him that his life has an inevitable end. He's had them in his possession for a long time. When he was in his early twenties, he read an essay in which Michel de Montaigne praised the ancient Egyptians for their custom of bringing a dried skeleton of a man into the room at the height of a party to remind the guests of life's impermanence. Impressed, he borrowed one of his surgeon father's skulls and kept it in his studio. In doing so, he was following Montaigne's advice: "A writer's working space ought to have a good view of the cemetery; it tends to sharpen one's thinking."

We were talking about life, death, and his skulls one morning not long ago as we were having our morning coffee in the area in our bedroom we call "the bistro." Let me set the scene.

Death with Coffee.

Our home is perched on a rocky ledge a thousand feet above sea level on a mountain in western Washington. Soaring pine trees stand like sentinels guarding the mountainside and dotting the valley and the town below. Beyond lies the blue grey water of the bay, home to pods of Orcas and salmon attracted by the rich nutrients that glacier streams deposit into the bay. It's not unusual to see a bald eagle soar through the skies. In the horizon, the jagged, snow-covered peaks of the Canadian Rockies create a vista that is so powerful it makes us feel at once ecstatic and insignificant in the face of such natural grandeur.

The view is best from our bedroom on the second floor. An open fireplace divides the room into two zones—one serves as a bedroom and the other as "the bistro." We've outfitted it with two microsuede swivel chairs and a rotating bookcase that serves as a table and lazy Susan in one. It's a perfect space in which to try to talk the universe into place, as we did that morning.

As is our custom, while I got dressed, washed my face and made the bed, David went downstairs to make coffee. I was plumping the bed pillows when I heard David coming up the stairs. That was difficult for him to do. He was still recovering from a knee replacement operation. For a while, we'd had our coffee downstairs to save him the trouble and the pain of climbing the stairs. Now, true to his warrior self, he refused to let pain or a reluctant body part stop him from doing what he wanted to do.

As he entered the room, I could smell the subtle aroma of freshly brewed Hazelnut coffee. I listened for the clink of two brightly colored Polish ceramic coffee mugs that had become the signal that our coffee klatch was about to begin. I noticed that David had prepared an unusually lavish breakfast. Instead of a boiled egg for me and a breakfast bar for himself, he had brought a plate with slices of dark bread, cheeses and prosciutto ham. Under the plate was his iPad. (He'd finally made the shift to reading the paper on the tablet instead of walking up the driveway to get the paper version.) In the corner of the tray was the hourglass he'd recently given me as a gift to celebrate my exploration of mortality and the meaning of life.

Sitting down, I said, "What a treat. Is this a special occasion?"

"Everyday we have together is a special occasion," he said.

David reached across the table and turned over the hourglass. We sat for a few moments watching the grains of sand fall through the glass. David broke the silence. "Your hourglass is like the skulls I keep in my office. They serve as reminders that we will die, and therefore should make the most of every living moment. Security is an illusion. The best we can do is to fight back by living life with vigor, passion and discipline."

"And that means spending as little time as possible on 'must do's', 'ought to's' and maintenance in general?" I asked.

"You've begun to understand me," he laughed.

"Your skulls have frightened away more than one cleaning lady," I said, smiling. "I could tell they spooked Paul when he painted your office."

"That's his problem. My skulls are only frightening to people who have not had the courage to confront their own mortality. As Frank Herbert said, 'To suspect your own mortality is to know the beginning of terror; to know irrefutably that you are mortal is to know the end of terror.'"

I nodded, pretending that I was familiar with the work of Frank Herbert. All I knew was that he was the author of *Dune*. I had never read the book.

David continued, "Life. Death. It's all part of the same story. It's the second law of thermodynamics. Everything, including the universe itself, is destined to disintegrate. Order will descend into chaos. Even the stars will one day go black. There is no way to beat it."

"Time is the undefeatable tyrant, and nature is ultimately destructive. Is that what you're suggesting?" I asked as I broke my promise to have only a single piece of bread with cheese, and reached over for a second.

"Not quite. I believe that those of us who get it right can get off the karmic wheel and reach a point of enlightenment or Nirvana. Then we can be free of the constraints of the ego, and enter a state of mindfulness where time has no meaning."

"I have read a lot about that but I really can't seem to get my head around it," I said.

"In that you are not alone," David responded. I could tell from the expression on his face that he was deep in thought, and on the verge of saying something profound or, at least, fascinating. He didn't disappoint me.

"I believe there is more to the universe and to nature than the second law of thermodynamics. After all, there is certainly a huge creative force in natural evolution. We now have conclusive proof that the dinosaurs that roamed this planet so long ago evolved into birds. The eagles that soar above us, the bluejays that have made our garden their home, the cranes that feed on the young frogs in our pond, and the owls we hear in the depth of night—all these creatures began as dinosaurs."

"The dinosaurs evolved into birds, but individual dinosaurs died," I said, trying to pull him back down from the intellectual stratosphere. Mankind may be evolving into cyborgs, but that's not going to save me or you."

"True," said David handing me yet another piece of dark bread with cheese.

Thinking what this was going to do to my calorie count for the day, I sighed and accepted his offering.

"Death is real," he continued. "Nothing is permanent. Everything is in a state of change. There is no such thing as stability or security or safety.

We become attached to things, to people and even to our own bodies at our peril. That's why I give away things when I get too attached to them. I once gave away four valuable pre-Columbian figures because I was so fond of them. That was before I met you."

"That's too bad," I said. "I'm glad you kept the ones you did. And, you haven't given me away. Does that mean you're not attached to me?"

Smiling, he said, "I confess I am very attached to you, and I could never give you away." Then he paused. His face grew serious. "Are you ever sorry you married me?"

Seeing an opportunity, I responded, "Only when you get crusty, paranoid and impatient like you did when you were taking that pain medication after your knee operation."

"But that was the medicine talking, not me."

I let it go. I decided not to ruin breakfast by pointing out once again that David was not aging gracefully. He flared easily and often, and got terribly impatient with me when my COPD was acting up, making me easily fatigued. He was equally impatient with his own flesh, resenting those periods when some part of his body was not performing as well as it did when he was younger.

David's a real enigma. He rages against aging and yet he has developed a richer and more complex philosophy about death than anyone I know. Perhaps that's because he's been contemplating death for a very long time. He was only six when he watched an old woman die in front of him.

When World War II broke out, his father shipped off to Europe with General Patton as the Third Army battlefield surgeon. His gutsy mother didn't intend to be left twiddling her thumbs in Manitowoc, Wisconsin. She put David, his brother and his cousin in a Cadillac, filled up several gas cans and begged or borrowed a bunch of gas coupons, and drove to Guadalajara, Mexico where they rented a house down the block from a walled mansion. It was there that David as a young boy witnessed death first hand.

"Tell me again about the death of the old Indian woman," I asked.

A natural teacher and storyteller, David complied.

"She used to come to the grand houses on the boulevard and beg for the food scraps the maids were going to discard. Then, she would wait at the bus stop right across the street from the gate to the mansion. Often she had to wait a long time. I would sit with her, and talk to her. She'd tell me about her village. Sometimes she was hard to understand because she'd slur her words and fall asleep in the middle of a story. My mother explained that sometimes the maids from the big houses would give her shots of tequila in addition to the food scraps. I decided that was probably a good thing."

In my mind's eye, I pictured the photograph of David with his mother taken in Guadalajara. He looked so curious, and yet so innocent. At six, he had been an adorable child. Looking at him, I could still see the remnants of the young boy in his seventy-eight-year-old face.

"One day I was in our yard. I saw the peasant woman on the sidewalk. She was swaying and talking loudly. I was thinking about talking to her when the bus started coming down the street. She didn't wait for it to reach the bus stop. As was the custom among agile Mexicans, she tried jumping up onto the moving bus. I watched as she fell backward off the bus and split her head open on the asphalt. Blood seeped out of the back of her head and spread out in a pool beneath her.

"It took a long time for the ambulance to arrive. I watched these people in white coats stuff her body into a bag and whisk her away. Minutes later, the gardener came out of the mansion with a hose and washed all traces of the old lady into the storm sewer. It was as though she had never existed. She was just gone."

"That must have been traumatic for you to witness," I said.

"Not as traumatic as learning a year later that my mother was dead from a brain tumor. But, yes, it changed me."

"I would have liked your mother, "I said

"And she would have liked you; especially the strong you."

Ignoring that little dig, I asked, "Are you afraid of death?"

"Everyone's afraid of dying. It's hard-wired into the species," he said. "I would be lying if I told you I had no fear of death. However, I have a greater fear of being buried alive."

"I thought you wanted to be cremated," I said.

"Don't be so literal. What I am afraid of is being burned alive. When I die, I want you to have my body embalmed before you burn it. That way, you'll be making sure I'm dead before you subject me to the flames. And don't forget you promised to burn my journals—all of them, without reading them."

"I will keep my promise," I said.

"Anyway, it's not death that's terrifying, it's life," David said, standing. "Or, rather, life when you get old. Youth is rife with the sense of potential. Age brings disillusionment. Anticipation is replaced with dread. As a friend of mine says, getting old is a shipwreck."

"That's putting it mildly," I suggested. "At times, I agree with Philip Roth who said, "Old age is not a battle. Old age is a massacre."[2]

The Curse of Old Age.

Like David, I find getting old and sick to be much more frightening than death itself. I know that we are not alone in this regard. When my Australian friend's husband died of cancer at the age of sixty-nine, she said to me at height of her grief, "At least he didn't have to get old." She wasn't smiling and she wasn't kidding. In spite of the fact that she fills every day with a dizzying series of activities as though to distract herself from death, she still believes that aging is the greater enemy.

I think about it this way: when I'm dead, I either won't know it, in which case it won't hurt, or I'll be in a better place, in which case it will feel good. Getting old is a different story, particularly when you have a disease with the word "progressive" attached to it. Then, simply holding onto your baseline becomes an enormous challenge.

But even people like David who do not have a defined disease suffer the indignities of aging. Knees that were overworked during the running years begin to give out. The aging heart develops atrial fibrillation. The eyes grow cataracts. No wonder that when I remind David that he is fortunate not to have a progressive disease, he responds, "Oh, but I do. Aging is certainly a progressive disease."

He's right. It's only going to get worse. Our faces will sag, and the wrinkles will deepen. The elasticity in the lens of our eyes will continue to worsen and to turn yellow. We are likely to develop a fear of falling. Our hearing is likely to get worse. Our short-term memory could begin to fade. If we are one of the 5.1 million Americans over sixty-five who have Alzheimer's or other forms of dementia, we are even at risk of outliving

---

[2]Phillip Roth, *Everyman*. (Boston, New York, Houghton Mifflin Company, 2006), 156.

our ability to remember who we were, and, therefore, who we are.

I am seventy-one years old. While my mind is still intact, my body is breaking down. I can no longer keep up with the Jane Fonda Challenge programs I once did religiously. I don't have the flexibility or the stamina for those moves (and I doubt she does, either). I'm twenty-five to thirty pounds heavier than I was twenty-five years ago, and I wear a Large instead of a Small or Medium. I still have blond streaks put in my hair, but now my hairdresser has to cover the grey with a light-brown dye before she applies the streaks. As a result of all the chemicals, my once fine, soft, shiny hair has become coarser and duller.

Hairs on my chin are appearing at an alarming rate. I can't take estrogen to slow their growth because of my heart condition. While my chin and upper lip are getting hairy, my eyebrows are thinning. Putting myself together in the morning takes twice as long as it once did. Now I have to worry about covering up age spots, putting a potion on fungal-infested toenails, and other not-so-wondrous activities.

My arms have grown flabby since I stopped using our weight machine to do chest compressions—my doctor told me to stop so I didn't risk dislodging the wires from my ICD implant. I only wear shorts in the privacy of my home since my varicose veins make my once shapely legs look diseased. I ride a stationary bike or walk on a treadmill forty-five minutes a day, five or six days a week, but I have to take supplemental oxygen lest exercise makes my oxygen saturation levels fall too low.

It's not a pretty picture, is it? And yet, not too long ago, I was regarded as a very attractive woman, and as a person who had boundless energy. Well, to be honest with you, maybe it was a long time ago. Now, I find the idea of having to clean the house as challenging as climbing Mount Everest. The idea of putting up a Christmas tree without the help of a younger person is intimidating. Putting on a dinner party for eight seems like a gargantuan task.

Our friends seem to feel the same way. We are issuing invitations less often and to fewer people. Because we live in a small town where going to other people's homes for dinner is the predominant form of socializing, we see fewer and fewer people. Sometimes I think we spend more time with our doctors than with our friends. And the number of friends we have is diminishing. Many are sick. Some have died.

That puts my David and I increasingly at one another's mercy.

Without others to distract us, or claim our attention, we begin to meddle in each other's affairs, making uninvited comments about everything the other does and fails to do. That's really irritating, and does not endear us to once another. We lose our tempers, and say things we later regret. That didn't happen when we were younger.

I met David when I was forty-two and he was forty-nine. I was living according to Helen Keller's belief, "Life is an adventure or nothing at all." I had posted that quote on a 3x5 card above the telephone in my kitchen. It described my philosophy and my life. I was willing and able to travel anywhere at anytime in pursuit of an opportunity or an adventure. Even traveling to see my family half-a-world-away in Western Australia didn't daunt me. Jet lag was for other people.

So were medical cautions against imbibing too much wine and smoking too many cigarettes and staying up all night talking with friends. These cautions applied to others, not to me. I was invulnerable and unstoppable. A vigorous morning workout was all it took to keep me lean and trim in spite of my indulgences. I was in control and certain that I would always be in control.

I have now learned that is not so. My body has deteriorated, as has my sense of optimism, my courage, and my readiness for wild exploits. David has aged, too, but his desire for adventure continues unabated. Now and then we have to go our separate ways so that David is not restricted by my physical limitations, and so that we can take a break from our overly meddlesome selves.

But we can't always get away from each other. The variety of maladies that seem to afflict the aging body makes us increasingly dependent on one another. A year ago, when David had a knee replacement, he was at my mercy for months. Now that he has healed, my nomadic husband is planning a trip to Hong Kong and Bali. Due to a lung condition that worsens in hot humid climates, I can't join him. As a result, before he can depart, he has to not only make sure he is well enough to tolerate the trip, but also that I am healthy enough to manage for a month on my own.

He was in the midst of planning for his trip when I threw him a curve ball. I did an over-vigorous workout, and sprained the muscles in my lower back and thigh. It was so painful that for five days I could scarcely walk across the room. Getting downstairs was a real challenge. In that condition, I could not have managed on my own. I have recovered now and he is once again free to go, assuming something else in his body or mine doesn't break before he takes off.

Recently I was comparing notes with my college roommate about the unfortunate state of our bodies. She said, "Getting old is not for the fainthearted." That is putting it mildly. It is the biggest challenge I have ever faced, and I was totally unprepared for it, in spite of the efforts of learned people who tried to brace me for what would occur.

When I was in college, one of my psychology professors decided to help his students understand what it felt like to age. He tied all nine of us together with a rope, and told us to perform certain basic tasks like tying our shoes, pouring dry cereal into a bowl, and removing a book from the bottom shelf of a bookcase. He progressively shortened the length of rope until it was so short we could hardly move. Basic tasks became impossible to complete.

As a result of the experiment, I learned what it felt like to age on an intellectual level, but I didn't internalize the lesson. Somehow, I didn't think it applied to me. I was young. Time was on my side, and would forever be on my side. Death was something for old people to worry about, and I would never be old. Aging was an abstraction, or something that happens to other people. I felt bulletproof.

Even after my body starting betraying me, I continued to believe that I would prevail. I would do the impossible and reverse my cardiomyopathy. Even though COPE (Chronic Obstructive Pulmonary Disease) is progressive, I would be the exception; I would beat it. I defied and denied aging and mortality until I was at the edge of the river with barely enough energy to make it across. Discovering that I was mortal, vulnerable, and sick came as a big shock.

In his eye opening book *Being Mortal*, Dr. Atul Gawande sheds light on why the whole awful process is inevitable, and on why so many of us succeed in ignoring or denying the fact that age is taking a terrible toll on our bodies. He refers to the work of Leonid Gavrilov, a researcher at the University of Chicago, who argued that human beings are like complex systems with multiple backup systems and redundancies that keep them going a long time even when a fragile component fails. But ultimately the accumulated damage is too great, and the system breaks down,

The human body, he and Gavrilov conclude, works the same way. "We have an extra kidney, an extra lung, an extra gonad, extra teeth. The

DNA in our cells is frequently damaged under routine conditions, but our cells have a number of DNA repair systems. If a key gene is permanently damaged, there are usually extra copies of the gene nearby. And, if the entire cell dies, other cells can fill in. Nonetheless, as the defects in a complex system increase, the time comes when just one more defect is enough to impair the whole, resulting in the condition known as frailty… one too many joints are damaged, one too many arteries calcify. There are no more backups. We wear down until we can't wear down any longer."[3]

And then we die, but before we reach that final point, we become increasingly dependent on other people to help us with the daily activities of living. For many that means spending a significant amount of time during the final years in nursing homes or assisted living facilities. These are generally structured to keep us safe even at the expense of our ability to make our own decisions about how we spend our days and nights. They deprive us of the chance to author our own life stories and, in doing so, they render our old age meaningless. Our hospitals intensive care wards collaborate, denying us even a chance to die. The doctors put a heart defibrillator into the chest of a ninety-year-old woman who is suffering from dementia and can't recognize her own children. They put an old man suffering from incurable cancer on a respirator.

And why do we let this happen to us? Why don't we anticipate what the ravages of old age will do to us and prepare accordingly? Perhaps it's because our bodies haven't yet begun to deteriorate and aging remains an abstraction. Or perhaps we think we will be the exception like Jauja Singh who completed the London marathon when he was 100 years old, or Johanna Quass, the eighty-six-year-old gymnast who is still capable of doing amazing feats on the balance beam. We don't realize even these extraordinary people can't ultimately outwit the hourglass. Their bodies will break down, too.

Perhaps the answer to our willful ignoring of the reality of human frailty is that we have been over-protected. We have not had to spend meaningful time with the old or with the sick or with the dying. We cling to our illusions that life is all about delights as did Guatama before he ventured forth from the palace to mingle with the people. His father, the King, failed in his attempt to keep the gods from forcing his son to witness

[3]Dr. Atul Gawande, *Being Mortal: Medicine and What Matters in the End.* (New York, Metropolitan Books, Henry Holt and Company, 2015),33.

18

that life is a great deal more than youthful and sensate delights. In his book, *The Masks of God*, Joseph Campbell retells the story as written by the poet-monk Asvaghosa, circa 100 a.d.. [4]

On the first day when the Prince ventured from the palace, the gods sent forth an old man. When the Prince saw him, he asked his charioteer, "Who is that man there with the white hair, feeble hand gripping a staff, eyes lost beneath brows, limbs bent and hanging loose? Has something happened to alter him, or is that his natural state?"

"That is old age," said the charioteer, "the ravisher of beauty, the ruin of vigor, the cause of sorrow, destroyer of delights, the bane of memories and the enemy of the senses."

"And will this evil come to me too?"

"Without doubt, by the force of time," said the charioteer.

So upset was he by that news that the Prince returned to the palace.

On the second day, the gods sent a man suffering from a horrible disease. "The Prince said, "Yonder man, pale and thin, with swollen belly, heavily breathing, arms and shoulders hanging loose and his whole frame shaking, uttering plaintively the word 'mother' when he embraces there a stranger: who is that?"

"My gentle lord," said the charioteer, "that is disease."

"And is this evil peculiar to him, or are all beings alike threatened by disease?"

"It is an evil common to all," said the charioteer.

Again the Prince chose to return to the palace, discomfited by what he had seen.

On the third outing, the Prince had occasion to ask, "But what is that, borne alone there by four men, adorned but no longer breathing, and with a following of mourners?"

"This, my gentle lord," the charioteer said, "is the final end of all living beings."

The Prince's view of mankind would never again be as it had been before he ventured from the palace. He asked, "How can a rational being, knowing these things, remain heedless here in the hour of calamity?"

And thus began the training of the man who would become Buddha. Like him, we can no longer afford to remain heedless of the ravages of

---

[4] Joseph Campbell, *The Masks of God, Volume II, Oriental Mythology*. (San Anselmo, CA, Joseph Campbell Foundation, Digital Edition, 2014), location 4834-4846.

aging now that it has become a common precursor to death. When Montaigne was writing in the late-sixteenth-century, few people died of old age. Disease often killed people well before their hair turned grey. Thus, he could say, "To die of old age is a death rare, extraordinary, and singular, and, therefore, so much less natural than the others; 'tis the last and extremest sort of dying: and the more remote, the less to be hoped for."

Given the miracles of modern medicine and technology, dying of old age is now a widely shared affliction. That which Montaigne described as a privilege afforded by Mother Nature to very few has now become commonplace. Therefore, we must be prepared. We need to clarify our wishes to those who are likely to end up making decisions on our behalf. We should put into place arrangements regarding where we will live when we can no longer function independently. Only then can we begin to regard getting old as a gift rather than a curse.

The Gift of Old Age.

Later in the book, you'll meet ninety-year-old Kitty Manigan. The last time I spoke to Kitty, we talked about the tragic death of her son, and the shock of learning only days later that her son-in-law had suffered a fatal heart attack. She told me her once brilliant husband hadn't been able to leave the first floor of their multilevelled home in years and now was rapidly losing his memory. She reminded me that she, too, had an implanted defibrillator in her heart and had recently survived a quadruple bypass.

Kitty was highly aware of the challenges of aging, and yet she was neither angry nor despairing. She said, "Living is a complex process. Each day of life is a gift, whether that day is filled with joy or with grief. I am grateful that I have lived for as long as I have. Gratitude. That's what I feel. And joy. I am joyous and grateful for having lived so long."

Recently, I came across a wonderful poem written by Henry Wadsworth Longfellow called *A Psalm of Life*. The thrust of the poem is that while we must confront aging and death, we must not let those confrontations deprive us of even a moment of life. Kitty Manigan understands this.

A PSALM OF LIFE

What the Heart of the Young Man Said to the Psalmist

TELL me not, in mournful numbers,
Life is but an empty dream! —
For the soul is dead that slumbers,
And things are not what they seem.
Life is real! Life is earnest!
And the grave is not its goal;
Dust thou art, to dust returnest,
Was not spoken of the soul.
Not enjoyment, and not sorrow,
Is our destined end or way;
But to act, that each to-morrow
Find us farther than to-day.
Art is long, and Time is fleeting,
And our hearts, though stout and brave,
Still, like muffled drums, are beating
Funeral marches to the grave.
In the world's broad field of battle,
In the bivouac of Life,
Be not like dumb, driven cattle!
Be a hero in the strife!
Trust no Future, howe'er pleasant!
Let the dead Past bury its dead!
Act,— act in the living Present!
Heart within, and God o'erhead!
Lives of great men all remind us
We can make our lives sublime,
And, departing, leave behind us
Footprints on the sands of time;
Footprints, that perhaps another,
Sailing o'er life's solemn main,
A forlorn and shipwrecked brother,
Seeing, shall take heart again.

Let us, then, be up and doing,
With a heart for any fate;
Still achieving, still pursuing,
Learn to labor and to wait.[5]

As Kitty so beautifully explained, being old can be a rich and fruitful part of life. Aging presents enormous challenges, but it only becomes a massacre if we define it that way. Nor does death have to loom so large over our daily lives that we live in fear. Although the magic of the spell of potential no longer entrances, we can relish a lifetime of memories. This is especially true if we have lived well and have few regrets at the end of our lives.

Randy Pausch, professor of computer science and author of *The Last Lecture,* died at the age of forty-eight of pancreatic cancer. He wrote, "We cannot change the cards we are dealt; just how we play the hand." [6] In large measure, how we play the hand depends on our MAM, our Mindset about Aging and Mortality.

Mindsets About Aging And Mortality.

At every waking moment we have a MAM, a Mindset about Aging and Mortality. This is true even if we are totally engrossed in the task in front of us, and not thinking about getting older or dying. Think of it as the lens in a pair of eyeglasses. Some are made of rose-colored glass and are designed to refract the light in such a way that the darkness is dispelled, allowing us to deny aging and dying. Others are made of clear glass that permits no illusions. The stark reality of decay is vividly apparent. Still others are made of darkened glass. The end of life looms like a giant shadow over our days, making us feel anxious or timid. Some are multi-focal, permitting the viewer to see clearly and respond quickly regardless of changing circumstances. Others are able to change with the light, softening the harsh light of day and increasing visibility at night.

---

[5]Henry Wadsworth Longfellow, *A Psalm of Life*, first published in *Knickerbocker Magazine*, 1838. Now in the public domain.
[6]Randy Pausch, *The Last Lecture*. (New York, Hyperion, 2008), 17.

Birth, Death and The In-Between

Our MAM affects our world view, and influences the decisions we make about how we invest our time, our energy and our money. It helps determine which opportunities we seize and which we let go. Our mindset influences the pace we adopt as we go about our days. It has an impact on the way we relate to others: to parents, to children, to mates, and to friends. It defines the way we interact with members of the medical profession, and the way we cope with illness and disability. Our mindset even affects our emotions: the way we feel most of the time, and the way we respond in a crisis. And, it affects the way we manage the challenge of aging and cope with the reality of our own demise.

Like life itself, our MAM is changeable, shifting in response to what is happening in our lives, and the impact of those events on our sense of well-being and our ability to meet the challenges or seize the opportunities. Our MAMs are a function of who we are and the circumstances in which we find ourselves.

On any given day, all of us fall somewhere on the continuum *Feeling Helpless and Vulnerable* to *Feeling Empowered and Confident*. At the same time, we are positioned somewhere along the continuum *Anticipating or Experiencing Good Fortune* to the opposite pole, *Experiencing or Anticipating Adversity*.

Putting these dimensions together yields four fundamental MAMS: the **Castaway**, the **Stargazer**, the **Warrior**, and the **Celebrant**. And then there is the fifth MAM that represents a blend of the attributes of the four primary MAMS. That is the **Sage**.

People whose predominant MAM is that of the Stargazer tend to be childlike in their response to the universe. They expect to be amused, entertained, and delighted. They prefer to see only the positive. They don't like to think about aging, and certainly not about dying. Aging Stargazers will often avoid the company of the elderly, preferring to surround themselves with younger people.

The Stargazer element within us helps us make a leap of faith and believe in God or Christ or something greater than ourselves that we cannot see, touch or even truly define. Trust in the ultimate goodness of the universe and belief in that which cannot be proven makes life a joyous experience even when tragedy strikes. My mother spent most of her life perceiving the world through the lens of the Stargazer and managed the impossible: she remained in denial of death to the moment of her last breath. That is an amazing accomplishment. You'll meet the Queen of Denial later in the book.

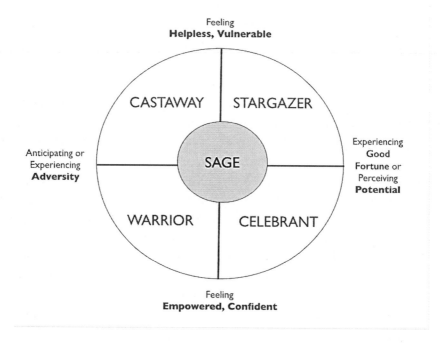

Celebrants dwell on the creative force that is God or nature. They celebrate the Mystery, the great unknown, and trust there is a larger scheme of things that mankind cannot and should not understand. The Celebrant mindset makes people feel confident of their own capabilities. Adept at finding the silver lining in even the darkest cloud, Celebrants remain optimistic even in the face of tragedy, loss, aging and death.

The other day I observed an aging couple at the grocery store. It quickly became apparent that both had adopted the mindset of the Celebrant. She was sitting in her walker poised to push a large shopping cart. He, in turn, was in position to push the walker. Ready to navigate up and down the aisles with their ready-made train, they appeared confident and in control of the situation. *Where there's a will, there's a way,* I thought as I smiled at them. She smiled back, and said to her husband, "Let's do the fruit first."

Natural Warriors are confident and courageous people who know that life as an aging mortal will be a battle, but a battle they intend to win.

Birth, Death and The In-Between

When people see the world through the lens of a Warrior, they often refuse to think about death and focus instead on extending their lives through vigorous exercise. When faced with a challenge, the Warrior focuses on meeting it with courage and conviction.

When it becomes apparent that the challenge cannot be overcome, or the disease cured, Castaways accept it and attempt to keep going, though with less vigor and enthusiasm. They anticipate having to endure life's vicissitudes with as much grace as they can muster, and are more prone to seeing the negative than the positive. Castaways console themselves with the thought that when they no longer exist, they won't know it. They react like the person who has had a gun held to their head for a long time. After a while, the gun ceases to terrify. "If you're going to shoot me, then shoot me. I will no longer give you the satisfaction of being able to terrify me."

Sometimes the mindset of the Castaway is the portal for adopting the perspective of a Sage. Sages manage to transcend the boundaries of their own ego, experiencing a sense of being connected to all other living things. They understand what George Lucas, the director of Star Wars, meant when he said, "The only reason for life is life. There is no why. We are. Life is beyond reason."

While people appear to have a predominant mindset, circumstances often force them to experience life through a different lens. When we are young, and life is rife with potential, we are often Celebrants or Stargazers. The challenges of aging and the experience of loss propel many of us to adopt the mindset of the Castaway. That can be positive, and a precursor to thinking like a Sage or adopting the more empowered orientation of the Warrior or Celebrant.

The key to living a rich life, to aging gracefully and to dying well is to move around the wheel, changing mindsets as circumstances change. As she lay dying, my friend Katherine smiled, twirled her hand in air and whispered, "Life is change, only change and always changing."

Part of that change is a shift in mindset. We need to learn to go with the flow when circumstances change and we are faced with new challenges or opportunities. Its important to accept these shifts in mindset and to understand that we are likely to behave differently, to make different decisions, and to perceive events differently as a result. Even the strongest among us sometimes feels vulnerable. Even the most optimistic sometimes despairs. Even the wisest of us can become frustrated and behave like a petulant child. We need to let that happen. What's important is to avoid getting "stuck" at the negative or extreme pole of any of the mindsets.

Each of the MAMs has both a positive pole and a negative pole. Stargazers can be self-absorbed, manipulative, and childlike. Celebrants can lose sight of reality as they become Pollyannas. Warriors can get rigid and defensive as they develop a bunker mentality. Castaways can slip into despair and the bog of relentless pessimism. Sages suffer from existential melancholia. The likelihood that people will conflict appears to be intensified when one or both are stuck at the negative pole of their respective mindset.

This is all apparent in the stories I will tell you. They are derived from my life, my parents' lives, my husband's life, and the lives of others I've known. The names of the members of my immediate family have not been changed. Similarly, I use the real names of public figures and authors whose work is quoted or referred to in the book. All other names have been changed. Though their names are fictitious, their stories are true.

Through these stories, we'll look at the devastating impact aging poorly can have on friendships and marriage. We'll consider ways to age gracefully and preserve a loving relationship in spite of the ravages of disease and the disabilities of age. We'll discuss how to deal with doctors who become ever more present in our lives as we get older. We'll figure out how to continue living well even when the body betrays, and we'll talk about how to die well.

In the next chapter, we'll take a closer look at each of the MAMS and their impact on the way we age and die. Before we continue, you might want to complete a short questionnaire to help you determine your mindset. You'll find the questionnaire at the back of the book on page 281.

2: MIND MATTERS: Placebos and Nocebos

There is a growing body of evidence that the mind influences the way the body ages and the way it responds to disease. In 1981, Harvard psychologist Ellen Langer conducted a small study involving eight men in their seventies who were in good health but feeling their age. For five days they lived in a converted monastery that had been equipped to make them believe the last twenty-two years had not happened. They were instructed to behave as they would have over two decades earlier. Astoundingly, at the end of the five days, each of them scored significantly better on measures of aging such as dexterity, memory, hearing and vision, cognition and flexibility. Mind clearly mattered.

Langer's later studies demonstrated the enormous power that labels and biases can have on the mind and, therefore, on the body. In 2010, she did a study in which she discovered that cancer survivors who described themselves as "cured" had a better quality of life than those who described themselves as simply "in remission."

Langer has also demonstrated that **placebos** (substances that have no actual therapeutic effect) work because people believe they will. Similarly, negative placebos, or **nocebos**, can prime the mind to make the body weaken. A doctor's diagnosis can function as a nocebo and make someone sicker than the body alone intends.[7]

David often comments, "All the body is in the mind, but all the mind is not in the body." In that single statement he is reflecting a philosophical argument that has gone on since the seventeenth century when Descartes

---

[7]Bruce Grierson, "What if Age is Nohing but a Mind-Set?" *The New York Times Magazine.* (Oct. 22, 2014). 1-2.

declared that the mind and body are made of different substances. He argued that the mind is "immaterial" and the body is "material." As such, the mind is capable of thinking and feeling; the body is not. Neuroscientists have now joined the debate. Many of them argue that the brain is part of the body, and that consciousness is simply a biological process.

There may never be a definitive answer to the question. Regardless, whether consciousness is of the body or distinguishable from the body, there is little doubt that it has a significant influence over how the body functions. The mind influences whether we age gracefully or poorly. It affects the way we view ourselves as mortal beings.

Two dimensions of our thought processes appear to make a fundamental difference: the extent to which we anticipate good fortune (vs. adversity), and the extent to which we feel empowered (vs. vulnerable). Let's begin talking about the empowered mindsets.

THE WARRIOR AND THE CELEBRANT.

People with either of these mindsets are confident that they will prevail. The difference between the two lies in their projection of the

28

future. Warriors anticipate adversity. Celebrants foresee good fortune on the horizon.

Celebrants love life, and believe, "Life is good." They are confident that opportunity can be found in even the most challenging circumstances. Good things will happen because they have the resources and the will to insure that it does. Celebrants are energized people who embrace each day enthusiastically. They manifest a persistent "can do" attitude, and are eager to seize the opportunities that they believe are about to present themselves. Expansive and expressive, these optimists embrace projects, people and programs with vigor born of love.

Warriors, on the other hand, believe that adversity besets every human being. They stand ready to attack or defend to minimize or remove the threat. The hallmark of the fighter is courage, or tenacity in the face of fear, and strength in the face of pain. Warriors feel empowered, in control and confident, and ready for battle. They are convinced that they will be able to meet the challenges and overcome the obstacles that are on the horizon. Confident of their ability to succeed, these soldiers thrive on challenges. Action-oriented, they can be impatient. When threatened, they are more likely to get angry than to feel fearful.

Raging Against the Dying of the Light.

Determined and independent, Warriors can become stubborn and resistant when told what to do by others. A strong self-preservation instinct coupled with well-honed survival skills render these fighters at once cautious and courageous. They seek to exert control over otherwise debilitating circumstances. That includes aging and death.

Chaos is disturbing to this mindset because it implies loss of control. When faced with chaos, Warriors will do all they can to introduce order. They are efficient, and they are focused. They set ambitious goals for themselves, and will not tolerate failure. If they do fail, they turn their anger on themselves.

Admiring strength and intolerant of weakness, Warriors push people to realize their full potential, and get impatient with those who are weak, tired, lazy or self-indulgent. They will often directly confront such individuals, unconcerned about offending them. Many Warriors do not care what other people think.

Preferring to move to the beat of their own drum, they establish their own deadlines in order to avoid being subjected to the time constraints created by others. Warriors are often in a hurry, and impatient with others who walk slowly, or speak slowly, or take too long to make their point.

Bear Stearns was led by a most impressive Warrior. Alan Greenberg, better known as "Ace," was a brilliant trader who grew the firm from a scrappy trading house to the fifth largest investment bank. I had the pleasure of knowing and working with him when I served as the Senior Managing Director of Marketing in the 1990's.

Ace's expertise was arbitrage, or the simultaneous buying and selling of securities to take advantage of price differentials. In that business, seconds make a difference between profit and loss. Urgency, immediacy, and being constantly on the alert were prerequisites of survival in his business, and in the firm he led. He celebrated personal ambition, the passion to make money, and the unyielding drive to win. In a real sense, Ace instilled within the whole firm the culture of the Warrior whose sole purpose was to protect "the golden goose."

He had problems with me because I ran a department that did not contribute directly to the bottom line. I survived because I found ways to be of service to him like writing his lines and sitting with him in the Green Room when he appeared on the talk show, *The View*, with his long-time friend, Barbara Walters. After the demise of Bear Stearns, Ace joined JP Morgan Chase rather than retire. At the time, he was eighty-one years old. When he died of cancer six years later, he was still an active trader and member of the management team.

As Ace illustrated, the Warrior is a very independent type of person. As such, aging which often forces a person to depend on the help of others, is particularly offensive. These troopers attempt to defy aging and struggle to remain independent and active. They resist retirement. If forced to leave the action because of company policy, the Warrior will typically become an active member of several boards, turn community service into a full time occupation, or seek consulting assignments.

Neil Gilliatt was an older friend and mentor with whom I co-authored several articles on marketing and strategic planning. He had once been the Vice Chairman and Chairman of the Executive Committee of the major advertising conglomerate, Interpublic Group. In this role, he traveled around the world advising other corporate chieftains. Coca Cola was his main client for many years.

Mind Matters

Other great examples of aging troopers who are attempting to defy the ravages of time are provided by men and women who continue to compete in sporting events long after their peers have quit. A decade ago, I went to San Diego to support my daughters when they ran in the marathon. I watched a man in his early eighties cross the finish line. The crowd cheered so hard and for so long that one might have thought we were applauding a hero who had stopped a meteor from hitting earth.

Defiant by nature, people with the mindset of the fighter even try to defy death. I have a friend who was diagnosed with breast cancer. Her oncologist advised a partial mastectomy followed by radiation and chemotherapy. Instead, she opted for a total double mastectomy, removing the healthy breast along with its cancerous sister.

Warriors are fixers. They are determined to fix their own problems, and to provoke or enable others to take care of themselves. Sometimes spouses or children of the dying are the fighters, and will attempt to force their loved one into fighting back. Luna, a Warrior and medical doctor, got impatient when her husband Stavros lay dying of multiple myeloma, and refused to work with a physical therapist. She couldn't accept that her once dominant mate was willing to surrender.

Dylan Thomas wanted his own father to fight back. A year before his father's death from pneumonia, he wrote a now famous and often quoted poem. The final two lines express the spirit of the fighter confronting death.

Do not go gentle into that good night.
Rage, rage against the dying of the light. [8]

While Warriors regard doctors as important weapons in their arsenal against aging and mortality, they are not awed by their authority. They regard physicians as functionaries to be consulted, but will readily challenge them and ignore their advice. If given a negative diagnosis or prognosis, people with this mindset are likely to believe they can prove the doctor wrong. Failing to do so, some will declare war on terminal illness, maintaining control over their own destinies by taking their own lives. David is such a Warrior.

---

[8]Thomas, Dylan. 1951 *Protest Song.*

David is determined to make his body do what he wants it to do, in spite of age. He stubbornly refuses to let his body slow him down or impede him in anyway. When he suffered from pain in his knee due to the deterioration of the cartilage, he didn't slow down. Instead, he forced himself to work out, enduring even more pain. "Pain will trigger growth hormones," he told me when I expressed concern. (Unfortunately, that didn't work out as well as he planned. He finally had to have a knee replacement.)

When David decides it's time to lose weight or reset his metabolic rate, he goes into boot camp mode. He fasts for five to ten days, and then goes on a strict diet for another couple of weeks. Though he thoroughly enjoys his martinis and his wine, when he decides it is time to detox, he simply stops imbibing. End of story. Warriors are willful and disciplined.

They are also cautious. Strategic in his quest for victory, David does not take unnecessary risks. When faced with a whiteout on the slopes, David returned to the lodge rather than hurtle blindly down the slopes and risk injuring or even killing himself. When threatened with the rumblings of an emerging kidney stone as he embarked on another journey through Australia's parched and relentlessly hot northwest searching for Bradshaw rock art, he gave up the quest and returned to Perth.

While David displays the positive characteristics of the Warrior mindset most of the time, he is capable of going to the negative pole. There are times when he becomes very defensive, and lashes out at perceived aggressors for little or no reason.

In the Bunker.

When stuck at the negative pole, the Warrior takes everything personally, and assumes others will take advantage or do them harm if given the opportunity. In this state, they remain on high alert, becoming rigid and hyper-efficient in an often-fruitless attempt to regain or retain control over a hostile universe.

I have a lot of this mindset in me and, when severely stressed or frightened, I move into a hyper-control mode. When my siblings and I gathered to help our mother die, I moved to the negative pole. As such, I was hyper-efficient at a time when others were hyper-emotional. And, I was paranoid, certain that their lack of appreciation of my efforts represented a personal affront. At the same time, my youngest sister, Joy, moved to the extreme pole of the Celebrant mindset. If I was a pit bull, then she was an emotional tsunami. The clash of mindsets was at times deafening.

MINDSET	Warrior
Major Attribute	*Courage*
Major Attribute Shared with the Celebrant	*Resilience*
Major Attribute Shared with the Castaway	*Realism*
At the POSITIVE Pole	*Resistance Defiance* *Focus Discipline* *Fighting Spirit*
At the NEGATIVE Pole	*Defensiveness Fear of Failure* *High Control Impatience* *Bunker Mentality*

For example, twelve hours before my mother died, I sat on the floor of her bedroom with an open suitcase and forced her to decide what she was going to take with her to the dreaded nursing home. I will regret that for the rest of my life. I was the unbridled Warrior at her worst. If I had been more compassionate and less efficient, more patient and less insistent on being in control, I would not have put her through that unnecessary anguish. Joy told me so, but I couldn't listen.

Unbridled Warriors can't hear Celebrants, particularly those who have moved to the negative pole and become a "see no evil, hear no evil" Pollyanna. If we had understood that conflicting MAMs were operative, perhaps we could have avoiding hurting one another. I'll tell you more about all of this later in the book.

The disadvantage of the Warrior mindset at the negative pole is an overuse of the will, and a tendency to be so driven by a sense of purpose that it becomes very hard to stay in the moment. When they travel, for example, they can be so preoccupied with the need to check off every item in the guidebook that they never actually experience or "feel" the new surroundings.

This preoccupation with a single purpose can be manifest in other unhealthy ways. I have a male friend in his mid-sixties who has become a slave to his workouts. His son, who is now an adolescent, has grown up believing his father to be a decade younger than he is. The father is determined to sustain that illusion. It's not unusual for him to report that, in a single day, he played several sets of tennis, ran ten miles, and scored points playing hockey. David and I are concerned that one day he will push himself too hard and his aging body will rebel. If that happens, he's likely to regard his breaking body as a personal failure.

Warriors "in the bunker" hate to fail. It makes them feel vulnerable and that, above all, is to be avoided. In an attempt to disguise these feelings, they will sometimes lash out at others. This can become particularly pronounced as the Warrior ages, making people want to distance themselves from him or her. In this regard, the Celebrant, even when at the negative pole, has a distinct advantage.

Life is Good.

Celebrants are optimists who tend to be expansive in their thinking, and expressive in their words and gestures. Believing in the basic goodness of others, they are often generous and are inclined to give people the benefit of the doubt. Rather than measure their own or others' performance against preset standards of excellence, they stress the importance of individual targets. It's not important to beat the world's record. It is important to slowly improve with practice.

These hopefuls believe in investing their energy in solving problems, not in complaining about them. If they fail in their pursuit, they simply shift the goal. They focus on what can be done with the resources that are available rather than bemoaning the lack of equipment or assets required to reach a predetermined goal. Even when presented with evidence to the contrary, they will attempt to dismiss, overlook or even deny the evidence to protect their positive worldview.

This pertains even to information provided by physicians. Celebrants want to believe there is nothing wrong with their bodies. As such, they will deny or minimize symptoms. If a doctor renders a negative diagnosis or bleak prognosis, they will continue hoping that a cure will be found or trust that their remarkable immune systems will render the doctor wrong. For years, I felt this way until Dr. Herz stripped away all remaining illusions that I was in control when he told me I could drop dead at any moment.

Natural optimists, Celebrants do not expect to get sick. Surprisingly, they do manage to stay healthier than people with other predominant MAMs. An article that appeared in *The Wall Street Journal* discussed a study that compared medically related behavior and expenditures on the part of people who reported themselves as low in well-being (uncomfortable, unhappy) with those who reported themselves as high in well-being (comfortable, happy). Both groups were tracked for twelve months. The high in well-being group were about half as likely to visit the emergency room; half as likely to be admitted to the hospital; and, twenty percent less likely to spend money on prescription drugs. Finally, they spent approximately sixty percent less on health care.[9]

There is more than a self-fulfilling prophecy at work here. In his book, *Learned Optimism*, Martin Seligman offers convincing evidence that the mind, or mindset, can influence both the likelihood that a person will get sick, and the outcome of the illness if they do succumb. Hope saves lives while hopelessness and its first cousin, helplessness, destroy lives. In his words, "...learned helplessness doesn't just affect behavior; it also reaches down to the cellular level and makes the immune system more passive."[10]

One afternoon I had an appointment with my pulmonologist, Dr. Winden, whom you'll meet in the chapter, *An Apple A Day*. As I sat in her waiting room, I watched two overweight and obviously sick fifty-plus-year-old people flirting with each other. Both were using power chairs to get around. A plastic tube crisscrossed the woman's bloated face. An oxygen tank stuck out of the basket of her power chair. Because the nurse

[9]Patricia L. Harrison, James E. Pope, Carer R. Coberley, Elizabeth Y. Rula, "Evaluation of the Relationship Between Individual Well-Being and Future Health Care Ultilization and Cost," *The Wall Street Journal* (April 16, 2012).

[10]Martin E.P. Seligman, Ph.D., *Learned Optimism*. (New York, Alfred A. Knopf, 1991), 17.

invited them into the doctor's office together, I gathered they were "a couple." They may even have been a married couple. If so, then they were newly married. They were too happy, too flirtatious and oblivious to those around them to have been together very long.

Randy Pausch's moving book, *The Last Lecture,* is filled with pithy reminders of how to retain the hopeful mindset even when death is in the room. I particularly like this one: "You don't beat the grim reaper by living longer; you beat the grim reaper by living better."[11]

My friend Alan Gans (his real name used at his request) provides a wonderful example of the aging Celebrant. He is a life-long bachelor who loves art, travel and learning. His modern home on the edge of the sea is filled with artworks and artifacts he has gathered during his journeys to the world's most exotic destinations. In the upstairs hall just outside of the guest bedroom is a print by Goya entitled *Old Man on a Swing.* The old man is smiling.

When I think of Alan, I think of that print. He is my Old Man on a Swing. As Alan ages, he continues to explore what life has to offer. And, he keeps smiling. On his eightieth birthday he wrote a poem that captures the essence of the Celebrant who refuses to let the ravages of age take away his optimism.

ON TURNING 80

I do not breathe the thinner air
On aging's forlorn peak,
Nor drink a pallid distillate
Of words I dare not speak.

I shed my past detritus
Like a winter coat in spring,
And marching into realms unknown
I savor Life-whatever it may bring.

Alan Gans, April 15, 2008

---

[11]Randy Pausch, "Carnegie Mellon Commencement Speech," 2007.

Celebrants tend to be loving, giving, compassionate people. I have friends who continue to celebrate life even as they move into their eighties, and experience the deterioration of their bodies. It's not unusual to find an old friend who now suffers from dementia at their table. Their entryway has been modified to accommodate their friends who are now confined to wheelchairs. In spite of having a large family, they always invite those who would otherwise be alone to share their Christmas dinner.

There is a negative aspect to this glorious, life-affirming mindset. When something bad happens, some Celebrants cling inappropriately to their positive outlook. They move to the negative extreme and begin acting like Drama Queens or Pollyannas.

Drama Queens and Pollyannas.

Ginger ale people can feel a sense of euphoria when faced with the opportunity to rescue an unfortunate other. When at the extreme of the mindset, they sometimes get so filled with the drama of the rescue and the potential of the moment that they become insensitive to the needs and desires of the person they are attempting to save. When that happens, performance replaces authenticity. The thrill of the rescue becomes the focus. The Celebrant as director and lead actress or actor expects others (including the victim) to play their requisite parts. Those who shy away from participating or can't quite find the ecstasy in the moment are discounted as being unable to share the vision.

Some Celebrants at the negative pole become Pollyannas. Regardless of what is going on around them, they pretend nothing bad is happening. When forced to admit that a crisis is at hand, they find the silver lining and focus on that. The name Pollyanna comes from the heroine in a series of children's books about an orphan girl who learns to play "the glad game."

The game consists of finding something good in every situation, no matter how bleak. When carried to the extreme, Pollyannas are blinded by their own need to see only the positive. They deny the existence of the negative, and in so doing, render themselves ineffective in action, tedious in conversation, and dwarfed in emotion. The valence of life is weakened. The light dims because it is no longer in contrast to the dark. Every Celebrant I have known, including my former self, manifests some degree of Pollyannaism. They underestimate the likelihood of failure, loss or adversity, and they overestimate their ability to manage the outcome. Further, they are less likely to achieve their goals than are those with a more realistic outlook.

MINDSET	Celebrant
Major Attribute	*Love*
Major Attribute Shared with the Warrior	*Resilience*
Major Attribute Shared with the Stargazer	*Optimism*
At the POSITIVE Pole	*Expansive Enthusiastic* *Innovative Compassionate* *Confident*
At the NEGATIVE Pole	*Scattered Pollyanna* *Drama Queen Heroic Rescuer* *Unprepared for Trouble*

Gabrielle Oettingen, a professor of psychology at New York University and the University of Hamburg, conducted a study with a group of women who needed to lose weight. Before the onset of the program, she asked each to rate how positively or negatively they felt about their chance of succeeding. A year later, she conducted a follow-up. She found that the more positive the ratings, the fewer pounds the women had lost.

She and her colleagues repeated the study with other groups of people attempting to achieve a goal, such as hip-replacement patients hoping to get back on their feet. In every study, imagining happy or successful outcomes had a negative effect. She explains, "Fantasying about happy outcomes, about smoothly attaining your wishes, didn't help. Indeed, it hindered people from realizing their dreams…dreaming about the future calms you down, measurably reducing systolic blood pressure, but it also can drain you of the energy you need to take action in pursuit of your goals."[12]

Part of the reason that some Celebrants fail to achieve their goals is the tendency to flit from one task to the other. While the Warrior at the extreme is overly focused, the Celebrant at the extreme is scattered. Since so much of life is inviting, he or she bounces from one activity to another, never quite completing one before moving to another.

This increases the likelihood that the Celebrant will fail. Unfortunately, because of their insistence on believing that life is good, and will only get better, they are often ill-prepared to deal with a negative outcome. In this regard, Celebrants who sit on top of the world are in a more precarious position than the Warriors in the bunker or behind the castle wall who are better prepared to deal with misfortune.

Because of their differences, the blend of the Celebrant and Warrior mindsets is powerful. The life-loving Celebrant makes it less likely that the Warrior will end up in the bunker. The realism and focus of the Warrior makes it less likely that the Celebrant will become a Drama Queen or Pollyanna.

Bouncing Back.

When both MAMs are present, and the courage of the Warrior meets the love and passion of the Celebrant, then we have a remarkably *resilient* individual. Celebrant Warriors bounce back. They try again. They will not be defeated. They recover more quickly than others. They embrace life with vigor in spite of knowing that life as an aging mortal necessarily entails suffering. People with these combined mindsets are both realistic and optimistic, courageous and expansive, determined and able to "go with the flow." They are strategic in their thinking, inspired and forceful as the "will do" of the fighter is combined with the "can do" of the optimist.

Consider the poignant story of thirty-nine-year-old Polett Villalta who

---

[12]Gabriele Oettingen, "The Problem with Positive Thinking," *The New York Times Sunday Review*, (October 14, 2014), 25.

has been paralyzed from the chest down since the age of twelve when she dove into the water from the shoulders of a friend and landed on her head. Refusing to have her wings clipped, she has learned to deep scuba dive. Skydiving is next. In the water and in the sky, she can move without restraint. [13]

MINDSET	Celebrant	Warrior
Combined Major Attribute	Resilience	
Major Attribute	Love	Courage
At the POSITIVE Pole	Expansive Enthusiastic Innovative Compassionate Confident	Resistance Defiance Focus Discipline Fighting Spirit

I am sure there have been many times when Polett's mindset was less optimistic, and less courageous. A sudden loss such as experienced by Polett can render the Celebrant no longer hopeful or optimistic, and make the Warrior feel suddenly helpless. When this happens, the mindset shifts to that of a Stargazer or Castaway.

[13]Elizabeth Bernstein, "Researchers Study Awe and Find it is Good for Relationships," *Wall Street Journal*, (Feb. 23, 2015)

STARGAZERS AND CASTAWAYS.

These mindsets have one important characteristic in common: both feel vulnerable and exposed. They believe they are at the mercy of others to take care of them, or rescue them, or protect them from harm. Because they are dependent, they believe they deserve or must accept that which comes their way. Their fundamental difference lies in their expectations of what the future will bring.

Like shipwreck survivors, Castaways expect to be thrown about or even battered by life. Aware that nature can be punishing and that every life ends in death, they anticipate misfortune. They often perceive that the people on whom they must depend are themselves vulnerable, and therefore potentially unreliable. The important thing is to accept life as it is, on its own terms. Like shipwreck survivors, Castaways accept Buddha's first noble truth, "Life is suffering."

Stargazers, on the other hand, believe it's a wonderful life, and that the future will bring good fortune and happiness. Nature is beautiful and to be enjoyed. The people on whom Stargazers depend can be trusted to do what's right and what's good. Life is not only pleasurable; it is at times wondrous.

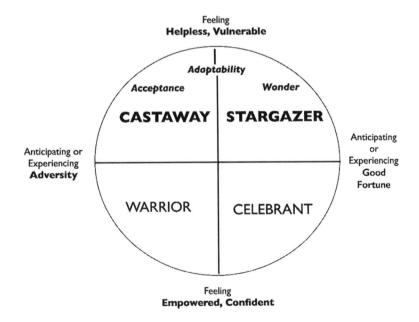

Acceptance renders the Castaway agile in the face of adversity. *Wonder* makes the Stargazer open to finding happiness. The individual who tends to shift between the two vulnerable mindsets is, therefore, highly *adaptable*, or able to adjust quickly to changing circumstances.

Daydreamers.

We are all born Stargazers, vulnerable and yet joyous. Many of us sustain that mindset until the social and psychological pains of adolescent disrupt our sense of well-being and begin to erode our innocence. Some of us, the lucky ones, manage to carry a bit of our natural child, our daydreamer mindset, into adulthood.

Stargazers are like perpetual children. They are often dreamers, idealists who are entranced with all the possibilities that life has to offer. Many seek immediate satisfaction and have little tolerance for deferred gratification or pain of any kind. They like their creature comforts. Some are even hedonists.

People with this indulgent mindset can be delightful. They can be playful and spontaneous. Trusting and innocent, they are naturally seductive. People simply want to help them. It is a pleasure to be in their company. Their wonder and delight can be infectious, making the serious burdens of life temporarily recede into the background.

Stargazers tend to be sociable, seeking out others who love to laugh and to play. Popularity is important. Not being invited to a party can make them very unhappy even if the gathering promises to be boring or tedious.

They tend to seek the approval of others, and will go out of their way to impress or to make others happy. Giving and receiving presents are important to people with a strong element of this MAM. Preferring everyone to get along, they can be conflict averse. Any sign that they have offended or displeased another person will cause the Stargazer great anxiety. Their desire for approval often extends to authority figures. People in positions of authority are not to be challenged. Like "good" children, they comply with the rules.

Stargazers tend to regard their doctors as godlike or final authorities who are to be obeyed without question. Often, they neither understand nor want to understand their own bodies or its frailties. Most are quite comfortable with doctors who say little, especially when the prognosis is dire. Death is something they prefer not to think about. Many believe that if their desire to live is strong enough, they can hold death at bay. They agree with Lord Byron who said, "'Tis very certain the desire of life prolongs it."

Many Stargazers are religious and have put their faith in a benevolent God. Many believe that when they die, they will go to Heaven and be reunited with loved ones. Their belief renders dying less frightening. Like trusting children, they close their eyes, say a prayer and let go. The Bible even directs believers to adopt the mindset of a child if they want to enter Heaven. Matthew 18:3 in the King James Version reads, "Verily I say unto you, Except ye be converted, and become as little children, ye shall not enter into the kingdom of heaven."

Fantasy Island.

Less religious Stargazers will often attempt to distract themselves from having to think about their own mortality. The retirees living in a community in Florida called The Villages provide a good example. Aging is ignored. Death is denied. I am told that when someone in The Villages dies, the ambulance comes to pick up the corpse in the middle of the night when everyone is asleep.

To help residents avoid thinking about aging and dying, The Villages makes it possible to fill every single waking moment with communal activity. It appears members of this community have taken the words of Marcel Proust to heart: "We say that the hour of death cannot be forecast, but when we say this we imagine that hour as placed in an obscure and distant future. It never occurs to us that it has any connection with the day already begun or that death could arrive this same afternoon, this afternoon which is so certain and which has every hour filled in advance."

The schedule posted on their website for a Monday is typical:
8:00 A.M. Clog Hoppers Show Team
9:00 A.M. Bridge or Body Shaping or Technology of Color Pencil and Ink Workshop
9:30 A.M. Book review/Non Fiction
12:00 Noon Creative Writing
1:00 P.M. Shuffleboard or Mahjong
2:30 P.M. Giggles and Shakes Exercise

4:30 P.M. Quilting or Tai Chi
7:00 P.M. Line Dance

After the line dance, many men and women continue their frolicking in The Village bars. My daughter, Monica, described an encounter while visiting her in-laws who are happy residents there. "A seventy-five-ish blond chick dressed in tight pants and a sequined top was sitting at the bar sipping a glass of wine. An aging cowboy entered the room and sauntered up to the bar. Within minutes they were flirting like people in their twenties. Well, not their twenties; more like, their thirties."

My mother would probably have enjoyed living in The Villages. She was very sociable, a great bridge player, and among the best at the art of denial.

The Queen of Denial.

My mother, Rosemary, was kind and generous and she loved to laugh. She insisted on seeing only the best in people. And, she was a natural seductress. People, even strangers, liked her, and they liked to look at her. She smiled a lot. And, she was very beautiful. In her youth, she had been a ravishing young woman who once dated Mickey Rooney and was often mistaken for Elizabeth Taylor. She learned at an early age that her beauty was a powerful currency, especially when coupled with an aura of innocent helplessness that made everyone, even her own children, rush to take care of her.

Like a true Stargazer, Rosemary so wanted to please those around her that she even drove her car into a swimming pool. Here's what happened. Shortly after they moved into their home in Perth, Western Australia, my parents invited the neighbors for dinner. The merry widow who lived next door asked for a glass of rosé wine. Because Rosemary had none to offer, she jumped into their orange Volkswagon Beetle and raced to the liquor store. In a hurry to return home, she inadvertently put the gearshift in reverse. She stepped on the gas, and panicked when the car shot backwards. Instead of putting on the brake, she accelerated. The car jumped the curb, crossed the road, crashed through a picket fence, and plunged into a swimming pool. Needless to say, my father was not pleased.

Stargazers often displease or upset others. They can be very manipulative, using their childlike charms to cajole others into doing their bidding. If that fails, they often become passive aggressive. Let me give you an example.

MINDSET	Stargazer
Major Attribute	Wonder
Major Attribute Shared with the Castaway	Adaptability
Major Attribute Shared with the Celebrant	Optimism
At the POSITIVE Pole	Trust Innocence Playfulness Natural Seductiveness
At the NEGATIVE Pole	Self Absorption Manipulation Denial Petulance

My parents' came to visit me at my home in LaJolla, California just months before my father's death. After he died, whenever my mother wanted to exert some form of control over me, she would smile sweetly and remind me that, as a result of that visit, my father had said, "In the future, we'll let the children come to us. We won't impose ourselves on them."

She knew how upsetting these words were to me. I had tried my best to make their ten-week-long visit a good one. But it was a difficult and complicated time in my life. Monica was leaving for college. I was flying back and forth across the country on business. The man I had been dating and his spoiled daughter were temporarily living in my house. All the changes in our routines had upset Melissa who responded by becoming anxious and withdrawn. I wanted to scream and I needed to cry. I could do neither. By the time I composed myself, Momhad moved onto other happier subjects.

You'd think I would have been able to withstand her attack. After all, I had published two books on the subject of non-assertiveness (or passive aggression) and aggression.[14] In the workshops I led as an organizational consultant, I had trained managers to be assertive (as opposed to aggressive) and responsive (as opposed to passive aggressive or non-assertive). Intellectually, I understood that her poison dart was her way of making me feel guilty, and thereby exercising some form of control. Emotionally, I was still vulnerable.

Rosemary frequently engaged in the non-assertive to aggressive swing. In that, she was behaving like many aging Stargazers who find asserting their true wants and feelings to be too scary. They are afraid of antagonizing the other person on whom they feel dependent. And yet, they do get angry and aggressive when their wants and feelings are ignored. The aggression, however, is perceived as dangerous, forcing the Stargazer to retreat and hide once again behind their "nice," non-assertive self. The process starts all over.

Sometimes Rosemary involved others in her game. Like a clever child who has learned how to pit one parent against another, she was adept at motivating one caregiver by subtly mentioning the deficiencies of another. My siblings and I continually made sacrifices in order to care for Mom. In her later years, this was particularly true of my brother, Clyde, who was the only one of us still living in Perth. To his face, Mom expressed gratitude. She complained to her friends, however, claiming that she could never count on him. That seemed to encourage them to do even more for her.

That she had maligned us became apparent whenever one of us had to escort our mother to a function where her friends had gathered. Their attitude and demeanor said it all. They believed "poor Mom" had been

---

[14]Pamela Cuming, *The Power Handbook:A Strategic Guide to Organizational and Personal Effectiveness.* (New York, VanNostrand Reinhold, 1984)

Pamela Cuming, *Turf and Other Corporate Power Plays.* (New Jersey, Prentice-Hall, Inc.,1985)

ignored by her faithless and ungrateful children. That made us angry, but we quickly got over it. It was impossible to stay angry with Mom even when her manipulative ploys became apparent. It was our job to adore her, not to criticize her. It fell to us to protect her innocence even after she had revealed she was not innocent. She was at once our mother and our beautiful child.

Mom was beautiful and she knew it. Like a child, she loved looking at the reflection of herself in the mirror. Age did nothing to lessen her vanity. Until the end of her life, she was able to deny that she had aged and that her body was deteriorating. One night around her eighty-sixth birthday she said to me, "I guess I've always had a bad heart. I mustn't need it, since I've gotten along fine all these years." Maybe she was joking. Somehow, I doubt it. She believed she would live to be 115 because her doctor had once told her so. Like many Stargazers, she never doubted the authority of her doctors nor questioned their ability to do magic.

In that, she was unusual. Aging and the threat of dying force many of us to give up the innocent wonder of the Stargazer, the optimism of the Celebrant, and the courage of the Warrior and to adopt the mindset of the Castaway. We lose what David calls the magic of the "spell of potential." We realize that things we had hoped to do or to accomplish will never happen. Our bodies begin to break down, reminding us that the future is not a field of infinite possibilities. That makes us feel vulnerable. We know that, physically, the worst is yet to come. The trajectory is all downhill. At the end lies death. Our mindset shifts to that of a Castaway. We then have a choice to make. We can *accept* that this is what life is all about, or we can fall into *despair.*

Caught in Despair.

When caught at the negative pole of the mindset, Castaways have given up. They are pessimistic, despondent, without hope. The future is bleak and there's absolutely nothing that can be done about it. Their worlds begin to feel groundless. Nothing is solid. Nothing is secure. They are caught in despair, the victim of a shipwreck, clinging to the raft and watching anxiously as the current of life bounces them around like pieces of driftwood.

Some become all suffering, and wrap themselves in a blanket of self-pity. Their moans are deafening. Their bleakness is like a black hole that drains energy from anyone who has to spend time in their presence. Castaways at the negative pole typically experience the world as a scary place. They fret about every little thing, exaggerating the importance of insignificant and easily solved problems. They begin to greet friends, relatives and caregivers with a hysterical litany of concerns.

Sometimes age and immobility push people to the point of the despairing Castaway. Other times, it's sickness or loneliness. Yet other times, it happens as a result of being preyed upon by others. That's what happened to my mother. She had managed to hold onto her Stargazer mindset even as her heart weakened and even after she crashed her car and had to give up driving. She took all of that in her stride until two young drug addicts made her afraid. Here's how it happened.

After Mom could no longer drive, she began to keep a lot of cash on hand to pay the old man who tried his best to maintain her small garden, her housecleaner, and the friends and neighbors who picked up groceries for her. Whenever my brother, Clyde, took her out shopping, she insisted they stop at an ATM machine. One time, two young hoods observed her drawing out cash. They followed her home. When they figured out she lived alone, they began to regard her as their private bank account.

Mom was asleep when suddenly she was awakened by a crash and the sound of glass breaking. She heard male voices shouting, "Take the fucking purse, and see what else the old bitch is hiding." Thinking she'd just had a bad dream, she fell back into an uneasy sleep. It wasn't until the next morning that she realized something was terribly wrong.

Going into the space that doubled as a living and dining room, she saw that the sliding glass doors to the patio had been shattered. Her heart racing, she peered out into the backyard. Outside the window to her bedroom were two empty dresser drawers. Her bras, girdles, panties and half-slips were strewn all over the parched grass. Gasping for breath, she stumbled through the duplex in search of her purse. It was gone, along with the five hundred dollars she'd withdrawn the day before. Shaking, she called Clyde.

It took him fifteen minutes to get to her place. He calmed Mom down, and then reported the robbery to the police. By the end of day, he had gotten the glass doors replaced and arranged to have a security system installed. In spite of the demands of his job and his own family, he stayed with her for several nights until she had regained enough peace of mind to be left on her own. Still, she was fearful, and more cautious than she had been before the robbery. When she went to bed, she brought her purse with her, and locked her bedroom door. Unfortunately, confounded by the technology, she did not arm the new security system.

Ten days or so after the initial break-in, the perpetrators (whom the police had tentatively identified as drug addicts in their late teens) returned in search of more easy cash. Again, they smashed the glass doors. When they saw that their victim had not left her purse in open sight, they flew into a rage and began smashing her dining room table. Their rage unspent, they kicked open the bedroom door and grabbed the purse out of their victim's trembling arms.

The weeks passed. The police failed to make an arrest even though they knew the identity of at least one of the addicts. As a result, Mom lived in fear that they would make another attempt. She became increasingly timid. She laughed less often and less heartily. Because she wasn't sleeping well, her energy waned. She grew unsteady on her feet.

She was perpetually anxious. At the slightest problem, she would break down. It got to the point where she would stand at the front door, waiting for me or my brother to arrive. As soon as we got out of the car, she would open the door and start wailing, "The credit card company said I didn't pay the bill last month. I did. I know I did. Oh dear, what should I do." "Oh dear. Something has happened to the screen door. It won't close." "The gardener hurt his leg. He can't come for two weeks. Everything will get overgrown. The grass will die. Oh dear. Oh dear." "The sky is falling. The sky is falling."

Just like Chicken Little, Mom had begun to believe disaster was imminent. The despairing Castaway mindset had taken over, replacing childlike innocence with anxiety and hysterical cries for help. The Warrior in me found her behavior hard to tolerate. I became impatient with her, accusing her of making mountains out of molehills. My accusations only made her more timid.

I understand that now, but it eluded me then. Now, it's me who periodically slips into the mindset of the despairing Castaway. It's David as Warrior who tells me to get over it. To show you what I mean, let me invite you to eavesdrop on a snippet of conversation that occurred between David and me at another of our morning breakfasts in the bistro.

"We begin in diapers and end in diapers," said David. "Well, not me. I'm not ending up in diapers. I'll use my Glock before I'll end up like that."

I decided not to point out that we owned a Beretta, not a Glock. He had given me the pistol for my birthday a year earlier. I had never taken it out of the box. Instead, I said, "You are a Warrior."

"I wish I could say the same thing about you," he said as he put a piece of cheese and ham on a slice of bread and handed it to me. "I don't like it when you get timid. I like it when you walk strong. Can I get us another cup of coffee?"

"Yes, thank you," I said. "Would you like me to get it so that we can give your knee a rest?"

"My knee does not deserve a rest," he said defiantly.

I swiveled my chair around so that I could look out the window and thought about his comment about "walking strong." I didn't like him comparing my present self to my youthful self. I simply could no longer walk as strong as I once did, and I didn't like him making me feel bad about that.

He, however, had no intention of leaving it alone. Putting down the steaming cups of coffee, he said, "It's important that you remember who you were. You were powerful and courageous. I think sometimes you forget that."

"I don't forget that, David. I am now a different person—not lesser, just different."

"I remember when I met you, you would get up early every morning and do those Jane Fonda tapes. You were really something."

"David, I am trying my best to stay in shape. But, as I said, I am now a different person. I am trying to learn to love my aging body as I loved my younger self."

"You're still an attractive woman," he said, as though trying to make peace. It didn't work. I didn't let him off the hook. "I hope one day you will learn to value the person I have become as much as you respected the strong and optimistic woman you married."

"I love the person you have become. You're a fine writer. I just don't like it when you get timid and anxious."

"I am neither timid nor anxious. I am simply accepting the fact that I am seventy-one years old. I am accepting the limitations imposed by two very real physical problems. I am doing the best I can with what I've now got."

That got to him. "Yes, of course you are. And you're right to bring me up short when I forget that."

David's attitude changed when I moved away from timidity, anxiety and despair to the positive pole—to acceptance of what life as an aging mortal means. While he probably would have preferred me to resume the mindset of the Warrior, he could tolerate the accepting Castaway better than the Castaway stuck at the negative pole of defeat.

Some Castaways demonstrate their acceptance of the human condition through humor. In *Jokes: Philosophical Thoughts on Joking Matters*, Ted Cohen writes: "When you make a joke about those more powerful than you, and even those who control your life, it is a way of striking back, of taking a kind of control over those people. It is a poor substitute, perhaps, for real power, but it may be all that is available."[15]

Perhaps because people feel so vulnerable in the face of death, there are a number of jokes intended to put even the Grim Reaper in his place. Here's one example that I particularly enjoy.

The Last Will

Moshe was on his deathbed and raised his head gently. "Mendel are you there?"

"Yes, Moshe, I am here."

A moment later Moshe said, "Izzi, are you there?"

His son, Izzi assured him he was by his side.

"Joshua," said the ailing Moshe, "Are you there?"

"I'm here Poppa," said Joshua taking his hand. "We are all here."

Moshe raised himself on his elbow and demanded, "Then who the hell is minding the shop?"[16]

While this is a Jewish joke, you don't have to be of that faith or culture

---

[15]Ted Cohen, *Jokes: Philosophical Thoughts on Joking Matters*. (Chicago, The University of Chicago Press, 1999), 44.

[16]"The Last Will", http://www.jewishmag.com

to turn to humor in the face of mortality. My friend Luna often relied on humor after Stavros was diagnosed with multiple myeloma. In an email to family and friends following his stem cell transplant, she wrote: "Before you know it, spring will be here...this year spring is Bad News because Stavros has been told he cannot do any yard work whatsoever for the next YEAR...Stavros is over the moon. If I had known this, I would never have let him go for this transplant. Clearly the side effects are completely

MINDSET	Castaway	
Major Attribute	Acceptance	
Major Attribute Shared with the Warrior	Realism	
Major Attribute Shared with the Stargazer	Adaptability	
At the POSITIVE Pole	Empathy Endurance	Tolerance Serenity
At the NEGATIVE Pole	Despair Anxiety Rage	Pessimism Panic Victim

unacceptable."

To acknowledge that adversity is an integral part of life is not to view life through the lens of the victim, but rather from the point of view of someone who understands that a vital part of living is facing challenges. As M. Scott Peck wrote in *The Road Less Traveled*, "Life is difficult...Once we truly know that life is difficult—once we truly understand and accept it—

then life is no longer difficult."[17]

Acceptance enables people with the Castaway mindset to learn from failure, feel compassion for fellow suffers, and adopt realistic strategies to cope with loss. As David is fond of reminding me when his Sage mindset is predominant, "As Buddha said, 'Life is suffering.' We must accept that everything is impermanent, and that life is loss. Only when we do so can we truly live."

This belief appears to be an inherent part of the Japanese culture. Stories abound about the heroic attempts made by thousands of Japanese to help their fellow citizens during the March, 2011 earthquake, catastrophic tsunami and nuclear reactor meltdown. The triple tragedy killed more than fifteen thousand people and uprooted hundreds of thousands more. The Japanese culture encouraged the survivors to adopt the mindset of the Castaway and to be acceptant, compassionate, and to remain connected to one another. Often repeated Japanese idioms reflect that mindset. 'Shikata ga nai" means 'it can't be helped.' 'Sho ga nai' means 'it's out of your control.' 'Gambatte' means 'to try harder, to persevere.' The Japanese coped by helping one another maintain perspective and a sense of inner calm in the midst of outer turmoil. They accepted, but they did not surrender, and they did not despair.

Perhaps that is why Castaways at the positive pole are able to age gracefully and to die with dignity. Accepting the limitations of the aging body and the reality of death, they are free to focus on living. This is the dark gift of this mindset.

The Dark Gift.

A woman in her early fifties rendered immobile by rheumatoid arthritis described her illness to author Oliver Burkeman as "a dark gift." In *The Antidote*, he writes, "Jocelyn...said her illness had proven to be a 'dark gift', and that once she'd learned to ignore the people telling her to 'fight' it or to 'think positive,' she had come to understand her dependence on others as a kind of blessing. She seemed serene..."[18]

---

[17]M. Scott Peck. *The Road Less Traveled.* (New York, Simon and Schuster, 1978), 15.

[18]Oliver Burkeman, *The Antidote: Happiness for People Who Can't Stand Positive Thinking.* (New York, Faber and Faber, Inc., 2012), 40.

Jocelyn found serenity because she had stopped denying or fighting against the reality of her situation. She acknowledged her illness. She accepted her immobility. She recognized a future in which she would likely get even worse. But she did not despair. Instead, she began to focus on other aspects of her life. In a similar vein, depression can free people to live richer lives.

In my mid-twenties, I had the opportunity of working with Dr. Frederic Flach. He was a prominent psychiatrist with a private practice in midtown Manhattan. His specialty was the treatment of depression. He taught me that giving in is not the same thing as giving up. He showed me that we can emerge from crises and loss as more aware human beings.

In *The Secret Strength of Depression,* he explains. "Any event or change in our lives that forces us to break down some of our defenses, for whatever reason, is going to be painful. To experience acute depression is an opportunity for us not just to learn more about ourselves, but also to become more whole. "Falling apart" not only affords us a chance for insight, but it can accelerate the process of reordering one's life after a serious stress... Becoming depressed is an inevitable concomitant of letting go—of a person, a position, a piece of oneself. The greater the attachment, the more involved it is with one's self-esteem and dependency needs, the greater the reaction will be."[19]

The threat of losing our very existence as physical beings is so great that few of us manage to avoid adopting the mindset of the Castaway when we finally break through the veil of denial. Despair is often our first response. Those of us who manage to move to a state of acceptance have a chance at walking through a portal and learning to perceive life and death through the lens of a Sage.

BECOMING A SAGE.

David and I had a Japanese friend who left a thriving strategic consulting practice when he learned he had advanced prostate cancer. Leaving his family and his business behind, he became a Buddhist monk.

---

[19]Frederic Flach, M.D., *The Secret Strength of Depression, Fourth Revised Edition.* (Hatherleigh Press, 2009), 34.

As a penance for previous indulgences, he walked the entire perimeter of Mt. Fuji, demonstrating the Castaway's amazing power of endurance.

At the end of Michi's journey, his incredulous physicians declared that his cancer was in remission. Now a deep believer that miracles can happen if faith is strong enough, Michi began traveling to share with others his vision and his faith. Dressed in the robes of a monk, complete with beads and sandals, he came to New York. David and I were able to spend an evening with him.

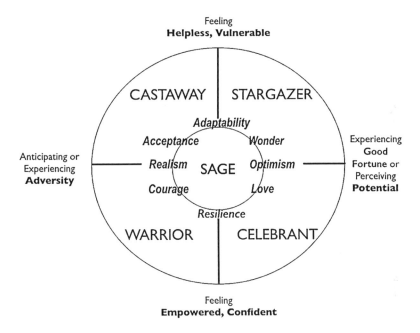

As he sat in our living room massaging his beads, he told us that his brush with mortality had changed him as a man. Once a striving, ambitious, consultant to the chieftains of Japanese industry, he had become spiritual and compassionate. He had shed his Warrior's armor and embraced the wonder, hope and optimism of the Stargazing Celebrant. His purpose now was to help others lead richer lives. In doing so, he was driven not by the desire to control, but by the desire to understand. Wisdom, not power, was his goal.

A few years later, he learned that his cancer had metastasized. Stripped of his Celebrant's optimism, and his Stargazer's natural joy in life, he was thrust into the depths of the Castaway mindset. Despairing, he began to ask the questions that most people are too busy or distracted to ask. Where do we come from? Where are we going? Can life have meaning if it is filled with pain and suffering and must end in death? How can we free ourselves from the fruitless quest for permanence and security, and from the fear of death and so live richer lives?

He kept asking these questions until he was able to accept his mortality. Eventually, he reached what he described as, "Enlightenment and a feeling of oneness with the universe and every living soul." He began to move with the currents of life, unfettered by petty grievances, frustrated ambitions, or the desire to possess what cannot be possessed. He was no longer enslaved by the passing of chronological time. The hourglass lost its power to terrify. He had so completely immersed himself in the experience of the moment that time had become irrelevant. All that mattered was NOW.

He had rid himself of the preoccupation with the ego that makes us grasp our body, our assets, our loved ones and mistrust or envy that which is not ours. Resentment towards others who enjoyed more wealth or better health had fallen away. He had learned to accept pain and suffering, and even death, as an essential part of the experience of living. Now, he neither raged nor fell into despair as his body weakened. He freed himself from the futile attempt to resist change, or to render permanent that which is impermanent.

Michi began to experience himself as deeply connected to all sentient creatures, and in so doing, to exalt life in all its forms and dimensions. He was awed by the wonders of the universe. The vast mountains, deep gorges and surging oceans humbled him and made him feel small and insignificant. That, in itself, was freeing. He no longer had to bear the burden of believing himself to be the center of the universe.

Michi learned to integrate the best attributes of each of the MAMS and, in so doing, to adopt the mindset of a **Sage**. Though *acceptant* that pain and suffering are inevitable, he was able to experience the *wonder* of a child. That all life, no matter how passionately lived, must end in death did not defeat his sense of *optimism*. He developed a sense of compassion for those beings who were unwell or facing misfortune or were "stuck" in defensiveness, pessimism, dependency, self-absorption, frenzy, or illusion. His compassion stemmed from an understanding of the human condition, and from the ability to *love* all other living creatures in spite of, or even because of, their imperfections.

Michi retained the *courage* that had always characterized his Warrior self. When combined with his optimism, this made him very *resilient*, and able to bounce back each time he received a disturbing medical prognosis. Because of his *realism*, he knew when it was time to surrender. In his last years, Michi became the embodiment of wisdom in the Hindu sense of the word. "Wisdom is all about outgrowing hunger—be it physical, emotional, intellectual or social."[20]

He had learned to transcend the demands of his own ego; to suspend disbelief and imagine other planes of existence or higher powers. He was able to envision death as part of life, or even as the defining moment of life. "Nowhere is Life stronger than at the moment of Death, the peremptory going-forth; it is stated not as a paradox but as a matter of experience of men throughout the religions, throughout the centuries."[21] That made Michi serene even as he waited for death. And, it made him able to soothe others who were sick and afraid of dying.

David also has that ability. I listened as he talked to his dying stepmother on the telephone, soothing her fears and easing her regrets. His cousin later told him that by the time she put down the phone, she was smiling and able to say, "I am no longer afraid." I watched as he helped my friend, Katherine, The Miracle Girl, die. You'll get to know her later in the book. David and she would sit for hours looking at the DVD of her artwork he had made for her. Together they would contemplate the paintings of Frankenthaller, and talk of how Katherine's work compared to the artist's. He helped her fill her mind with colorful images until the end.

The Sage Warrior.

David's path to embracing the mindset of the Sage began with the death of his mother when he was eight. That tragedy initiated a search for the meaning of life that would quickly set him apart from others. By the time he was thirteen, he preferred modern classical music to rock and roll, and he had turned to literature in his search for the meaning of life. While

---

[20]Devdutt Pattanail, *Sita:an Illustrated Retelling of the Ramayana.* (London, Penguin Books, 2013), 294.

[21]Bhiksu, *Bakti Yoga.* (Chicago, The Yogi Publication Society, 1930), 198.

---

his high school peers were reading *The Blackboard Jungle,* David was studying Thomas Wolfe, Ernest Hemingway, Andre Malraux and T.E. Lawrence.

In high school David was introduced to the writings of George Gurdjieff, a hands-on philosopher who believed that most people live their lives not fully awake. He proposed that people need to make a conscious effort to wake themselves up, and to stop behaving like robots and automatons who go through the motions but understand little.

Gurdjieff's teachings resonated with David. Like the nineteenth century romantic poets, Shelley and Keats, he embraced the belief that life was a process of "soul making," not "soul saving." He committed to a life of continuous learning and developing an ever-deeper insight into himself, the human condition, and the nature of the universe.

His search never stopped, even when he served in Special Forces as a demolitions expert. On missions, he carried in his pack what he regarded as his two essential guidebooks. One was his demolitions manual—key to the Warrior's survival. The other was the *Bhagavad Gītā,* a 700-verse Hindu scripture that is part of the ancient Sanskrit epic, the *Mahabharata.* That fed the soul of the Sage, and reminded him that the point is not to win or to lose, but only to do what has to be done.

Embracing the Spanish philosopher Jose Ortega y Gasset's belief that "I am myself plus my circumstances," David decided that his biggest enemy was stagnation, sameness, routine and maintenance. He vowed to keep changing his circumstances to force himself to keep evolving and, through evolving, to developing a deeper understanding of the universe both within himself and without. He sharpened his thinking by following the teachings of Carl Jung who sought to unleash the creative unconscious through the active imagination. He began using meditation and dreaming to access the contents of his unconscious and to put him in a better position to, in Jung's words, "give shape to himself."

Occasionally his ongoing search stalls, and he gets "stuck," entrapped by the mundane and the routine aspects of life. He becomes like Kazantzakis' Odysseus after he's finally returned to Ithaca, killed off his wife's suitors, and resumed his rightful place at the table and in her bed. It doesn't take long before Odysseus is bored out of his mind. David hates to be bored. With boredom comes ennui and a suspicion that life may have no meaning at all. Existential angst begins to torment him as he moves to the negative pole of the Sage mindset.

The Dark Night of the Soul.

When David is in this mindset, he falls prey to what philosopher Gerald Heard calls "involutional melancholia." He begins to suspect that death is no more than the end of a senseless and sensate time on earth. During these dark moments, he believes Emerson was right when he said: "Like sick men in hospitals, we change only from bed to bed, from one folly to another; and it cannot signify much what becomes of such castaways—wailing, stupid, comatose, creatures—lifted from bed to bed, from the nothing of life to the nothing of death."

MINDSET	Sage
Major Attribute	Enlightenment, Wisdom
Major Attributes Shared with the Other Mindsets	Adaptability, Wonder, Optimism, Love, Resilience, Courage, Realism, Acceptance
At the POSITIVE Pole	Transcendence Wisdom Serenity
At the NEGATIVE Pole	Existential Angst Involutional Melancholia

In spite of a lifetime of study, David begins to believe he understands nothing, or that all that knowledge is simply worthless. He was feeling this way a month or so ago. When we had sat down for cocktails before dinner, I could tell from the expression on his face that he was not happy.

"What's wrong?" I asked.

"What's right?" he answered. "As the nihilists say, 'I don't know. I don't care and it doesn't make any difference.' It has all been a failed experiment of self-indulgence. Like Faust, I think life is without purpose, without hope and without meaning."

"You're existentially depressed. That will pass," I said.

"And when it does, I'll be like Don Quixote—a nutty old man who lives in a fantasy world and tilts at windmills." He paused and then added, "I think of the two, I'd rather be Don Quixote than Faust. At least he has the energy to tilt at windmills." I laughed and then noticed that he wasn't even smiling.

David always recovers from these bouts of existential angst. Sometimes it takes a day or two, and sometimes a week or two, but it does lift. It does so more quickly if he can travel and have contact with people who lead lives very different from his own. In that regard, he is like Kazantzakis' wonderful character, Zorba the Greek. Like Zorba, David is contrarian, despising routine and complacency. He is passionate and hungry for experience. He will not be subdued. He is a fictional embodiment of the author's advice presented in *The Saviors of God*. "Be always restless, unsatisfied, unconforming. Whenever a habit becomes convenient, smash it! The greatest sin of all is satisfaction."[22]

If smashing a habit doesn't do the trick, David resorts to other methods for pulling himself out of the existential bog. In the chapters that follow, we'll talk about some of these methods. We'll also talk about some of ways we can avoid getting stuck at any of the negative poles as we age. We'll talk about what it means to age gracefully. We'll consider ways in which we can keep our relationship with our mate vital as we get older. We'll talk about dealing with doctors and about dying with dignity. We'll consider ways to stay open to new ideas. In the next chapter, we'll look at the tensions that exist between the young and the old in our changing world, and what we can do about it.

---

[22]Nikos Kazantzakis, *The Saviors of God: Spiritual Exercises*. (New York, Simon and Schuster, 1960), 68.

3:THE WAR OF THE AGES:
Confucius Be Damned

As we get older, many of us move to the extreme pole of our predominant mindset. Castaways become whining, pessimistic downers. At the least sign of trouble, they whimper and cower. Stargazers become manipulative and childlike in their dependence. Some begin to despise the people on whom they are dependent, and lash out in subtle but highly effective ways. Those who manage to hold onto at least the vestiges of the Celebrant mindset can become Drama Queens, insisting that their aches and pains consume the center of the family stage. That can be very tedious. Sages suffer through periods of existential despair that are so black that others are drawn into the void along with them.

The young are often Celebrants, eager to embrace life and all it affords, or Celebrant Warriors, intent upon the privilege of accumulation. They want to focus on the right side of the mindset circle, on the side that anticipates good fortune. They don't want to be fettered in their pursuit of happiness or held back as they march forth to realize their potential. The problems of aging and confronting mortality are abstractions to them. The television writer Andy Rooney once said, "Death is a distant rumor to the young." They regard it as somebody else's problem. They look into the future and see a long trajectory. Unlike their elders, they are filled with the spell of potential.

The defensive, aging Warriors who refuse to get out of the way can be particularly upsetting to the rebellious or ambitious young. Rather than retire to their gardens, they insist on remaining in control long after their expertise is viewed as relevant. In the process, they deprive the restless young of their turn at the helm.

In *The Five Ages of Man*, philosopher Gerald Heard explains what happens: "The damage that, today, the rebellious young can do to the community is great. It is smaller, though, than that harm that can and must be wrought by the growing mass of a new class of elders who have a greater sense of political power and a deeper selfishness because they have a more profound, far better founded hopelessness and fear toward a tomorrow that holds for them no promise, only negation."[23]

If the young had their way, they would treat older folks like the Struldbrugs in Jonathan Swift's *Gulliver's Travels*. Struldbrugs appear normal but are immortal. Unfortunately, while they never die, they do age. As they age, they fall into despair, and become argumentative and unpleasant. As they approach eighty, they are consumed with avarice and the unremitting desire to possess and control everything and everyone. They cannot be allowed to prevail. Because they can't see or hear and suffer from dementia, they are not fit to lead. If they were allowed to fill positions of leadership, the whole society would collapse. To avoid this from happening, when they reach the age of eighty, Struldbrugs are declared dead under the law. They cannot own or rent property. A small amount is put aside to cover their care in a shabby public facility (read nursing home). The rest of their fortune is given to their heirs.

Safety vs. Autonomy.

Gulliver's Travels was written in 1776. Even then older people had a fear of the "public facilities" designed to accommodate the aging. In those days, the facilities were usually poor houses. Nursing homes came later and were developed in response to the hospital's need to find a more efficient way to look after the long-term sick. Nursing homes were built on the same model as hospitals. Safety was promoted over independence, and predictability over autonomy. In short, their goal was to take care of the elderly rather than enabling the elderly to continue making their own decisions.

In his insightful book, *Being Mortal*, Dr. Atul Gawande makes it very clear that the medical model that drives nursing homes and most assisted living facilities is detrimental to the quality of life of its residents. He quotes the sociologist Erving Goffman who, fifty years ago, drew an analogy between prisons and nursing homes. According to Goffman, both

---

[23] Gerald Heard, *The Five Ages of Man*. (New York: The Julian Press, Inc., 1963), 154.

are "total institutions"—places largely cut off from wider society.

"A basic social arrangement in modern society is that we tend to sleep, play and work in different places, in each case with a different set of co-participants, under a different authority, and without an overall rational plan. The central feature of total institutions can be described as a breakdown of the kinds of barriers ordinarily separating these three spheres of life. First, all aspects of life are conducted in the same place and under the same single authority. Second, each phase of the member's daily activity will be carried out in the immediate company of a large batch of others, all of whom are treated alike and required to do the same thing together. Third, all phases of the day's activities are tightly scheduled, with one activity leading at a prearranged time into the next, the whole circle of activities being imposed from above through a system of explicit formal rulings and a body of officials. Finally, the contents of the various enforced activities are brought together as parts of a single overall rational plan purportedly designed to fulfill the official aims of the institution."[24]

As Dr. Gawande explains, in spite of the fact that the official aim of the nursing home is "caring," residents feel more like prisoners or patients than people who are being "cared for." He talks about Alice, once a spirited, independent, elderly lady who had to move into a nursing home after a series of falls. "All privacy and control were gone. She was put in hospital clothes most of the time. She woke when they told her, bathed and dressed when they told her, ate when they told her. She lived with whomever they said she had to. There was a succession of roommates, never chosen with her input and all with cognitive impairments. Some were quiet. One kept her up at night. She felt incarcerated, like she was in prison for being old."[25]

Alice rebelled using the only strategy at her disposal—she stopped cooperating. She refused to eat, or to participate in activities, even those she once would have loved. Her caregivers responded to the "feisty" resident by further reducing her autonomy. Unable to continue writing

[24]Erving Goffman, *Asylums: Essays on the Social Situation of Mental Patients and Other Inmates.* (Anchor Books, 1961)

[25]Dr. Atul Gawande, *Being Mortal: Medicine and What Matters in the End.* (New York, Henry Holt and Company, 2015), 73.

her own story, Alice began to believe she had no place in this world. She died a despairing Castaway, her feistiness and other Warrior-like tendencies gone. The nursing home had managed to eliminate any sense of personal empowerment that Alice had before her "incarceration."

Dr. Gawande concludes that most older people do not behave like empowered and angry old folks who refuse to give up the helm. They do not behave like Strulbergs. They have no sense of political power, or power of any kind. What they do have is an increasing sense of hopelessness as the power to make their own decisions is denied them. "As people become aware of the finitude of their life, they do not ask for much. They do not seek more riches. They do not seek more power. They ask only to be permitted, insofar as possible, to keep shaping the story of their life in the world—to make choices and sustain connections to others according to their own priorities. In modern society, we have come to assume that debility and dependence rule out such autonomy."[26]

Why do seniors allow themselves to be put in this position? Many make the mistake of relying on their children to make life-changing decisions for them. Apparently, this has become the norm. Nursing homes and assisted living facilities now market more to the needs of the grown children than they do to the needs of the elderly who will become their residents. They make the children feel good about the brightly lit lobby, and the entertainment center. They tout the family dining room as a place where visiting relatives can share a meal with their old folks.

I fell for their ploy. When it came to looking for a nursing home for Mom, I scarcely even noticed that the beautiful lobby was empty of residents, the entertainment center was quiet, and no one was in the family dining room even though it was the noon hour. When my guide showed me the rooms, she took me first to a large, well-furnished space with glass doors that led to a small patio. In a darkened corner sat a very old woman with long white hair. She stared at me, but it was a blank stare. I don't think she was even aware that we had invaded her space. It felt as though no one was home in that body.

We hadn't even left the room when the guide said, "We have no more rooms with outside access available, but one should become available

---

[26]Dr. Atul Gawande, *Being Mortal: Medicine and What Matters in the End.* (New York, Henry Holt and Company, 2015), 146.

soon." What she didn't say was that the majority of the rooms not only didn't have outdoor access, they didn't even have windows. Though well-lighted, roomy and new, they were all interior spaces. I agreed to look at the two interior rooms that were currently available.

As she showed me around, the guide focused on how "safe" the rooms were. The beds had bars that the staff could raise if, in their opinion, this was necessary to restrain or control the resident. The toilet seats were painted black to make them more visible and distinguishable from the white rim below. There were no rugs on the floor, and no other falling hazards. There weren't even thresholds at the doorway that might trip an unwitting resident who decided to leave the safety of his or her room to explore the public areas.

I'll tell you more about the episode of the dreaded nursing home in the next chapter. Suffice it to say, I bought their sales pitch, and signed a contract to secure the room. In doing so, I was responding more to my own need to find a "safe" place for Mom, a place that made me comfortable; a place that eased my anxieties, not hers. In looking at the situation through my own lens instead of hers, I was not unique. My own daughter, Monica, is now doing the same thing as she tries to influence where I will lay down my head when I am frail.

For a while David and I contemplated giving up our home in the Pacific Northwest and moving to Florida where we would be on the same coast as Melissa and in the same state as Monica. After a lengthy visit, we changed our minds. Monica was particularly upset. She called me one morning and said, 'Mom, I want you to rethink this. It would be so much better for me if you were closer. I mean, I want to spend more time with you and all but, on top of that, you're being so far away as you get older makes me really anxious. I don't like feeling that way."

I know that Monica loves me, and wants the best for me. Regardless, she cannot get into my shoes and see life as I see it. She is middle-aged. I am old. She's a Celebrant who thinks about the future and is still under the spell of life's potential. I am alternatively a Castaway and a Warrior who focuses on overcoming the great adversary known as Age. She wants to be autonomous, and yet she would prefer that I be "safe." She can't understand that for my life to be meaningful, I have to write my own story as I want it to be told. I have to be able to take chances, to take risks, to live life the way I want even if that means I don't live as long.

Monica hasn't mentioned the move or her anxieties again. I am sure she is still worried, but we avoid that in our conversations. Similarly, I avoid talking about my concerns regarding the future. As my heart and lung problems progress, I will become more dependent on others to help me through my days. When that happens, unless David continues to be strong and healthy, living high up on a mountain on a secluded road will probably not be feasible. It will be out of the question if he also succumbs to old age and needs help himself.

Not a pretty picture. So what do we do? For as long as we can, we avoid thinking about it. We don't bring it up. When Monica asks me how I'm doing, I say, "Great. I feel great," whether it's true or not.

Double Blind.

When the challenges of aging become severe, the rules of engagement between parents and their children blur. Confusion sets in as the roles shift. Children are accustomed to perceiving their parents as sources of strength and support. They are used to being the dependent ones in the relationship. It's devastating when age or illness takes its inevitable toll and turns the strong parent into a fragile creature who needs care. The feeling of loss is immeasurable.

The young grieve both for their aging parents and for themselves. Grief, in turn, manifests as guilt or anger and confounds the relationship. Often, the caregiver's emotional dilemma is, "I resent you because you need me, and I feel guilty because I resent you."

The parent, too, is caught in an emotional maelstrom. "I need you, but I don't want to need you. Therefore, I am angry at you."

Hoping to avoid these feelings, the old and the young collaborate in a double blind. Older folds go through a period of false independence reminiscent of the way we behaved as toddlers. We tough it out, pretending that everything is just fine and we don't need or even want any help. Rejecting the notion of helplessness, we cling to the belief that we are masters of our own destiny and will forever remain so.

Our children often encourage our pretense or our illusions because they don't want to be responsible for us any more than we want them to assume control over our lives. Their need to deny is intensified by their desire to believe in perpetual youth. They don't want to get old themselves, and they don't want us too, either. It's easier to pretend it's not happening, or to minimize how difficult it will be when it does happen.

Double blind appears to be the norm. In her touching book, *A Bittersweet Season*, Jane Gross writes, "My mother wasn't going to burden me or my brother by explaining any of this, ask our assistance, or even welcome it if we offered it unsolicited. All of these were problems she preferred to solve on her own. But how could I not have seen that this independence was really stoicism in the face of considerable pain? Why didn't I pay more attention to her suffering, notice what was going on sooner?"[27]

Part of the reason she didn't notice it sooner is that medicine and technology have combined to alter the pace at which the body ages. There used to be a period of relative health followed by a sharp downward trajectory when illness invaded or an organ failed. Now, new medicines, pacemakers and the like have changed the rate of decline.

Dr. Gawande explains, "The road can have vertiginous drops but also long patches of recovered ground…increasingly large numbers of us get to live out a full life span and die of old age. Old age is not a diagnosis…But in truth no single disease leads to the end; the culprit is just the accumulated crumbling of one's bodily systems while medicine carries out its maintenance measures and patch jobs. We reduce the blood pressure here, beat back the osteoporosis there, control this disease, treat that one, replace a failed joint, valve, piston, watch the central processing unit gradually give out. The curve of life becomes a long, slow fade."[28]

The long, slow fade makes it easier for the child to remain blind to what is happening and for the parent to continue pretending. Ultimately, however, the day does come when the disease has progressed to a point where it can't be denied, or a failed organ can't be repaired, or a damaged joint can't be replaced. When that happens, the parent has no choice but to seek help, or the child suddenly realizes "things" are not the same as they have always been. At that point, there must be a change in the

---

[27] Jane Gross, *A Bittersweet Season: Caring for Our Aging Parents - and Ourselves*. (New York, Alfred A. Knopf, 2011), 16-17.

[28] Dr. Atul Gawande, *Being Mortal: Medicine and What Matters in the End*. (New York, Henry Holt and Company, 2015), 27.

---

relationship.

On Facebook, I found the following sentimental entreaty written by an unknown author. A lot of people had pushed the "like" button, and the "share" button. These are the passages that resonated the most with me.

My dear girl, the day you see I'm getting old, I ask you to please be patient, but most of all, try to understand what I'm going through.

If when we talk, I repeat the same thing a thousand times, don't interrupt to say, 'You said the same thing a minute ago'... Just listen, please. Try to remember the times when you were little and I would read the same story night after night until you would fall asleep.

When I don't want to take a bath, don't be mad and don't embarrass me. Remember when I had to run after you making excuses and trying to get you to take a shower when you were just a girl?

If I occasionally lose track of what we're talking about, give me the time to remember, and if I can't, don't be nervous, impatient or arrogant. Just know in your heart that the most important thing for me is to be with you.

And when my old, tired legs don't let me move as quickly as before, give me your hand the same way that I offered mine to you when you first walked.

These are beautiful sentiments, but almost impossible for either the daughter or the mother to implement, especially over the long haul. The mother will get crusty and excessively demanding if she's in her Warrior mindset, or whiny, frightened, and terribly needy if she's in a Castaway frame of mind. The daughter, meanwhile, has a lot on her Celebrant plate—a job, a house to maintain, maybe children of her own to care for. She doesn't have the time nor the desire to patiently listen to the rantings or complaints of her aging mother. She can't deal with the seemingly endless demands. If she fails to do so, however, she feels guilty. If she forces herself, she feels resentful. Neither is in the spirit of the author's sentimental appeal.

I'm guessing these words were written by a mother who has just begun to notice the signs of aging, but has not yet lost her grip or her mobility, or at least has not lost the power to pretend. And, I'm imagining the daughters who read these words were envisioning some time in the future when they, indeed, would behave in just that perfect way.

Borrowing a line from My Fair Lady, "Oh, wouldn't it be loverly" if it could be so. It generally cannot, especially when dementia is part of the equation as it is in the case of five million Americans, or half of those over the age of eighty-five. When that happens, the aging parent becomes as dependent and as difficult to handle as a petulant child.

Gratitude Deficit Disorder.

As Dave Shiflet says in his *Wall Street Journal* article about living with his dying father, "Dementia is a terrible disease that robs its victims of their memories, their good nature and much of their dignity. Children of suffering parents will see many things they wish they hadn't, and they may learn things about themselves that aren't always flattering."[29]

He describes the year his father lived with him and his wife in brutally honest terms. "One morning I heard Dad crying from the upstairs bathroom. There is no pleasant way to describe what I discovered. He was standing in his own excrement, which was scattered widely about. Cleaning up was no picnic, especially when attending to his soiled body, which puts one in frightfully close contact with the apparatus instrumental to your existence."[30]

He talks about "Gratitude Deficit Disorder" and wonders whether he suffered from it during those times when his stiff upper lip concealed grinding teeth. Nonetheless, he concludes by saying that taking his father into his house not only brought he and his wife more life, but actually made them better people. "As Dad's flame flickered, ours burned brighter. As his life faded, it brought our lives closer together. The challenge of caring for him also made us stronger."[31]

My friend, whom I'll call Charity because of her generous nature, would say the same thing. She took her ninety-year-old mother into her home after she was diagnosed with dementia. The Queen Mother, so called because of her narcissistic nature and need to control, initiated the

[29]Dave Shiflett, "Life Lessons from Dad: Caring for an Elderly Parent," *The Wall Street Journal*, June 27, 2014.

[30] Ibid.

[31] ibid.

move. She asked Charity and her husband, Brett, if she could live with them. In exchange, she offered to contribute a substantial amount of money to the household as well as her expensive collection of art and custom-designed furniture. Charity and her husband agreed. They moved the Queen Mother into a suite of rooms in their home.

Together they bought a piece of land on Long Island Sound, hired an architect and began designing a new home in which all three would live. The project excited all of them, and helped alleviate the tension created by the mother's endless demands for attention. They were even able to laugh at the nicks in the molding and the scuffs on the floor that her power chair made as she navigated across the house between her suite and the family room.

Once they moved into the new home, the tension began to mount. The nicks and scuffs were no longer the source of amusement. If Charity didn't find ways to continually entertain her mother, she would get sullen, making Charity feel guilty. When Charity and Brett were invited to the home of friends, the Queen Mother made it clear she expected to be invited as well. Charity tried to make that happen. The invitations became less frequent.

Charity stopped painting, gardening and having lunch with friends. The more Charity gave, the more the Queen Mother demanded, until Charity's own life was completely on hold. She couldn't put Brett on hold, however. Her marriage needed and deserved attention. In an attempt to create time for them as a couple, Charity hired caregivers to stay with her mother one night a week when she and Brett had their "date night." The Queen Mother managed to abort those plans several times by treating the caregivers like worthless servants. One after another announced they would not take the mother's abuse, and refused to come back.

Provoked by Brett, Charity finally reached her limit. She told her mother that she had to either change her behavior or they would put her in a nursing home. Apparently the mother believed her. The negative comments ceased. In their stead, silence reigned. Weeks passed. The daughter relaxed a little, and so did the mother.

The Queen Mother died peacefully in her room in Charity's home eight years after she moved in. Those were eight long, difficult years, rendered only slightly easier by the fact that there was enough money to hire a steady stream of people to dress her, undress her and deal with her messes.

I imagine the Queen Mother felt that her financial contributions gave her the right to be demanding. I don't believe Charity or Brett ever shared her point of view. They didn't really need the mother's money; they were quite comfortable without it. It was not money but rather generosity and compassion that made Brett and Charity tolerate those eight years.

Stories like these don't always have a happy ending. Sometimes elders give up their assets at their peril. Think about Shakespeare's *King Lear*. Lear decided to dispose of his estate while he was still alive. He assumed that the recipients of his wealth would be grateful and, therefore, eager to care for him until he died. He fell for the excessive flattery of his two least generous daughters, ignoring his youngest daughter's quieter but genuine statement of affection. He gave all of his assets to the two daughters who played most effectively to his aging ego.

As soon as they got their hands on his assets, both daughters began to neglect him, and to treat him with gross disrespect. He was deprived of his guards, and then of his servants. He was denied all of his indulgences, and stripped of his dignity. He had put himself at their mercy, only to learn that they were merciless. He became enraged, but could do nothing about it. As fury and impotence took its toll on the old king, the family disintegrated. Bloody feuds erupted between the daughters and between the daughters' husbands. In the end, they all died, alone and embittered.

In our society, there are aren't many like Charity and Brett who have the resources (time, space, money) coupled with the spirit of generosity and compassion. Similarly, the totally ungrateful children such as were portrayed in *King Lear* are the exception. The majority are middle-class families who want to do the right thing by their aging parents, but find their demands too taxing from a financial, emotional, and even familial point of view. They don't want to do it, and their elders typically don't want them to.

I know I would hate it if my daughters had to clean up my excrement when I failed to make it to the toilet. If I get to that point, and haven't had the courage to kill myself, then I would prefer that a professional paid caregiver do the dirty work. Somehow, that is more dignified. I imagine my daughters agree. I suspect you and your children also agree. At least the statistics would suggest that is true.

Whereas in early twentieth-century America, sixty percent of those over age sixty-five resided with a child, by the 1960s the proportion had dropped to twenty-five percent. By 1975, it was below fifteen percent. The pattern is true worldwide. Just ten percent of Europeans over age eighty live with their children, and almost half live completely alone, without a spouse. Clearly, the days of Confucius are over.

Confucius be Damned.

Even in the Far East, the Confucian belief that the elderly have earned the right to sit at the center of the family, to be respected above all others, and to be cared for—physically, emotionally and spiritually—has died. Recognition of the fragility of the Confucian ethos in the face of a "me ethos" may help explain why Beijing saw the need in 2012 to amend its laws on the protection of the elderly. Those laws had already criminalized nonsupport of one's elderly parents. Under the new law, elderly parents could sue their children for spending insufficient time with them.

Laws like these are unlikely to give the Chinese elderly much of a reprieve. On the contrary, the younger Chinese are likely to resent both the State and their parents for forcing them to pay the kind of homage they do not want to pay. It's probably better to be an aging parent in the West where Confucian values and traditions have never applied. At least the State won't get involved in what can become a very difficult family negotiation.

The marked shift away from the western family taking care of its elders occurred partly as a result of job mobility, increased longevity, and changes in property ownership. As the youth began moving away from home seeking better opportunities, the elderly began to live so long that they could no longer support the family homestead, either physically or financially. They sold or reversed-mortgaged the "family farm," in order to sustain themselves. The child who stayed at home to care for them no longer could expect to inherit the homestead when they died. As a result, fewer chose to make the sacrifice. Those who did struggled to take control. As Dr. Gawande explains in Being Mortal, "For young people, the traditional family system became less a source of security than a struggle for control—over property, finances, and even the most basic decisions about how they could live."[32]

I know all of this was true in my case. My mother had no "family homestead." Nor did she have a lot of money. What she did have was an aging body and the first signs of being unable to live alone. It all began in December 2002 when Mom was almost eighty-four. David and I had sold our apartment in New York, and put our things in storage, intent on exploring the world before settling down again. We planned to base in Perth, Western Australia and travel from there to Asia. We rented a funky three-story apartment in what used to be a train-switching station in Fremantle. It was one hundred yards from the beach, five minutes from my brother Clyde's place, and ten minutes from Mom's duplex.

The visit did not turn out the way we had planned. The SARS epidemic hit, making it unwise for anyone with compromised lungs to travel to Asia. The start of the war in Iraq and riots in countries protesting the war made travel less attractive. Then, in the early spring of 2003, Mom suffered a transient ischemic attack (TIA), a kind of mini stroke. She lost consciousness and crashed into an immense metal trash bin, barely missing a young mother with a toddler in hand and baby in a stroller.

Mom's driving days were over. For weeks, she grieved her loss of independence. Hoping to make her feel better, I put myself at her disposal and offered to become her driver. She didn't hesitate to take me up on my offer. She summoned me just about every day, leaving me very little quality time with David. That did not please him.

The one thing we did continue to do together was our morning bike ride along the coast. One of our routes took us past magnificent homes that sat high above the Indian Ocean. Because the U.S. dollar was strong, it would have been possible to buy an oceanfront home for a fraction of what a similar property would have cost in the United States. I began toying with the idea of buying a house and inviting Mom to live with us. Clyde vigorously supported the idea. David was less enthusiastic. Ignoring his disinclination, I called a realtor and arranged to look at properties. David reluctantly came along, but managed to find something wrong with each one.

One Saturday night, we got into a huge argument. David felt trapped

---

[32]Dr. Atul Gawande, *Being Mortal: Medicine and What Matters in the End.* (New York, Henry Holt and Company, 2015), 19.

by Australia, by my family, by Mom and by me. He raged and I raged back. I ended up sleeping in the guest room. When I got up the next morning, David was gone. So was his bike. I fretted and drank coffee for two hours before the phone rang. It was David. "Okay. I give up. If you want to buy a house in Australia and move your mother in with us, I am willing to do it. Let's just stop fighting. We'll do whatever you feel you have to do."

That call rendered me speechless. It was so loving, and so giving that I had no response. I realized how much energy I had been putting into resisting David. That had been my focus. I hadn't really asked myself if I could build a life in Australia. I got out my own bike, and rode down the coast twenty-three kilometers past public beaches, through the middle of a trailer park, and out onto Pelican Point, so named because it was a favorite meeting ground for those strange looking, aggressive birds.

I locked up my bike and sat for a long time on a boulder looking out at the ocean. I tried to visualize living in one of the fine oceanfront houses with David and Mom. I imagined her friends coming over to play bridge and having to interrupt my writing to make their tea sandwiches. I visualized the dinner hour. David and I couldn't talk when Mom was around. She had a way of colonizing the conversation. That's not because she was such a big talker, but because she managed to shift the focus of every conversation to herself.

My mother was a solipsist. She behaved as though she was the center of the universe. That stemmed not from a sense of superiority but from complete self-absorption. She was held captive by her own incessant preoccupation with how she was regarded by others. She was not able to put her focus on self at bay long enough to tune into the wants and feelings of those around her. It's not that she didn't want to do so. On the contrary, being liked was extremely important to her, as was being viewed a "nice" person. She simply couldn't get out of her own way. That made her difficult to live with.

Worse, she made me difficult to live with. David didn't like who I became or the way I behaved when I spent too much time with my mother. He often told me that when I got around her, I totally ignored him. "You get toxic," he said. "I love you, and I love your mother, but I don't like what happens when you are around her."

I knew what he meant, but I felt powerless to change. I could not deny the woman who presented herself like a child who deserves to be loved and protected. Sitting on that boulder, I realized that if I forced us to remain in Australia and to take Mom into our home, our marriage would effectively be over. Even if we stayed together, the spirit that inspired our sense of togetherness would have been squashed. I also realized that if I remained, I would never write the books I hoped to create. I hadn't composed a decent page since arriving in Australia. The culture which discouraged an open and frank discussion of bleak or depressing subjects made my brain feel like mush—not a state conducive to good writing. Finally, to remain in Australia was to put half a world between me and my daughters and their families. That was a sacrifice I could not make.

My story is unusual only in the geography involved. It is not the least bit unusual in terms of the thought process. I decided not to provide a home for my mother because of my wants. This is becoming more widespread. In an intriguing article about the global flight away from family responsibilities, Nicholas Eberstadt writes, "All around the world today, pre-existing family patterns are being upended by a revolutionary new force: the seemingly unstoppable quest for convenience by adults demanding ever-greater autonomy."[33]

That autonomy translates into not taking on an aging parent, and into having fewer children. The children that parents do have, however, frequently become the center of the family's existence, at least in western societies. It is not the oldest member of the family who is at the center, but rather the youngest. Everything and everyone takes a back seat to making sure that every waking moment of a child's life is rich, productive and, above all, safe. The needs of an aging parent, a reluctant spouse, a good friend, and even oneself are put in abeyance for the sake of the child.

Today, parents "hover" over their children, seeking to influence and to oversee everything they do. I have a friend who, until recently, ran a large distribution company. She told me that the parents of some of her employees had requested that they be invited to the performance review of their forever-child. Colleges are having to make room for increasing parental intrusion into what was once a dividing line between childhood and adulthood. The child-centric phase of a family's life has now extended

---

[33]Nicholas Eberstadt, "The Global Flight From the Family," *The Wall Street Journal*, Feb 21, 2015.

into early adulthood, leaving the parents of those children with little left to give their aging parents.

Sometimes the elderly resist, attempting to claim their due and exact their rights. This rarely works out very well. In the last months of his life, David's uncle Emil became furious when Esther, his wife of fifty years, was hospitalized with pernicious anemia. He couldn't forgive her for getting sick. He demonstrated his fury by taking away her wedding rings and then refusing to visit her. Her pleas that he return her rings were met with a stony silence.

Her death represented the ultimate betrayal. Flailing around, Emil called David, Esther's nephew, and insisted that he turn his back on me, and our business, and move to the Midwest to take care of him. When David refused, Emil decided to punish him. Wanting to deprive David and his brother of their small inheritance and to leave it instead to his own nieces and nephews, he buried the will in a pile of *National Geographic* magazines he and Esther had accumulated over a period of many years. He then instructed the caretaker of the property to burn the magazines in the event of his death.

A few weeks later, Emil took an overdose of sleeping pills and died. When David learned that he and his brother were to be cut out of the distribution of the proceeds of the small estate, he hired an attorney and got on a plane. He was still in the air when the caretaker began burning the magazines. He had burned about half of them and was throwing another pile onto the fire when a sheaf of paper fell out and landed at this feet. It was the original will.

Esther's wishes regarding the disposition of her share of their assets prevailed. That would have been very important to her. She had long regarded David and his brother like her own children. She had helped raise them when their mother, her sister, died when they were very young. When Esther died, photographs of David and his brother as young children still hung over her bed.

Emil's last act was to punish his wife's favorite nephews because they ignored his impossible request that they suspend their own lives in order to take care of him. A Warrior at the extreme end of the pole, he regarded their refusal as a rejection of his worth as a person. The same thing can happen when the aging Warrior does end up living with a child. The trouble begins when he or she starts to resent the grown child who is now calling the shots.

The Sad Story of Dr. No.

I have a friend I'll call Dr. No. who recently celebrated his eightieth birthday. In his prime, Dr. No had been a very influential psychologist and successful entrepreneur. He and I worked together for several years. Our collaboration led to a friendship that spanned more than a decade. Then a series of moves, job changes and new marriages intervened and we lost touch. Ten years passed during which time we did not communicate.

A few months ago, I found him on Facebook. We began emailing. He said he and his wife were living in the Midwest with her daughter and family. The last line of the email read: "Nobody wants to listen to an Old Phart." I sensed that he was waging war on his environment and the people in it, and that he was losing.

A few months later, he and his daughter-in-law got into a final battle. He provoked her and she shoved him so hard that he fell to the ground. He filed charges. She was arrested and he ended up living without his wife in a Veteran's Administration home—an unhappy outcome for an unbridled Warrior who refused to go gently into the good, good night. We communicated once after he moved into the VA facility. My other messages went unanswered.

Did that arrangement have to end so badly? Perhaps it did. It had all the provocations and none of the mitigators that can defuse or deflect the War of the Ages. Lack of money and space intensified the tension between someone who had once been important and those family members who were aspiring to be important. Because the daughter was Dr. No's wife's by a previous marriage, there was no sense of family history, or ties born of shared ancestry and long-established traditions to hold it together.

The War of the Ages.

The War of the Ages is real. It's fueled by tensions over pace, tempo, money, responsibility, focus, and, underneath it all, the differing mindsets toward mortality and the tendency of old people to get stuck at the negative pole. It's provoked by the desire on the part of the young and middle-aged to take the helm, and reluctance on the part of the old to give it up. It's intensified by youth's quest for unrestricted autonomy at a time when the old are living longer and, therefore, becoming increasingly dependent. It's exacerbated by the essential conflict between keeping the elderly "safe" and leaving them free to continue to write their own life stories.

Is there a solution? I suggest that rather than rant and rage or wallow in self-pity because we have been ignored, we content ourselves with watching our children and grandchildren evolve and then retreat to our own space where we can keep our own counsel. This was beautifully stated in a message that is beginning to make its way around the world. It's entitled *When We are Old, Who Do We Depend On? Ourselves, Ourselves, Only Ourselves.* It came to my attention through a very savvy ninety-year-old woman.

The writer talks about four stages of aging, and cautions that regardless of our stage, it's essential to:

"Have your own abode.
No matter what, do not lose it, until your death!
If you have an old companion,
Keep each other good company."

The segments from the stages themselves that had the biggest impact on me were these:

1ˢᵗ Stage:
Just after retirement, between 60 to 70 yrs old,
Our health will still be comparatively good
So too our financial means.
Do not be hard on yourself
Our days are numbered
So, grasp the opportunity.
If the kids are well off, It is their business...
If the kids are filial, They have good traits....
We need neither decline financial help from our kids.

The War of the Ages

Nor decline their respect.
But we should remain independent &
Live our own life well.

2nd Stage:
If no mishap and illness strike after we are 70,
We will still be able to take care of ourselves.
Not a major problem.
However, we must realize we are really getting old.
Gradually, our body and mind will give way.
Our reflex will slow down with time...
We can no longer put on a front, we have to look after ourselves!
Do not meddle anymore with this and that, or control the kids!
We have intervened our entire life, It is time for us to be a little selfish.....
Take hold of ourselves. Life must come full circle.

3rd Stage:
Our health begins to fail ....
We have to request help from others ....
We have to be mentally prepared for it.
The majority of us cannot escape this hurdle.
We have to prepare ourselves, emotionally, to accept that:-
Be prepared for it in advance and we will not be too depressed.
The idea is not to add to the kids' burden, emotionally, increase their
chores & their financial commitments.
Try our best to overcome -
What hardship has our generation not endured?
What disasters have we not experienced?
Trust us to take life's last lap in our stride.

4th Stage:
When our quality of life has deteriorated drastically...
We must be courageous enough to face death!
Insist that the family not try to prolong our life ....
Do not incur unnecessary expenditure ....

WHEN WE ARE OLD, WHOM DO WE DEPEND ON?
Ourselves, ourselves, ONLY ourselves.
Amen!

Ourselves, Ourselves, Only Ourselves.

Sometimes David and I talk about what each of us would do if the other were to die. I really don't know what I would do. Would I want to live with either of my daughters? If I lived with Monica, I would have to get up very early to attend her sunrise yoga sessions on the beach. I'd have to embrace her health food crazes. The televised sounds of football, basketball and lacrosse games would permeate the house. It would be hard for me to find a quiet place to write.

Would living with Melissa work any better? I close my eyes and imagine living with her, her husband Ted and my two young grandsons. In Melissa's home, there are clear rules of engagement, most of which she establishes and enforces. In other words, she runs a very tight ship. Even though she has two rambunctious young boys, her house is tidy. There are never dirty dishes in the sink, and the kitchen counters always look like the housecleaner just left. Her closets are organized. Even the laundry room is bin sorted. While I admire that, I cannot emulate it. My lack of order would probably drive her crazy. She'd try to restrain herself but ultimately she'd flip out and yell at me. She has a very sharp tongue when she gets angry. Afterward, I'd feel hurt and she'd feel awful.

The only way I could live with either of my daughters is if it she had a "granny flat" at the far end of the property so that I could live with her in name only. I need my own space. I need to be free to establish and maintain my own routines in response to my own interests and abilities. Above all, I need to be the one to decide how to spend my time.

I want to be welcome in my daughters' homes as a visitor, and I want them to look forward to visiting me in my home. I do not want them to have to deal with me and my agendas hour after hour, day after day. Nor do I want to constantly deal with theirs. In maintaining separate lives, we increase the likelihood that the love and mutual respect that binds us will grow with time, and not wither under the stress of excessive familiarity or the clash of different mindsets.

In wanting to maintain my own space, I am like most other seniors. Dr. Gawande reminds us, "Given the opportunity, both parents and children saw separation as a form of freedom. Whenever the elderly have had the financial means, they have chosen what social scientists have called "intimacy at a distance." [34]

Fortunately, it's possible these days to live separately even when you're sick or disabled. As Paula Spam points out in *When the Time Comes*, "In theory, almost everyone could stay at home. Short of surgery, virtually any form of healthcare can be delivered in a private home. Companies have sprung up to modify homes for safety and accessibility; they install grab bars and tilt risers, ramps and stair lifts … Since capitalism abhors a vacuum, the growth of a more affluent group of seniors, and other disabled people determined to remain independent, has fostered a raft of new businesses. Is your parent doing pretty well at home, except that she can't handle the bill paying any longer? Or drive to the supermarket? Or manage small chores like changing lightbulbs? You can hire firms...to do all these things."[35]

As a result of these services and advances in healthcare, as of 2009 when Paula Spam published her book, nearly a third of the elderly, and half of women over the age of seventy-five lived alone. For those who still had community ties, and were mobile enough and healthy enough to stay connected, this was good news. It was also good news for those less robust seniors who preferred to remain at home even if that meant living in one room of an eight-room house, and never going upstairs.

---

[34]Dr. Atul Gawande, *Being Mortal: Medicine and What Matters in the End.* (New York, Henry Holt and Company, 2015), 21.

[35]Paula Spam, *When the Time Comes.* (New York, Springboard Press, 2009), llc 696.

Thomas the Chaplain, so called because of his ministerial aura, had a father named Nathan who until recently lived in a small town in Wisconsin in the same two-story house in which he and his wife raised Thomas and his four sisters. The house represented stability to Nathan. He resisted changing anything about it. He even kept his dead wife's things in the bedroom just as she had left them thirty years earlier. Nathan was very close to his five children. Until a year before his death, he spent several weeks each year visiting each of their homes. He was always happy to see them, but even happier to return home again.

Two years ago, Nathan was forced to spend several months in a rehabilitation center after he fractured his hip. He slipped into a quiet depression because he missed his home. The attention of caring nurses and the company of other seniors who were drawn to the old man with the ready smile and twinkling eyes couldn't compensate for not being in his own place.

Even though Nathan's mobility was so limited that he could no longer climb the stairs to his bedroom or the only bathroom in the house, he chose to return home. He lived in the living room. A portable toilet and daily sponge baths provided by hired caregivers sufficed to maintain his personal hygiene. Once a week, a service for the elderly picked him up and took him to a spa where he had a whirlpool bath. Every Wednesday, one of his daughters came to visit. She stayed overnight and cooked up a storm, leaving his refrigerator filled with his favorite dinners.

Content to be home, Nathan healed faster than anyone imagined possible. He even got to the point where he could climb the stairs on his own, with supervision. In the evening, he would sit by the window enjoying a single martini as he observed the comings and goings of neighbors, all of whom held him in special regard given his long tenure on the block. He then heated up one of dinners, and watched sports on television, unless of course it was the special night of the week when one of his daughters came to visit.

Nathan lived to celebrate his hundredth birthday. Family members flew in from London, New York, and Florida. Our good friend, Thomas the Chaplain flew in from the Pacific Northwest. Nathan was elated and able to take in all of the festivities in spite of a small stroke that had occurred weeks before. A week after the birthday celebration, as Thomas had predicted, Nathan looked fondly at the few family members who lived nearby and had come to see him, smiled, and died. Thomas described it to me as "an incredibly beautiful death."

Thomas returned to Wisconsin to take part in a memorial service. Like so many other families who come together after the last parent dies to grieve, to mourn, and to figure out what happens next, they found that disagreements and petty squabbles threatened to intrude upon the grieving process.

This appears to be inevitable as people in grief tend to go to the negative extremes of their mindset. They can then no longer understand or accept the values and priorities of their siblings who are demonstrating the extremes of a different mindset. Warriors hate the lethargy of the Castaway. The Castaway can't tolerate the efforts of the Celebrant to rescue the situation. The Warriors are fixated on regaining control of the uncontrollable, and have a hard time with the self-indulgence of the Stargazer. And so it goes when we are forced to move to the front of the line.

4: THE FRONT OF THE LINE: Ashes, Ashes, We All Fall Down

When we gather with our siblings to say our final goodbyes to our last living parent, we hope that in coming together we can make each other feel less naked and exposed. We want to mute the fear that comes from realizing we are now at the front of line, and that there is no longer a generation standing between death and us. Sadly, it is often not comfort but rather distress that we inflict on each other. This happens as sadness, stress and regrets push us to the extreme of our predominant mindset.

Stargazers don't like to be discomfited. By definition, death is a discomfiting situation. Some will try to avoid spending too much time in the presence of the dying. Their siblings can resent what they perceive as their failure to pull their own weight. It can be especially irritating when the Stargazer minimizes the seriousness of the situation. "Dad is not afraid. He believes in Heaven. He prays every night. We have to accept that he's going to a better place." Those who are not true believers and have witnessed Dad's palpable fear find these assurances hollow and annoying.

Determined to bring compassion to the gathering, Celebrants play the part of the big-hearted rescuer. They try to remove negative feelings from the room and replace them with "positive vibes." Some get so high on the drama inherent in the death scene that they become insensitive. Performance replaces authenticity as the theatrics become more important than the dying or the observers. Armed with unbridled optimism, they will often offer to do the impossible in order to make facing the end of life more tolerable. Their misplaced heroics create chaos.

The Front of the Line

When faced with a dying parent, a Warrior is prone to moving into hyper-efficiency mode as grief is shunted aside in the interest of a desperate attempt to retain control and keep fear at bay. They believe that, without their efforts, the family would descend into utter chaos. Unlike the Celebrant "rescuer" caught up in the drama, the Warrior tries to be the "fixer." Realism, not optimism, is his or her contribution.

That contribution is not welcomed by either Stargazers or Celebrants who prefer innocence and optimism to reality. When his or her siblings reject the attempt to fix things, the Warrior begins to feel under-appreciated, misunderstood, marginalized, and even paranoid. Raging against the Celebrant's tendency to create chaos and the Stargazer's self-indulgent attitude, they can tolerate only the Castaway and the Sage.

Accepting that death hovers nearby, and that the end is near, Castaways neither rage against death like the Warrior, nor attempt to make everyone feel loved and loving like the Celebrant. They grieve quietly. They observe. They tend to follow the lead of others. This works out fine as long as the others are not in conflict. If they are, they will attempt to pull the Castaway in different directions. Regardless, some functional Castaways are able to act as mediators or arbiters between their Warrior and Celebrant siblings. Listening to both sides, they consider the perspective of each before making a recommendation. Using humor, they deflect and diffuse the tension that inevitably accompanies the death of a parent.

Sages are quietly acceptant, recognizing that death cannot be defeated. They try to help their siblings understand that death is an inherent part of life, and should be neither feared nor regretted. They can lend a perspective that is at once calming and nurturing to their siblings, and even to the dying. They bring to bear the compassion of the Celebrant without the drama, and the realism of the Warrior without the compulsion to control and introduce order at a time of inherent disorder.

Let me tell you a story that illustrates what happens when siblings with different mindsets come together to bury the last parent. My mother, Rosemary, and her sister, my Aunt Jill, died within a week of one another. Rosemary died of a seizure in an emergency room in a hospital in Fremantle, Western Australia. Jill died of a stroke in the middle of the night in her small duplex in West Sacramento, California. When they died, my mother was eighty-seven; Jill was eighty-six. They were the last of their generation to die in my family.

I was close to both of them. Jill never married nor had children. When I was a child, she lavished attention on me. As she aged, I did the same for her. While my siblings sent her the occasional photograph and a gift at Christmas, I was primarily responsible for making sure she was all right.

My brother, Clyde, was the primary caregiver for our mother after my sister, Gay, left Australia. In the final years of my mother's life, Clyde was the only one of her four children who lived in that part of the world. The rest of us were scattered across the United States.

Given the vast distance, Clyde called and asked for our help only when it was critical. Early in September 2006, Mom was hospitalized after experiencing yet another transient ischemic attack. The attending cardiologist decided it was time to replace her aortic value. Because the surgery was very risky, and because Mom would need a lot of post-operative care, Clyde called his three sisters.

It took me a day to accept that I had no choice; I had to go to her bedside. It was a difficult decision. Daughter Melissa was pregnant with her first child, and expected to give birth within a month or so. She would need me on the East Coast of the United States, half a world away from Mom's hospital bed, to nurture her and help care for the baby. But there were others who could do those things for her. Mom's situation was different. Afterall, I was the family "fixer." Even Mom regarded me that way. "What would we do without you?" she said so often that my siblings began to resent it.

Joy also decided she needed to make the journey, in spite of the impact on her struggling Cape Cod architectural practice. As I learned later, she had an intuition that Mom could be nearing the end of her life.

Gay decided not to join us since only weeks before she had returned to the States after spending the entire summer in Australia. She was a professor of early childhood education, and the semester had just started.

Two days after Clyde's call, David drove me to Seattle to board the flight to Perth. Just before boarding, I called Aunt Jill to tell her what was happening. Minimizing the seriousness of Mom's medical prognosis, I said to her, "I am sure I will be back in plenty of time to come see you in October."

Death Watch.

We were still in the air when Mom fainted, falling to the floor of the hospital and triggering a Code Blue alarm. Her doctor concluded it was too risky to operate. When Clyde objected, he suggested we get a second opinion. The hospital agreed to let Mom stay until Clyde found another surgeon willing to review her case. Clyde managed to get an appointment with Dr. French, a world-renowned cardiac surgeon at one of Perth's finest private hospitals. (Although he was trained in the United States, he had a French name and spoke with a slight French accent). Not surprisingly, we had to wait to see him.

Mom remained in the hospital six days after Joy and I arrived. During that time, both of us stayed at her villa. Joy slept in Mom's bed and I stayed on the pullout couch in the adjoining room. Those were good days for us. We retrieved the bikes David and I had left in Clyde's shed after an earlier visit, and spent every morning cycling up the coast. We visited Mom together and then wandered through the markets, buying each other whimsical gifts and matching tee shirts. We took turns driving the white pick-up truck that my friends, Geoff and Jessie Fairfax, had lent me for the duration of my stay. We were both manifesting the mindset of the Celebrant.

Halfway through the week, we decided to look for an apartment. After all, we reasoned, the villa was small and Mom had always liked her privacy. True to our Celebrant selves, we allowed ourselves to believe that the second surgeon would operate and Mom would return home ready to resume her life. Since I was in better financial shape, I agreed to sign the lease and pay for the rental. We quickly discovered that we had few options. We settled on the only place that would rent to me for only a month or two.

It was a unique though rundown residence hotel less than a fifteen-minute walk from Mom's villa. It offered oversized, one-bedroom units with full kitchens and private balconies. Most of the renters were young families who lived and worked on farms and ranches in the interior. They made the journey to Perth once or twice a year to play in the ocean and barbecue amidst the tropical plantings that made the hotel look like it belonged somewhere in Latin America. We jokingly referred to it as "the Copacabana."

The manager and I struck a deal. I agreed to pay $2400 Australian dollars for a unit on the second floor for one month with an option to renew for a second month. Joy and I returned to the villa, packed our things, and moved into our new apartment. We allowed ourselves to believe we were about to embark on a shared adventure, at the end of which Mom would emerge healed.

The visit with the second surgeon changed all of that. It marked the end of Mom's hope for more life, crushed my Celebrant mindset, and pushed Joy to the extreme of hers. It was one of those mind-altering, life-changing meetings that sometimes happen when we see doctors.

From the beginning, Dr. French presented himself as a superior being. He was at the top of his game, and he knew it. Though he realized Mom was frail and had been taken directly from the hospital to his office, he kept us waiting for almost two hours. When we were finally ushered into his inner sanctum, we felt like petitioners facing an executioner.

Dr. French was standing when we entered. "Hello. I'm Dr. French," he said gesturing for me to park Mom's wheelchair beside his immaculate desk. "Please take a seat," he said pointing to three small chairs on the opposite side of his desk. Sitting down, he opened a skimpy manilla folder and scanned its contents. Then he looked at Mom. She had cocked her head in her ingenuous way and was smiling sweetly at this latest authority figure. She had already put complete trust in him, because that's what Stargazers do.

"I cannot give you longevity because, at eighty-seven, you already have that," he said, smiling at his own cleverness. "And I cannot replace just one valve. I would have to replace all three. You would have to be on a heart-lung machine for a long time—five hours or more. I can tell from the palor of your skin that you wouldn't survive the surgery. You are too weak. You are too frail. You have skin lesions that won't heal."

Dr. French was referring to a sore on her leg that, in fact, had begun to heal. The information in her file was out-of-date. I wanted to interrupt and correct him, but his style made me hesitate. He spoke like an actor on the stage. His delivery was eloquent, articulate and commanding. It certainly did not invite interruption, nor encourage dialogue.

"I could keep you alive on the table for five hours, or ten hours, or twelve hours. These days, it's possible to keep anyone alive in the operating room. But then you'd die in intensive care. Better that you go home and die there, with your family around you."

Mom's smile faded. She looked down at her lap and began playing with the fringe of the shawl we had draped over her black raincoat.

The doctor turned and looked at Clyde, Joy and me. After scanning our faces, his eyes settled on mine. Perhaps that's because I was clearly the eldest. Speaking as though our mother was not even in the room, the judge said, "The good news is she will not even know what happened. There will be no pain, and no suffering. She will faint and never wake up." And then he embarked on a long story about a woman with Mom's condition who had almost dropped dead just as she was about to board a plane in Queensland. "She was lucky that I was right behind her. I saved her life. I'm afraid I can't do the same in this case. Now, if you'll excuse me..."

Clyde and Joy stepped back. It was clear that I, as the eldest, was to have the honor of pushing Mom's wheelchair out of that office, down the corridor, into the elevator, across the cold, immaculate lobby and out of the hospital. No one said a word until we were driving home. Mom was the first to speak. She whimpered, "He wasn't very encouraging was he?"

When neither Clyde (who was driving) nor Joy answered, I said as calmly as I could, "No, he wasn't."

We never again mentioned that meeting to Mom. Instead, we focused on getting her released from the hospital and resettled in her own home. In the process, we met with an officious young Chinese nurse who said, "If she has a seizure, don't bring her back here. There is nothing we can do for her." We learned later that the nurse had no right to bar us from returning to the hospital. At the time, however, it made us feel isolated and abandoned in our deathwatch.

We felt a little less forsaken when we met with a social worker who described all the services available to families who were facing end-of-life care. She explained that Mom needed to have someone with her twenty-four hours a day because she would die if she tried to walk even five feet. She told us to rent a hospital bed and to borrow a toilet chair from the hospital. She said that someone would be coming by to teach us how to get Mom out of the bed and onto the toilet chair. She informed us that yet another official would pay a visit to make sure the villa was properly equipped and configured.

We moved into hyper mode. Within twenty-four hours, we had installed a hospital bed in Mom's room, moved her double bed into the guest room, and put the pullout couch in her bedroom so that visitors would have a place to sit. To enable us to wheel Mom into the shower, Clyde removed the bottom ledge and replaced the door with a curtain. Joy and I raced into town and bought several sets of bed sheets. An hour before we were due at the hospital, Joy moved her things out of the Copacabana and into Mom's tiny guest room. We had agreed to take turns, with one of us staying with Mom and the other sleeping in the apartment. Every few days, we would switch places.

The morning after Mom came home, Wendy, queen of the social workers, arrived to assess our needs for assistance. That meeting marked the beginning of the breakdown in communications between Joy and me. I found Wendy so intrusive I didn't want her help. Although I was unaware of it at the time, I had already moved to the extreme pole of the Warrior mindset. Mom's villa was the bunker, and I was on guard.

Joy, on the other hand, found Wendy empathetic and responsive. When Wendy hugged her as she was leaving, Joy embraced her as though they had been friends for years. She had moved to the extreme of the Celebrant mindset. Life was a rich drama and Wendy was an important part of the unfolding play.

For a while, we succeeded in muting the tension that had begun to build between us. I arrived early every morning before Mom was awake. When we heard Mom stirring, we'd take her to the bathroom and then give her juice, coffee, cereal and her morning medication. We'd talk with her until the woman from the Silver Chain arrived to help her shower.

We spent the afternoons taking turns keeping Mom company. While Joy and she played Scrabble, I worked on my novel. While I watched soap operas with Mom, or read her pages from my book, Joy sat in the lounge room and answered the myriad of emails she had received from her architectural colleagues, her clients and her employees. Clyde dropped in several times a day.

In the evening, we'd give Mom her medication and then microwave one of the frozen meals we'd had a service prepare. After she'd eaten a few morsels and pushed the rest around the plate, we'd put her in the wheelchair and bring her to the lounge room or the back porch. She'd nurse a single glass of white wine until it was time to return to bed. When she was asleep, the three of us would pour more wine and order dinner from a local Thai restaurant, or make do with cheese and crackers. We fell into a nice routine that lulled us into a false sense of complacency.

Demonic Possession.

That evaporated the night Mom had a violent seizure. It was her fourth night back at home. Clyde, Joy and I were in her room saying goodnight. Standing at the foot of the bed, I watched her face morph into a reptilian mask, her muscles stiffen, and her arthritic fingers claw the air.

"Hold her legs" Joy shouted, climbing onto the hospital bed behind Mom and clasping her around the chest.

I reached for her legs. Suddenly Mom swung her right leg into the air, hitting the side of my head. I managed to grab her leg, but she pulled it away from me. "Clyde, help me," I shouted. Together, we managed to contain the strange beast the seizure had unleashed.

"God loves you," I said, hoping that her belief in God and in Jesus Christ would calm her. After all, she had been an avid churchgoer most of her life. "We love you," I hastened to add in case the reference to God was not enough.

"I don't care about all that crap," she shouted in a guttural voice none of us recognized. The crazy person in the bed bore no resemblance to our mother.

By the time the paramedics arrived, Mom lay limp and inert. They measured her vital signs and then wrapped her in the bed sheets and put an oxygen mask on her face. As they wheeled her to the ambulance, she summoned what little energy she had and tried to remove the mask. Joy and Clyde followed the ambulance to Fremantle Hospital. Badly shaken by the experience, I returned to the Copacabana to call David.

"Mom's possessed by some evil aboriginal spirit," I said. "I know it sounds crazy, but I saw it with my own eyes. Something possessed her.

On her own, she never could have summoned that kind of strength."

David listened to me. He didn't tell me I was crazy. Instead, after we hung up, he called our friend, Dr. Peter Whybrow, a neuroscientist who heads the Semel Institute for Neuroscience and Human Behavior at the University of California in Los Angeles. Peter assured David that Mom was not possessed. He explained that pieces of her stenotic heart value were breaking off and going to her brain. That was causing the seizures and explained the odd reptilian mask and behavior that seemed to overcome her. He told David that the end was near. David relayed Peter's message to me the next day.

From that moment on, I sensed the presence of death in the villa. It was there taunting us, teasing us, tormenting us. I understood Mom could have another seizure at any moment, and that it could be the final one. The idea of having to deal with it so terrified me I could no longer be alone with Mom. I knew I could never have done what Joy did when the seizures began. Climbing onto the bed and holding Mom was more than I could do either physically or emotionally. I confessed to Joy and Clyde my misgivings, and suggested I remain in the apartment and that Joy stay at Mom's villa. Then, in a Warrior's desperate attempt to convince myself that I was still in charge and playing an important role, I nominated myself the chief errand runner.

That worked for a while. The sick and the dying generate a lot of errands. Joy, Clyde and I often commented on how astounding it was that our bedridden, little mother was able to keep the three of us and a battery of other caregivers so busy.

A False Reprieve.

A few days after Mom's seizure, cousin Liz came to visit. Joy and I retreated to the walkway in front of the villa so that we could talk without being overheard. We had barely begun when Clyde arrived. We huddled together and tried to console each other. Our sad conversation was interrupted when Mom's primary physician, Dr. See, paid an unexpected visit.

"What's all this?" he asked. "This is no time for sad faces. Remember, your mother has a remarkable immune system. I was in the neighborhood and thought I would stop by to see her."

"She's in the bedroom," Joy said.

"Go right in," I said.

Doctor See nodded, touched his turbaned head, and disappeared into the villa. Ten minutes later, he came out smiling. "As I said, this is no time for sad faces. Your mother has fooled the cardiologists before, and it appears she is doing so again. It is time for all of you to begin to pool your resources. I'll stop by again in a few days." With that, he disappeared, leaving us confounded.

"What did he mean, pool our resources?" asked Joy. "What resources?"

"Resources, where are you?" joked Clyde, twisting his head and looking behind his back.

Ignoring their attempt to lighten the mood, I said, "I think he means we need to figure out how to pay for a nursing home."

"They're called aged-care homes here," said Clyde.

"If Dr. French is right, then we need a hospice facility, or perhaps no facility at all," I said. "Who should we believe?"

"Let's hope Dr. See is right," said Clyde. "Anyway, it's not really up to us. A doctor from Sir Charles Gairdner Hospital will be coming to evaluate Mom. That doctor will certify whether she is ready for hospice or an aged-care home. Without that document, she can't go into either one."

Weird, I thought to myself, but said nothing.

The next morning we got a telephone call notifying us that the doctor would be coming that afternoon. We called Mom's hairdresser and asked her to come to the villa. After showering her, we dressed her in a brand new pair of deep burgundy lounging pajamas. When the doctor arrived, Mom was sitting up in bed, playing a game of solitaire. She looked absolutely regal.

In hindsight, I realize we made a terrible mistake. The doctor's evaluation was based largely on an interview with Mom. The physical examination was cursory. Because Mom was in denial, she was quite convincing when she told the doctor that she felt wonderful. Her appearance corroborated her story. The doctor decided she was a candidate for long-term care in an aged-care home, not short-term care in a hospice.

Two doctors had said Dr. French was wrong. The Warrior's bugle had sounded. I had to get to work fixing things. Mom was not going to die, but she was immobile. She needed care on a 24/7 basis, and that meant an aged-care home. I knew she would hate the idea, but I figured it would be better to get her into the home as soon as possible. I wanted to get her used to her new environment before I had to return to the United States. I assumed that once she had made new bridge buddies, she would adjust. She might even like the chance to have meals with other people. She was, after all, a highly social creature.

The fixer had a mission. I put on my suit of armor and set out to do battle with the world of aged-care homes. I began by calling my friend Emilia. She told me that she had nothing available in any of her homes, and that I would be fortunate to find a single room anywhere in Western Australia. She also confirmed that these facilities were expensive. I realized there was no way Mom could afford to keep her villa. When I shared that realization with Clyde and Joy, neither disagreed.

We talked about the best way to tell Mom that she was going to have to move out of her villa and into a nursing facility. "I think you should be the one to tell her," I said to Joy. "She trusted you to find her a new home when she had to move out of her duplex. When you told her you wanted her to put in an application for this villa, she happily complied without ever even seeing it."

"I agree," said Clyde. "I am the handyman. Pam is the moneymaker and you, Joy, are the architect. Architects create homes. Yes, you should be the one to tell her."

Joy reluctantly accepted the unpleasant task, and promised to break the news to Mom. Days passed and she did nothing. Nor did she want to revisit the subject. Instead, she kept suggesting ways to keep Mom amused. "I think we should take Mom to the Porongorups for a few days," she said. "She's gets really bored just lying in bed all day."

"Are you crazy?" I countered. "What would we do if she had a seizure down there, when we're forty-five minutes from the nearest hospital?"

"Well, then, let's take her to the casino. Let her play the slots. She always loved doing that."

"Joy, she can't walk. If she takes five steps, it will kill her. We can't take her to the casino."

"At least we could take her out to lunch," Joy said, refusing to be dissuaded.

"Yes, I guess we could manage that," I agreed.

We decided to take her to lunch at a chic new restaurant on a nearby street known for its upscale shops. Joy lifted her in and out of the car, and I pushed the wheelchair. We lingered over lunch for more than two hours. The outing definitely lifted Mom's spirits. Joy had been right.

It was that night that Joy found an opportunity to talk to Mom about the nursing home. It was after ten. Clyde and I had just left and Mom was still wide-awake. Failing to find anything of interest on the television, she and Joy were playing Scrabble. Joy was winning, but not by a wide margin.

"Mom, there's something I need to discuss with you," Joy said as Mom lay down five tiles that spelled "stung."

"Yes, darling, what is it?"

"The doctors have said that you need care around the clock."

"Yes, I know that. But I am going to get better."

"Pam, Clyde and I think it's best if you move to a place where you can have the kind of care you need."

Mom looked at her with a vacant stare. A smile remained on her face, but it was a frozen smile, a remnant from a feeling that had already gone.

"Mom, do you undertand what I am saying?"

"It's your turn, darling."

The next morning Joy told me what had happened. "She didn't react. I mean, she just lay sat there and stared at me. It was pretty awful."

"Maybe she just needs time to process it all," I said. "I suggest we leave it alone until we have pictures of an actual facility to show her. That will make it more concrete."

The Dreaded Nursing Home.

Joy and I began visiting facilities whenever cousin Liz or neighbor Sandy could stay with Mom. Some were too depressing to even consider. The nicer homes had no vacancies. Finally, we found an aged-care home that had recently opened. It was bright and cheerful with inviting public spaces where families could gather. We were told that two single rooms were available, but that the staff member in charge of room assignments was not there that day. If we wanted to see the two rooms, we would have to come back the next day.

Because Joy had an appointment, I went alone to see the available rooms. I've told you about that visit in an earlier chapter. You already know that I learned that both rooms were internal; neither had a window. I called Emilia. She told me I had been fortunate to find a single room at all. "Don't hesitate," she advised.

I chose the least offensive of the two rooms, and promised to return later that day with the signed contract and a check for ten thousand dollars to cover the down payment and the first month. I called Clyde. He told me that Mom's brokerage account had sufficient cash in it and that I should get her to sign one of those checks. He told me where to find the checkbook.

Armed with a blank check and the aged-care home contract, a cup of hot coffee and a biscuit, I ventured into the bedroom. Mom was still drowsy with sleep. She smiled and said, "Hello, darling. We are so lucky to have you. I don't know what we would do without you."

I waited for her to sip the coffee and nibble the biscuit. "Mom, we're trying to get things set up for you to make sure you get the care you need. I need your signature on some forms and on a check for ten thousand dollars."

"That's a lot of money," she said, as she signed the check and the contract. "But I'm sure you know what you're doing." Then she smiled again, and asked me to turn up the television.

I understood why Mom's failure to react had unnerved Joy. Mom had just signed a very large check without even inquiring about its purpose. In fact, she had done more than simply fail to ask. In turning up the volume on the television, she had made it clear that she was not ready to discuss the matter at all.

To clear my head, I went outside and walked around the block. When I returned, I could tell from the look on her face that the purpose of the form and the check had finally registered. Pouting like a little girl, she said, "I hate change. I've always hated change."

"I understand," I said. "I think most people hate change."

"I hate it more than most people," she said, turning her face away. When she turned it back, her eyes were tearing. "I don't want to leave my home," she said. "I want to stay here. Why can't I stay here?"

Before I could answer, she continued. "I can't stay here because I can't take care of myself. Is that right?"

"Yes," I said. That's right."

"Why can't I pay someone to take care of me? They can sleep in the next room."

I didn't have the heart to explain to her that she couldn't afford a live-in caregiver. If she sold her investments to pay for a caregiver, then she wouldn't have enough to live on. Nor did I want to explain that David and I couldn't give her the money because we anticipated that Jill was going to need our financial help when she had to move into an assisted living facility. I was still framing my answer to her question when she picked up the remote and turned up the volume on the television. Once again, she had indicated the subject was closed.

I could tell she wasn't really listening to the cooking show. She was using it as an excuse to stop talking to me. I decided to leave her alone. When I came back into the room a half hour later, the television was turned off, and Mom was asleep. I sat down and watched her. She looked so frail and so vulnerable I could barely stand it. I was still sitting with her when she awoke. She looked at me with a sad face and said, " I read somewhere that it's wrong to commit suicide."

"Perhaps you're referring to the Bible," I said.

"Yes, that's right. The Bible. I read it in the Bible."

That afternoon, I took Mom's check and the signed contract to the aged-care home. The next day, Joy went to take the measurements of the room so that we could plan the furnishings. Only then did she discover that I had committed to an interior room. Upset with me, she called Clyde to complain. He, in turn, alerted me. When Joy got back to the villa, I was armed and ready to defend myself.

"Emilia said I was fortunate to have found a single room and shouldn't take a chance on losing it. It may not have a window, but it's new and its spacious, and she doesn't have to share it with a complete stranger. And, by the way, I don't appreciate your calling Clyde to tell him you have a problem with something I did."

"When you decide to do something, there's no stopping you. You're a force of nature," she said. She wasn't smiling.

"Thank you," I said, pretending to take her comment as a compliment.

"I know you did what you thought was right," she said. "I just don't like it. I just can't imagine Mom being happy there."

"She'll be safe there, and she'll learn to like it when she meets a few people."

Joy didn't argue with me. Instead, she sat down at the table. Using the measurements she'd taken of the dreaded room, she created a scale drawing and figured out how to make optimum use of the space. The next day, she and I drove out to Ikea and purchased a wall unit that would give Mom a place for her treasures and photographs and, at the same time, protect her privacy from the man in the adjoining room. The Warrior was pleased. The Celebrant was biting her tongue.

Misplaced Heroics.

Five days later, we were again ready to move Mom. That night, while I was still at the villa, she had another seizure. Our response had become routine. I held her legs. Joy climbed up on the bed behind her. Clyde called the ambulance. Mom was raced to the hospital, only to return a few hours later.

"If I didn't know better, I'd think she was doing this on purpose," I said to Joy the next day when I got back from picking up Mom's medications and some groceries.

"I think it's her way of telling us we're going down the wrong path," Joy said, standing up straight and looking me directly in the eye.

"It's the only path open to us," I said, stiffening my spine and wishing she weren't two inches taller than me.

Joy looked away. "Last night, after you and Clyde left, I promised her she wouldn't have to go to the aged-care home."

"You what?" I asked, incredulous. "You had no right to do that! You know we don't have any choice. Your misplaced heroics are just going to cause Mom a lot more pain, unnecessary pain. What were you thinking?"

"I intend to make it work. I'd rather close my architectural practice, take a part-time job at the university, and move in here with her than put her in an aged-care home."

I wanted to strangle her. "Joy, that's just not realistic. In the first place, she wouldn't want you to give up your business and your life. In the second place, she needs care around the clock. She'll need more than somebody sleeping in the next room. What if one day you couldn't get home on time? What then? Or what if she had one of her seizures when one of the Silver Chain volunteers is here? I mean, they're wonderful people, but they're not medically trained. It just wouldn't work."

"I'll make it work," she said as she walked away. The rescuer was alive and well and ready to do battle with the fixer. Neither of us was going to back down. I was the oldest sibling and accustomed to calling the shots. It made me mad when she failed to behave like the compliant little sister. Joy was the youngest, but many years had passed since she'd taken orders from me. She was now an accomplished architect. She had been married and divorced. She had a full-grown son. She, too, was accustomed to calling the shots.

When Clyde arrived later that afternoon, we both accosted him, eager to tell our side of the argument. A natural mediator, he listened first to me and then to Joy.

"Joy, I think Pam is right," he said, though too tentatively for my liking. "Mom needs care around the clock. We can't afford to pay for that kind of care without selling the villa. It's unfortunate, but that's the way it is."

Joy crossed the room and stared vacantly at the backyard. Finally, she turned and said, "At least let me be the one to tell her. I'll tell her tonight."

What Joy failed to explain was that she believed, in spite of the doctors, that Mom did not need a nursing home because she was about to die. Unlike Clyde and me, Joy was intimately involved with the care of Mom's body. Ugly rashes from a candida yeast infection covered Mom's armpits and her crotch. Joy's attempts to get rid of it by serving Mom yogurt probiotics and getting her to drink more water had done nothing to stem the spread of the infection. Joy believed this was a sign that Mom's body was never going to recover; it had already begun to die. Unfortunately, Joy never shared that with us.

The next morning I arrived at villa before anyone was even awake. I used my key and let myself into the darkened living room. Hearing me, Joy got out of bed. I didn't give her a chance to wipe the sleep out of her eyes before I challenged her, "You did tell her, didn't you?"

"I did," she answered. "I felt like I betrayed her."

I stopped myself from pointing out that she wouldn't have had to betray Mom if she hadn't made a dumb promise in the first place. Instead, I said, "I thought I'd give her a chance to decide what to take with her. If she's involved, she might find the move easier to accept." I took Joy's failure to respond as tacit approval.

Joy busied herself making Mom a special breakfast of bacon and a toasted croissant. Mom had not been eating well, and had complained about how boring her meals had become. I watched as Joy brought her the treat, smiling as she played it on the bed tray. Her smile vanished as Mom pushed the food away and snarled, "What is this stuff? I want my cereal. I always eat cereal. Cereal with a banana."

We brought Mom her cereal, and sat with her, talking inanities and waiting for her sullen mood to pass. I went to the store for more cereal and bananas and provisions for lunch while Joy helped Mom brush her teeth, wash her face, take care of her toilet, and put on a clean pair of lounging pajamas. After lunch, I brought her well-worn suitcase into the bedroom, opened it, and sat down on the floor next to the low-lying bureau. "I'll be your hands, Mom. I'll hold up things, and you tell me whether to put them in the suitcase to take with you, or to put them in storage."

Mom looked at me quizzically. I persisted. I held up a half-slip that still had the tags on it. "I don't think you'll need this," I said. "I imagine you'll want to wear the lounging outfits I bought you last week."

She nodded, and said nothing. I held up three brassieres. "I think you'll need these," I said.

"I don't want to go," she whimpered.

"I know you don't. Once you get there, you'll like it. Your friends can visit. You can play bridge. There's a wonderful theatre with a huge screen. You'll see. It won't be so bad. You'll be able to have dinner every night with the new friends you'll make."

She looked at me like she wished I would vanish into thin air. Instead, I opened another drawer and held up a box of jewelry. "Shall we go through this, or would you like to take all of it?" I asked.

"It's just junk," she said. "You might as well throw it away. Throw everything away. Throw me away."

She turned her head away. I heard her sigh and thought she might be weeping. I wanted to say something but remembered neighbor Sandy's advice. "Your mother needs time to think, to reflect, to adjust to what's happening to her. Sometimes its best just to sit with her in silence."

Finally, she turned her head and looked at me. Her cheeks were moist. "I don't want to die in Australia," she said. "I don't understand how this has happened to me."

Again, I felt a desperate need to save her from sadness, pain, aging, and especially from death. I despaired because there was nothing I could do, nor even say. Perhaps if I had expressed these feelings to Joy, we could have been more supportive of one another. Unfortunately, the more vulnerable and out of control I felt, the more rigid I became. Now, my focus was on getting Mom prepared for the move. Before I could start again, she rescued both of us by changing the mood and distracting me from my purpose.

"Where's my blue silk coin purse? The piece of my tooth that broke off is in it." She stuck her arthritic finger in her mouth, pointing at her cracked tooth.

I stood up, removed her blue purse from her bedside drawer, and handed it to her.

"I really need to go see the dentist," she said. "Perhaps you could make an appointment for me."

This was not the first time we had gone through this ritual. She clutched the purse close to her body. Focusing on her chipped tooth seemed to help her stop dwelling on death and the dreaded nursing home. Thinking about seeing her dentist was to imagine life continuing as usual.

"They told me I wouldn't live past the age of thirty-six because I had a bad heart. I fooled them, and I will keep fooling them," she said as she handed me the purse and indicated I should put it back in the bedside table drawer. "I don't care what they say. I can take care of myself."

At this point, the telephone rang. Joy answered it. I heard her say, "I'm sure she'd like that very much." When she hung up, she came into the bedroom. Looking at Mom, she said, "That was Alicia. She and two of your other friends want to come over for a little bridge game. Would you like that?"

Before she could answer, I jumped in. "You can't be serious," I said. "A visit, maybe, but bridge? Mom's not up to that. Besides, we have to get her ready for the move."

"I'd like to see my friends, and I'd like to play bridge," Mom asserted with surprising force.

Moments later, Joy marched into the bedroom with the card table. Shoving the suitcase under the hospital bed with her foot, she gave me a stern look and set up the table. "Your friends will be here any minute,

Mom. Would you like me to make up some sandwiches?"

"Oh yes," said Mom, brightening up and sitting up straighter.

Her friends arrived within the hour. I sat in the lounge room listening to the women talk and laugh. Mom's laughter was hearty. *Joy was right*, I thought. *But so am I. This can't go on forever. It's just not viable. Something has to be done.*

Her friends left at around five. Clyde arrived shortly thereafter. Joy gave Mom her meds. I read out the list of frozen dinners that were in her freezer. She chose a cube steak with peas and mashed potatoes. When I served it, she turned up her nose, and complained that it was overdone. Criticizing the food we gave her had become Mom's new way of expressing displeasure with us and with life in general.

While she pushed the food around her plate, we sat with her in the bedroom and sipped white wine. I can't remember what we talked about. I do know we stayed away from the subject of the aged-care home. After dinner, we turned on *Bridget Jones: The Edge of Reason.* Mom nodded off, but woke up each time we tried to turn off the television.

The Death of the Queen of Denial.

I went back to the Copacabana around ten o'clock that night and quickly fell into a deep sleep. Shortly after eleven, my phone rang. "Mom has had another seizure," Joy said. "We're on our way to the hospital."

"I'll be right there," I said, struggling to wake up.

"I don't think you need to come. She came out of it even before the paramedics put her in the ambulance. I think she's just managed to delay the move again."

I didn't argue. None of it seemed real. I felt like I was trapped in an endless bad dream. I went back to bed. Just before two in the morning, the phone rang again.

"Mom has passed," Joy said. Her voice was calm and her tone, measured. "We're back at her villa if you want to come over."

I was stunned. Though on some level I had known since I arrived that we were on a deathwatch, the reality of Mom's demise was shocking. I could not understand how my childlike mother had summoned the courage to die! It was unfathomable.

I pulled on my jeans and yellow tee shirt, stumbled down the stairs and made my way past darkened windows to the parking lot. I drove through the deserted back streets to Mom's villa. When I pulled into the empty space assigned to her, the left-front bumper of the truck scraped the right rear of Sandy's carefully preserved navy blue sedan. The sound of metal on metal made me come to a complete stop.

Joy and Clyde came running out of the villa. They didn't even have to ask what happened. Clyde opened the door. "I'll park it," he said. "No worries."

"I've damaged Sandy's car," I said nervously. "I've got to tell her."

"In the morning," said Clyde. "We'll take care of it in the morning."

We stayed up all night. They described in graphic detail the events of the evening. "Mom came out of the first seizure," Clyde said.

"It was at that point that I went into the hall to phone you and tell you what was going on," Joy explained. The call wouldn't go through. I had a feeling that I should get back to Mom. I just barely made it before she went into another seizure."

"Yes, but first she smiled at us," Clyde said. "Her smile was so calm and peaceful. It seemed as though she'd accepted that she was about to die."

Clyde sighed, swallowed hard, and then resumed. "When she seized again, a team of five people began working on her. The lead doctor suggested that they try twice to revive her. We agreed. They gave her a shot of something or other, and began massaging her heart..."

"Lidocaine," I said, remembering the drug they had given my late husband. "It must have been Lidocaine."

"Lidocaine," Clyde repeated after me. "When they got no response, they tried again. Still nothing. There was no more they could do. Mom was gone."

"The doctors and nurses quietly left the room," Joy said in a hushed voice. "We stood on either side of the table and held her hands in ours. We watched as the wrinkles seemed to vanish from her face. She lay there, her white hair framing her serene face, like someone who was simply asleep. We stood there for a long time letting her quiet lingering presence soothe us."

Envying their sense of closure, I asked them to repeat the story of Mom's final hours. It was almost dawn when I got back to the Copacabana. I called David. "Mom died last night," I said.

David sighed. "I'm so sorry, but you do know it was time. As Peter said..."

I interrupted him. "Yes, I know it was time. That doesn't make it any easier to bear."

"Do you want me to come over there?"

"No, there's too much going on at home. You can't just leave all those workmen."

"I could if..." he said.

I interrupted him. "I dread telling Jill. She's going to be devastated."

"You sound exhausted. Let me call Jill."

"She'll expect to hear it from me," I said.

"I can do a better job of making her feel like she's not alone. I don't have to deal with the distance or with the time difference. I'll call her every few hours, and then every few days. If need be, I can fly down to Sacramento. Leave it to me. Just take of yourself."

I showered and put on fresh clothes and then returned to Mom's villa. Clyde was there. He had gone home to shower and change clothes and then returned. We agreed that the only way to manage the day was to stay together and to keep busy.

Crowding into the front seat of the truck, we drove to an industrial park on the outskirts of town where Ikea was located. We wanted to return the wall unit that we'd never even taken out of the bay. Then, we drove to the mall so that I could return the several sets of lounging pajamas that I had bought for Mom to wear in her new home. We then drove over to a nearby storage unit and rented a facility large enough to house Mom's furniture.

Feeling as though we'd accomplished some important tasks, we decided to treat ourselves to lunch at a restaurant on the water in Fremantle. We ordered fish and chips and white wine and sat there listening to the waves lap against the pier. We spoke again of Mom's final hours.

"Did they give you her rings?" I asked.

"No," said Clyde. "I didn't think to ask. I guess we better go back and find out what happened to them."

Later that afternoon, Clyde returned to the emergency room while Joy and I waited in the car. He learned that when Mom's body was sent to the morgue, her rings were still on her fingers. Because of her arthritis and swollen knuckle, they hadn't been able to remove them. The attendant suggested we retrieve the rings from the funeral director. When Clyde told us what he had said, we all understood the implications. They'd had to cut Mom's finger off to remove the rings. We chose not to speak of this, however.

While I retrieved Mom's ten thousand dollars from the aged-care facility, Joy and Clyde contacted Karracatta cemetery, scheduling Mom's memorial service for the following Thursday morning. At Gay's suggestion, they called the minister who had been a long-time friend of the family and arranged for him to conduct the service. They scheduled a meeting with him for the following Monday. Then they drove into town to Chippers, the funeral home that had managed Dad's funeral twenty years earlier. There, they chose a coffin and booked a date for the viewing.

When they told me all of this that evening, I felt left out. They hadn't even asked what I thought about a public viewing of Mom's body. If they had, I would have argued against it. The whole idea of an open coffin offended me. Only much later would I understand that, in Australia, it's common practice to give people an opportunity to view the body before it's sent to the crematorium. At the time, I felt neglected and marginalized which heightened my sense of vulnerability. That, in turn, led me to intensify my efforts to remain in control by focusing on the business of death.

The Emotional Tsunami and the Pit Bull.

Retrieving the ten thousand dollars from the aged-care facility got me thinking about all the things that had to happen before I could comfortably return to the United States. Mom's papers had to be sorted. We had to cancel her credit cards and her subscriptions. We had to get Reader's Digest to stop their incessant mailings of books that Mom hadn't wanted and couldn't recall ordering. We had to deal with her social security. Her overstuffed closets and drawers had to be emptied. Yes, there was a great deal to do. To prepare, I went to the grocery store and bought a box of oversize black garbage bags. The Warrior was armed and ready.

Arriving at the villa with the black plastic bags in hand, I announced to Joy that we were going to begin by sorting Mom's books. I told her Cousin Liz had called that morning and offered to pick up boxes of books and deliver them to the second-hand store. When she pitched right in, I had a momentary feeling that we were on the same page.

We hadn't even packed half a box when Clyde, Sue and their son, Darby, showed up. Clyde sat down in the lounge room with a cup of coffee. He turned his chair so that he was facing the credenza and the wall. It was obvious to me he needed a little quiet time in that room where he and Mom had spent so many hours. I didn't mind that he didn't offer to help with the books. I did mind when Joy decided to join Sue and Darby in the backyard, and engage Darby in a game of catch. Joy's playfulness was totally at odds with my need to attend to the business of death.

She never did help me finish sorting the books. I made the decisions, and packed several boxes for Liz to take. When she arrived, Clyde carried the boxes out to her car. Clyde, Sue and Darby left shortly thereafter. Joy opened her laptop and began answering emails. Even though I understood she needed to do this to keep her architectural practice running, I was upset with her. She seemed to delight in putting obstacles in my way. Her guitar and suitcases were piled in front of the file cabinets. I needed access to those to help Clyde deal with the business of the estate.

Making a face at her back, I went into Mom's bedroom and began looking through her crammed closets. I began making piles on the floor: a pile for Good Sammy's (like our Goodwill); a pile for Gay's daughters who were small like Mom; and a pile of things that were special treasures. One was a fuchsia pashmina shawl that Mom often wore. I put it around my shoulders. Her scent lingered on the cloth, making me feel sad and alone. I didn't want to fight with Joy anymore.

I dug out a multicolored silk shawl that I had bought for Mom at the Metropolitan Museum in New York. It was the shawl that we had draped over her black raincoat the day we took her to get the second opinion. Taking it into the lounge room, I handed it to Joy. "I thought this would look wonderful on you. I gave it to Mom not long ago."

Joy rubbed the fabric against her cheek. "Thank you," she said. She smiled, and her face softened.

That night we celebrated Clyde's fifty-fourth birthday at a trendy restaurant down the street from his home. Mom, Joy and I had agreed to chip in to buy him an iPod. That had been only weeks before. Now, we had to write Mom's name on the card because she couldn't do it herself.

Mom was dead. Dead. Her body lay in the morgue. And yet here we were, at a restaurant, celebrating Clyde's birthday in a futile attempt to pretend that life goes on. I didn't know how to think about it all.

We drank too much, as we had often done of late. Much of the conversation centered on the architectural drawings Joy was making for Clyde's remodel. Joy mentioned that she'd received an email from Gay with her flight information. I suggested Gay might like to stay with me at the Copacabana. Joy felt strongly that Gay would prefer staying with her in Mom's villa. Clyde didn't express an opinion. I had hoped that Gay's arrival would change the dynamics, making me feel less like an unwelcome third wheel. When I realized that was not going to happen, I moved deeper into the Warrior's bunker, becoming even more rigid and defensive.

The next morning, I arrived at the villa early, armed with my black plastic bags. I bagged up the clothes destined for Good Sammy's and then started in the kitchen. I expected Joy to offer to help me. Instead, she talked on the phone. She talked to her friends, and to Mom's friends. She spoke eloquently and with dramatic flair about the tragedy of Mom's passing. Even as she spoke of our loss, she was smiling. The smile disturbed me. It seemed to me that she was getting high on the intense feelings that surrounded Mom's death. Only later would I understand that her smile was an expression of relief that Mom's journey through life had ended when it did—in her own home, with her children around her. Given her immobility and increasingly violent seizures, her death had been a blessing.

A month or so ago, I happened upon an article that could have been written by Joy. Ann Patchett wrote, "If you were sure that God was waiting for your father, wouldn't you want him to go? Wouldn't you want him to go even if you didn't believe in God, because death is the completion of our purpose here? He's finished his job and now is free to send his atoms back into the earth and stars. Isn't that really kind of great?"[36]

---

[36]Ann Patchett, "Finding Joy in My Father's Death," *The New York Times*, February 27, 2015.

I also now understand that my black plastic bags made Joy as angry as her smile made me. If she was all emotion, then I was all mind. Oblivious to my own contribution to the tension, I finished the kitchen, and started thinking about what we could get rid of at the town's next curbside junk pickup. Scheduled to happen later that week, the pickup spot was conveniently located only a hundred yards down the road. That would spare us several trips to the town dump.

Joy was still on the phone when I finished. Hoping to clear my head, I decided to take a bike ride along the coast. By the time I finished my ride, my natural aversion to conflict had taken over. I called Joy and suggested we get takeaway Thai that night and eat it on the balcony at the Copacabana.

"I'm going over to Clyde's soon to talk about his renovation," she said. "I'm not sure what time we'll be done."

"Okay," I said, and then waited for her to suggest that I meet her at Clyde's and that we all go out for dinner. She did not.

That evening, I poured a glass of wine and called David. I told him Joy and Clyde were ganging up on me, and I wanted him to come over. Though he thought I was being a bit paranoid, he agreed to come. When we hung up, he called the Flight Center in Vancouver, British Columbia and booked a flight to Perth leaving the next day.

When I got to the villa the next morning, the front door was closed and locked. Thinking that Joy must still be sleeping, I used my key to unlock the front door. As I opened it, I heard her say, "Here she is with her damn black plastic bags." I knew she was talking to Clyde.

"I've asked David to come over," I said when she hurriedly hung up.

"I think that's a great idea," she said. She wasn't smiling.

I began to gather up things to take to the junk pickup spot. There was a floor lamp with a bent shade that hadn't worked for a while. There were old suitcases that smelled of mildew. There were blackened pots and pans that had seen better days. When I had accumulated everything outside the front door, I asked Joy to help me cart it down the road.

"Not now," she said dismissively. "I'll do it later. I have to answer some emails from people in my office, and then I'm having lunch with Liz."

"How nice for you," I said, irritated that she thought going to a social gathering was more important than dealing with the business of death.

Because I had buried my grief under a mountain of "must do's," I didn't understand that Liz and Joy needed to be together to share their grief over Mom's passing.

The two of them had enjoyed a special relationship ever since Joy arrived in that strange country at the age of thirteen. As Dad had grown increasingly concerned about finding work and as Mom had begun turning to wine to escape the reality of her new surroundings, Joy had turned to Liz for help and for comfort. The bond they formed was to be a lasting one. It was only natural that they would now want to spend private time together. But I didn't get that. Instead of supporting her or simply suggesting that I would like to join them, I attacked. "I suppose you think you can take the Fairfax's truck. Did it ever occur to you that I might need it? They didn't lend it to you, after all."

"Don't worry about it, Pam" Joy said. "I'll rent my own car."

"You can't afford it," I challenged.

"What I can and can't afford is none of your business," she exclaimed. "Take your damn truck. I'll ask Liz to pick me up."

Chastised, I looked away. "You can use the truck."

Joy sped off. When she returned several hours later, she was driving a rental car. Clyde was right behind her in the truck.

Early the next morning, Clyde and I met David's flight. Clyde dropped us off at the Copacabana and then headed off to work. Hoping to force his body onto Australian time, David suggested we take a long walk along the beach and then stop for breakfast. Later, he took a nap while Joy, Clyde and I met with the minister.

He asked us a number of questions to ascertain what kind of tone we wanted at Mom's service. "Mom loved ritual. I think she'd have wanted a formal service in a chapel or a church," I said.

"Gay suggested that, in addition to the hymns, we write a song about Mom that I can sing at the service," Joy offered.

"We don't have enough time to write a song," I argued. "I think it's more important that we focus on writing the eulogy."

"We can do both," protested Joy. "We want a service that is heartfelt, and not overly formal."

"Maybe we should hold it on the beach," I said sarcastically, envisioning all of us showing up in bare feet, wearing long flowing robes and wreaths of flowers in our hair.

"Of course we want a service in a chapel," said Joy, getting up from the sofa and taking a seat opposite me and next to the minister. "I was not suggesting we want sand between our toes. I do have some sense of propriety, you know."

Clyde looked from one of us to the other, not taking a position. The minister tried to intervene. "Now, now, I'm sure there is an acceptable middle ground."

David came in shortly after the minister left. He and I sat on the small verandah behind the villa. Only a sliding screen door separated us from Joy who was sitting at the table in the lounge room working on her computer. Clyde had retreated to the bathroom where he was replacing the parts of the shower he had removed when we made Mom's villa wheelchair-ready.

My cell phone rang. It was Jessie Fairfax. She was calling to welcome David and to invite us to dinner the following night. When she suggested we might like to bring Joy, Clyde and Sue along, I asked her to hold on, and referred the question to David.

"I'd rather we go alone," he said definitively. "After all, I haven't seen the Fairfaxes in a very long time, and we have a lot of catching up to do."

"No, we'll come alone, thanks, without them," I said to Jessie.

Moments after I hung up, Joy marched out onto the verandah. Her arms crossed over her chest in a gesture of definance, she looked at me and snarled, "What right do you have to cut us out of a dinner at the Fairfaxes? I heard you. I know what you did."

Joy marched back into the house. We heard the sound of the bathroom door slamming shut. I went inside and listened. Joy was berating me, telling Clyde what an awful, selfish person I was, and what a terrible thing I had done. That leaving them out had been David's idea made no difference. Only much later did I come to understand that Joy's hostility stemmed from feeling left out or shut out. It appears that both of us were highly sensitive and ready to perceive of the slightest affront as an attempt to sideline us.

David and I left an hour later. Over dinner, we talked about what had occurred that evening. Putting his hand on mine, David said, "I now understand what you've been telling me. I have to confess that I suspected you were over-reacting, and that you were probably driving everyone crazy with your hyper-efficiency. I mean, when you decide to solve a problem, you are like a pit bull. You just won't let it go."

I was about to defend myself when he continued, "I can see what's going on here. For whatever reason, Joy wants to be the center of this drama that's unfolding around all of you. I doubt she's even aware that her behavior is driving a wedge between you and Clyde. I am sure she has no desire to do that. She is not a cruel person."

David helped me to regard Joy's behavior as a result of stress, and not ill will toward me. We managed to put negative feelings aside long enough to pick out the clothing that Mom would wear for her final appearance on this earth. We chose the pink silk suit that she had bought for her grandson Tyler's wedding. We managed to write a eulogy we all liked. Our efforts to pen a song were less successful. In an email to Joy, Gay suggested that, instead, Joy sing "Lucky Child," a song she had written about Mom years earlier and used as the title song in her CD.

The day before the service, Clyde and Joy met Gay's plane, and brought her directly to the funeral home. Joy positioned herself next to Mom's open coffin and smiled her beatific smile at the mourners who came to pay their last respects. Gay sat in the back of the room. Clyde stood near the doorway. I sat in the adjoining room. I had viewed Mom's body once and couldn't bear to do so again. The eerie stillness of the figure in the pink silk suit that had been my mother frightened me. I couldn't stop from visualizing the missing ring finger on her hands tucked neatly under a white cover.

Every time someone opened the door to enter the viewing room, I could see the coffin and Joy positioned next to it. With wide eyes, she was awash in emotion. She took my breath away. It was as though she was an emotional tsunami that literally sucked the oxygen out of the air.

Because Gay's suitcases had not arrived, after the viewing Joy offered to take her to find an outfit to wear to the service. Clyde hates to shop, so I hoped he would prefer to spend the evening having a private dinner with David and me. I was hurt when he opted to go along with Joy and Gay.

In competing with each other for Clyde's attention and his allegiance, Joy and I made him part of the problem. In hindsight, I am not surprised that he chose the warm embrace of the Celebrant as opposed to the cold efficiency of the Warrior in the bunker. At the time, however, I saw his shift in allegiance as a betrayal.

The funeral procession began at 10:00 the next morning, October 5. It was a beautiful spring day. As family and Mom's many friends and admirers gathered, the cawing of magpies and the screeching of white cockatoos perched in the fragrant eucalyptus trees added a surreal backdrop to the hushed condolences. Geckos scurried across the warm pavement, oblivious to the human drama being enacted around them.

I was relieved when the minister told us the processional was about to begin. Because I was the eldest, I had the honor of walking with David directly behind the coffin, leading the long stream of mourners up the lane bordered on either side by tall, erect cypress trees. The trees lent a sense of the majestic to our solemn march to the chapel.

After the eulogy, Joy sang her song. Then we, the lucky children, circled Mom's coffin. Holding hands, we said our final farewells before the floor opened and the coffin dropped down and began its short trip to the furnaces. In that moment, I think we momentarily forgot our differences.

Ashes to Ashes.

That evening, David and I had dinner alone, and then packed our suitcases and got ready for the journey to the Porongorups. We were going to spread Mom's ashes in the same place as we had spread Dad's cremains twenty years earlier. Let me briefly pause my story to tell you a little bit about the mysterious place we call "the Porongorups."

In 1973, my parents bought ten acres in the forested foothills of the world's most ancient mountain range in the southwest corner of Australia, three-hundred-sixty kilometers southeast of Perth. Sixteen kilometers long and four kilometers wide, the Porongorups boasts thirteen granite peaks, the oldest of which is thirteen million years old.

The highest peak, Devil's Slide, rises twenty-two hundred feet into the air. Its name was derived from an aboriginal dreamtime story in which an evil male spirit tries to capture a young maiden who is frolicking on the slopes. As he reaches out to grab her, he slips and slides down the rock face. She escapes.

The aboriginals regarded the mountains as places of danger and mystery to be avoided if possible, especially at night. They preferred to do their hunting and gathering in the hills and valleys below the sacred peaks. They wandered through the karri forests finding bush tucker to fill their bellies and medicinal plants to heal their wounds. They hunted the western grey kangaroo, the brush wallaby, the honey possum, and even the deadly dugite snake. Overhead they'd hear the screech of the black cockatoo. As they approached watering holes, they'd be accosted with the croaking of hundreds of frogs.

Now the aborigines are gone. Tourists, bushwalkers and rock climbers have taken their place in an ancient land still lush with life. Remnants of vast karri forests continue to thrive on the moist upper slopes. Jarra and marri trees grow in the deep loam on the lower slopes. Fields of colorful wildflowers cover the landscape in autumn and early spring. Parrots, honey eaters, robins, tree creepers, wrens, chats, hawks, white-tailed black cockatoos and wedge-tailed eagles soar above, filling with sound the concert hall created by the ancient peaks.

Sadly, the Porongourups is much more domesticated than it was when Dad and Mom bought the property. The road leading to the Cuming stake is no longer a dirt road rendered red by the iron ore in the soil. It's a paved road. Yet once you turn off the street and make your way down the long and narrow rutty dirt passage dotted with four-foot-high termite mounds, you feel as though you have left civilization far behind. There, in the midst of the forest sits the house that Jack, my father, built. Behind it is the Australian bush where Mom's ashes would finally join with Dad's.

As I closed my suitcase, I was thinking about the property and Jill's telling me that she wanted her own ashes spread in the Porongorups so she could be with her sister. She had clung to that notion for several years until I convinced her that it was a strange, remote place with energies that were foreign to her. Finally, she'd agreed that her ashes should be scattered in the rivulet that cascaded down the mountain and through our property on its way to the sea. I worried that the death of her sister would rekindle her earlier wish. I was about to call her to tell her about Mom's service when Clyde, Gay and Joy arrived.

"We thought we'd come by for just one drink," said Clyde.

"I'm glad," I said, thinking to myself that sharing a single drink didn't make up for a whole evening of being the odd man out. "First, let's call Jill. It's seven in the morning her time. She'll be up and waiting for the call."

Jill didn't answer until the fifth ring. That was unusual. Because her place is so small, she usually picked up by the second or third ring. I tried to sound upbeat as I said, "The service was beautiful, Jill. More than two hundred people came."

"Rosemary had a lot of friends," Jill replied, her tone flat.

"We all missed you very much, and wished you could have been with us."

"Yes, that would have been nice," she said, still without any energy behind her voice.

"Jill, I want you to promise me that you'll take care of yourself. I'll be home soon, and I'll fly right down to see you."

"That would be nice," she said, still without enthusiasm.

"We're heading down to the Porongorups tomorrow to spread Mom's ashes. I can't call you from there, but I will call you on Tuesday when we get back."

"That's fine, dear. Don't you worry about me."

"You take care of yourself, Jill," I repeated. "Remember, it'll soon be your and my turn to have some fun together."

Clyde, Gay and Joy then took turns speaking briefly with her. They each reported that her tone was flat and her lack of vitality worrisome.

The next morning we headed south in three separate cars. On Friday night, the wine flowed freely. We argued, primarily about our children's vested interest (or lack thereof) in the holiday house and the property, and went to bed angry.

We got up early the next day. Putting aside all negative feelings, we gathered in the bush behind the house. We took turns taking handfuls of Mom's cremains and carefully spreading them on the ground as we had done with Dad's ashes more than twenty years earlier.

Early the next day, Clyde and Gay left for Perth. Gay had a plane to catch, and Clyde had to go back to work. Joy, David and I stayed for two more nights. The magic of the landscape the aboriginals regarded as sacred coupled with the pleasure of being together without having to deal with the business of death muted the tension that remained between us.

We got back to Perth Tuesday evening. David drove over to Mom's villa to drop off some things we'd brought back from the Porongrups. I checked to see if anyone had left a message on the hotel phone. There was one from Thomas, the Chaplain, our good friend and neighbor who had volunteered to water our plants while we were away.

"Hello, Pam. This is Thomas speaking. When I watered your plants this weekend, I noticed that you had a new message waiting on your answering machine. The sheriff's office in Sacramento is trying to reach you. They left this number: (916) 874-9320."

The Final Reunion.

My hand trembling, I punched the number. After four rings, I got a recorded message. "This is the office of the Yolo County Coroner. Our office hours are..."

I put the phone down, unable to process what I had just heard. Then my cell phone rang. Joy said, "When I got back, I found a message on Mom's answering machine. It's for you. The sheriff's office in Sacramento. I called the number."

I interrupted her. "I know. It's the coroner's office. I can't believe...David's on his way to the villa to drop off some stuff. Please tell him to turn around and come right back."

"Yes, of course I will," said Joy. "Pam, I'm so sorry. I..."

I didn't let her finish. I couldn't. I had to hang up the phone. I needed to scream. I needed to cry. I needed to force myself to think the unthinkable; to conceive the inconceivable. There was only one reason the coroner in Sacramento was calling—Aunt Jill was dead. But I couldn't let that thought into my conscious brain; at least, not yet.

When I finally reached the coroner several hours later, I still couldn't believe it was real. The call was a mistake, or some kind of bad joke. Jill had often complained of fatigue, but she had been basically healthy. The only medication she took was to lower her slightly elevated blood pressure.

In telling me the details, the coroner made it real. Jill had died of a massive stroke less than twenty-four hours after I had spoken with her. She hadn't shown up for her Friday morning appointment at the hair salon. Since she hadn't missed an appointment in ten years, the stylist was concerned and called the fire department. When they rang the bell and no one answered, they broke into the duplex. They found Jill on the floor, caught in her bedsheets after what appeared to be a final struggle to free herself. She had died within hours of her sister's funeral. She had died before her sister's ashes had even been spread. She had died utterly alone. That made me very sad.

Gay had only been back in the United States a few hours when I called to tell her that Aunt Jill had died. Though her body was weary from crisscrossing the globe, Gay had to be our emissary. She and her husband, Richard, got on a plane the next day and flew to Sacramento. My daughter, Monica, joined them, prepared to act in my stead and read a eulogy I had written for Jill. As Jill's executor, I signed and, with Clyde's help, faxed the legal documents authorizing her cremation. With each signing, her death became more real.

David and I spent hours talking about all that we wished we had done for Jill when she was alive. We had intended to give her a subscription to cable television, but hadn't gotten around to it. We had intended to drive down to get her and bring her back to our home for a visit, but the timing was always wrong. We regretted never telling her that we intended to move her to an assisted living facility near our home when the time came. I guess we were afraid she'd take us up on the offer before it was absolutely necessary. Unlike Mom, my grief over Jill's death was complicated by regrets that I had not done more to make her life richer.

And, it was complicated by my grieving the loss of a role that I had come to both treasure and to fear. I had made a commitment to Jill. I had promised that I would be her caregiver as she got older and more frail. I didn't know what that would entail from a physical, emotional or financial point of view. Jill's death meant that I would never have to fulfill my commitment to her. That filled me with a deep sadness, but also with a sense of relief.

I told Clyde and Joy about my ambivalent feelings, and learned that they shared them. They said they had always intended to help provide the care that Jill would need as she got older. "We weren't going to just sit by and let you and David do everything," Joy said.

"We're in this together," Clyde added.

I did have the feeling we had begun to come together. We weren't quarreling as often. I stopped swearing at Joy because her guitar and suitcase were still parked in front of the file cabinets. Somehow the shock of the second death made me aware that, no matter how hard I tried, I could not control the chaos either within me or without me. I stopped trying to fix things.

As I give up playing the fixer, Joy stopped trying to be the rescuer. Perhaps, like me, she realized that death would not be denied. She got quieter. She still smiled, but she no longer pulled the oxygen out of the air.

Joy was still in Australia when my sixty-second birthday arrived. It was October 13. It fell on a Friday that year, but it was far from an unlucky day. My grandson Will was born that day on the other side of the world.

Joy left the following Monday. Clyde and I turned our attention to dealing with the affairs of Mom's estate. David and I left Australia around midnight on October 30. A week later, we flew to Sacramento.

Remnants and Remains.

It was only when we arrived at Jill's duplex, and her smiling face was not at the kitchen window waiting for me that I really felt she was dead. From the moment we stepped into the place she had called home for more than thirty years, it was apparent that death had taken her by surprise. A stack of cancelled checks was on the kitchen table. A portable shredder sat on top of a plastic wastebasket next to the table. In the cabinet over the toaster were her plastic medication organizers. There were four of them— enough to last four weeks. Only two days worth of medicine had been dispersed. In the living room, her boots were tucked under the couch just as she'd left them when she got home from the senior center.

It took four days to empty Jill's duplex, gather her things from the coroner, and collect her ashes from the funeral home. When we left, Jill went with us in my red LongChamp bag. We got home close to midnight. David turned on our propane-fueled automatic fireplace, and poured us a cold glass of wine. I placed Jill's ashes on a shelf above the fireplace next to the two-foot-high ceramic church that the ambassador to Mexico's children had given David after their father's death. We raised our glasses and toasted Jill.

We hadn't even taken a sip when both David and I heard the sound of gypsy violins emanating from the next room. Puzzled, David stood up. "Did you turn on the stereo?" he asked.

"No. Maybe we left it on."

David went into the media room, or "the red room" as we had called it since painting it a deep red. "Everything's turned off in there," he said, as he returned.

"It must have been our imagination," I said. "Both of us are pretty exhausted."

Before David could agree or disagree, the music started again.

"I guess that's Jill's way of saying she's glad to finally be here," I said.

Postscript.

The following May, when Gay and Richard came for a visit, we spread Jill's ashes on our property. That summer, Clyde came for a two-week visit. We talked deep into the night, laughed a lot and put any residual bad feelings behind us. Joy came to visit a year later. We explored her "expansive expressiveness" and my pit bull tendencies. We began to reopen the wounds, hoping that they could then heal without scar tissue.

That didn't happen right away. In fact, because we live on opposite sides of the country, it took years to finally heal the wounds. We didn't fully realize our differences in perspective until I wrote about Mom's death in an early draft of this book. My rendition of what had occurred upset Clyde and Gay, and made Joy feel that her earlier attempts to reconcile had meant nothing to me. My words made her angry and they made her feel I no longer valued our friendship nor celebrated the bonds of sisterhood. Months passed without any communication.

Finally, we began trying to sort out our differences through a series of emails. She attempted to explain what upset her, and I suggested ways in which I might incorporate her point of view into the chapter. None of this eased the hurt. It wasn't until we could sit down together and go over the material paragraph by paragraph that we were finally able to write the story of Mom's death in a way that fairly represented both of our perspectives, our motivations and our feelings.

In the process, we learned a lot about how my being the eldest and she the youngest, and the twelve years difference in our ages, had impacted our view of our family and its dynamics. We learned that, although we had the same biological mother, she had had a very different psychological impact on the two of us. Finally, we realized we could have avoided a great deal of hurt and been more mutually supportive had we understood that we were operating at the extreme poles of very different mindsets.

If we had understood that an over-efficient Warrior seeking to maintain rational control could not tolerate an emotionally effusive Celebrant determined to effect a heroic rescue, we would have approached each other differently. We would have been less inclined to evaluate the other's behavior, and less likely to attribute motivation when we didn't understand. We might even have been able to laugh at our differences. In short, we believe we might have defused our conflicts before they threatened to undermine the very foundation of the family.

Now we are able to appreciate that, in the process of confronting death, we experienced each other at our best, and at our worst. We clashed and we hurt each other, but we have repaired the wounds. We now choose to stand together at the front of the line.

Nine years have passed since Mom died. Our grief has faded and been replaced by fond memories of the people we once thought of as the "older generation." Now, we are that generation. It is our turn to confront the challenges of getting old. Because we are reunited, we can help one another do just that. Joy recently suggested that if David dies before me, I should consider moving to Cape Cod to be near her. The idea is very appealing. In addition to offering to be "there" for me, she has assured me her town is "elderly friendly" and has excellent medical care.

In the next chapter, we'll look at how important that becomes as we get older. One of the greatest challenges we face as we age is navigating the medical care system, and managing the doctors and nurses who play an increasingly important role in our lives.

5: AN APPLE A DAY: Dealing with Doctors

As we age, we see more doctors, and we see them more often. In order to patch up our deteriorating bodies we have to see a number of specialists, each of whom has access to advanced technology. As a result, in addition to repairing what's broken, they often find new issues of concern. Given the medical imaging devices that exist today, it's astounding anyone walks out of a medical exam without finding out that something else is malfunctioning or about to do so.

Doctors are now able to identify the tiniest abnormality in our physical makeup. Having identified a problem, they are determined to treat it. The treatment often involves giving us a new medication or a new assistive device to help us breath better or walk better or sleep better. Having made an intervention, they have to monitor the effects. Thus, one appointment leads to another and another. If our maladies are such that we are seeing more than one specialist, our days get filled with medical appointments, our bathrooms start to look like pharmacies, and our bedrooms begin to feel like hospital rooms.

The better the doctor, the more likely this is to occur. Competent doctors are better able to find things that are wrong with us than are less competent doctors. That's the irony of it all. An ancient Arab saying comes to mind: "If you have a bad enemy, send him a good doctor."

As our doctors become a significant part of our lives, their attitudes and behaviors begin to shape our own. The larger and more powerful our physicians appear, the smaller and less powerful we feel. Sandra Gilbert writes: "While the patient is nearly naked, immobilized, frequently in pain, either partly or wholly ignorant of the implications of his illness, and basically unable to control his own condition, the doctor is clothed, mobile, healthy, educated in the meanings of illness, and at least superficially in control of the situation. At best, this asymmetry may replicate the relationship of infant to parent, with the patient in the role of helpless child and the physician playing the part of the wise caregiver."[37]

Stated differently, as we struggle with the physical decline that often accompanies aging, the perceived power of the doctor makes it more likely that our predominant mindset will be that of the Castaway—a person who needs to be rescued or saved. If that mindset takes over, then we are at risk of losing the courage of the Warrior, the faith of the Stargazer, the love of life of the Celebrant, and even the perspective of the Sage at a time when we most need those mindsets.

The power differential between the doctor and the patient was again evident to me when I recently had to undergo surgery to add a lead to my cardiac pacemaker in order to make the two chambers of my heart beat synchronously. Lying there, looking up at the masked face and gloved hands of Dr. Kepler as I began to lose consciousness, I felt totally powerless. I was at his mercy. Fortunately, I trusted him completely. Had I not, or had he been a stranger, I would have been terrified.

I am grateful to Dr. Kepler for implanting the device in my chest and, in so doing, giving me the gift of time and energy. I owe thanks to the anesthesiologist who made sure I felt no pain when they made the incision and while Dr. Kepler snaked the leads through my veins. I am beholden to my cardiologist, Dr. Caldus, who told me it was time for the procedure.

I am thankful, and yet I am wary. Why? Because doctors can change the trajectory of our lives, for better or for worse. Aging gracefully and dying well requires that we learn how to manage our interactions with the medical establishment. That begins with learning how to manage our own doctors.

FOUR TYPES OF DOCTORS.

I've been studying the behavior of doctors for a long time. During my consulting years, I worked with several medical practices to help them improve relationships between the nurses and the doctors, and between the doctors themselves.

---

[37] Sandra M. Gilbert, *Death's Door: Modern Dying and the Ways We Grieve.* (New York, W.W. Norton & Company, 2006), 189.

As I mentioned earlier, when I was in my mid-twenties, I worked with Dr. Frederic Flach, the renowned expert on depression. He hired me to work with him on a project designed to "humanize" the medical profession. It was Dr. Flach's thesis that the best schools of medicine were attracting bright young men and women who were more ambitious than compassionate; more interested in research and the objective study of the human body than in interacting with people. He observed a disturbing lack of empathy on the part of many interns and residents. They were unresponsive and unable to "tune into" patients. He recommended modifications in the curriculum and even a shift in the criteria for admission. Together, we designed workshops on interpersonal effectiveness for the medical students.

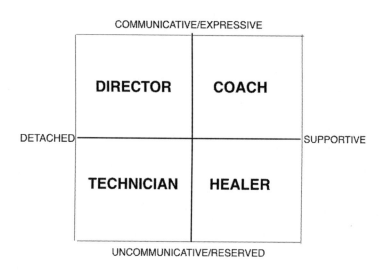

We did that work more than forty years ago. Did it make a difference? It's hard to tell. Medicine has changed a great deal in the interim. Doctors are increasingly specialized. The role of the family doctor as primary caregiver has been eroded. Often when a patient enters the hospital, he sees only specialists he has never met before. These specialists often know nothing more about the patient than the numbers generated by the tests they have ordered. If they are Coaches or Healers, they may take the time to ask questions, and to try to understand the preferences and concerns of the patient. If they are Directors or Technicians, they are likely to focus only on the test results. As a result, their interactions with the patient can be devoid of warmth and compassion, and their delivery of diagnoses shockingly harsh or frustratingly vague.

The Director.

Directors offer a lot of information in either an assertive or aggressive manner. The emphasis is always on them—on what they know and on how they believe treatment must proceed. Directors take the high ground and hold it. They position themselves as superior beings whose expertise entitles them to dictate to the patient. It is their opinion and their expertise that matters. The patient's job is to listen and to comply.

If the Director is assertive, and not aggressive, then the patient will not feel demeaned or devalued. The overriding message of the assertive Director is: "Because of what I know, you should do as I say." If the Director is aggressive, the patient is likely to feel as though he or she is in the presence of the judge or the executioner. The overriding message of the aggressive Director is: "Because of who I am, you will do as I say."

Whether assertive or aggressive, Directors make patients feel they are in the presence of a superior being who can save or rescue them. For that reason, Directors get along best with Stargazers and Castaways who are willing to defer to the power of a higher authority. They have trouble with Warriors who challenge their diagnoses or refuse to comply with their directives.

The Directors' worst nightmare are the Celebrant Warriors who deny anything is seriously wrong and believe that if they push their bodies hard enough, they can heal themselves. These "patients from hell" regard the doctor as an adversary to be manipulated in the interest of maintaining their illusions. Their doctors have no choice but to take the upper hand and force them to give up their pretenses. While Directors are good at this, they would prefer to avoid the drama. Resenting having to work to take control, they expect others to simply honor their right to command.

I have mentioned my friend, Luna, whose husband, Stavros, died from multiple myeloma and melanoma. A few months before his death, we had a sad lunch in her kitchen. As we nibbled on the fresh salad and sipped cold white wine, she told me horror stories of the months they had spent in the hospital in what she termed "medical land" while he endured two bone marrow transplants and then began treatment for a second cancer. She described the disconcerting behavior of one of the oncologists, a Director, who had such a high need for control that he refused to give Stavros' body a chance to adjust to his continuously changing protocol.

"It was like he couldn't stand it if things didn't go according to plan—his plan," Luna said. "Like a ship's captain who runs into high seas, he would turn the ship precipitously, desperate in his need to remain in control of the uncontrollable. In so doing, he put the ship in more danger than it had been before."

Directive oncologists made Luna and Stavros "medically averse," to use her term. This is particularly astounding since Luna is a medical doctor. She and her sick husband got to the point they didn't want to tell the doctors when something didn't feel quite right. They were afraid of triggering yet another test or precipitous change in medication. In short, they began to resist and resent the very experts they had sought out to help Stavros.

I've told you about the painful meeting we had with Dr. French shortly before my mother's death. I am not criticizing Dr. French because he refused to do the surgery. I am objecting to the way he delivered the news. As he pronounced Mom near death, he acted as though she wasn't even in the room, and spoke only to her children. Mom would have been less upset if Dr. French had been a reticent Technician whose reluctance to communicate would have made it easier for her to cling to her Stargazer mindset and continue to deny that the end of her life was fast approaching.

The Technician.

Like the Director, Technicians are personally detached. Unlike their forceful counterpart, they tend to offer little in the way of information. They tend to be most comfortable with patients who have the mindset of the Castaway. Castaways neither demand answers nor expect their physicians to befriend them. Technicians can be put off by the Warrior's demand for information and the Celebrant's expansiveness. The Stargazers' desire to be nurtured or "rescued" can also make them uncomfortable.

The cardiac surgeon my brother called "the Cowboy" because he wore cowboy boots even when wearing his white medical coat was a Technician who caused my family a great deal of anguish. He was the surgeon to whom Clyde turned when Mom was hospitalized after suffering one of her frequent "mini strokes," or trans ischemic attacks. He told my brother that surgery was necessary and that our mother's life depended upon having her aortic valve replaced. He agreed to do the surgery if a dental evaluation confirmed that her gums and teeth were healthy.

In spite of her clearance from the dentist, the Cowboy waffled after our mother suffered yet another "mini stroke." When Clyde approached him to ask about scheduling the surgery, he was brusque. "I haven't even decided whether I'm going to do it." He refused to explain the reason for his ambivalence. This went on for weeks as Mom grew perceptibly weaker. Finally, the Cowboy announced that he would not perform the surgery. Again, he refused to explain.

Not all Technicians are as aggressive as the Cowboy. Many are unassuming and nonassertive, positioning themselves as knowledgeable servants whose purpose in life is to take measures and make sure the machines that help us stay alive keep humming. My first cardiologist was such a Technician. In the interest of hiding behind results, Dr. Mountebank conducted unnecessary tests. He made me endure a stress echo every six weeks. During each of these appointments, he drew blood. After I switched doctors, I learned that the heart muscle changes slowly—so slowly that a stress echo should be conducted only once a year. Doing blood tests every six weeks is equally ridiculous.

Dr. Mountebank over-tested, and he under-reported. In the two years that I saw him, he never explained the nature of my cardiac distress, nor its probable cause. He talked to me like I was a child, cautioning me to avoid salt, but not explaining why. He prescribed a strong diuretic for emergency use "when the sponge is too full," to use his words. He called it a "silver bullet." The medication was so powerful my pharmacist was reluctant to fill the prescription.

Dr. Mountebank was not only reserved. He was so detached that he couldn't hear what his patients had to say. Toward the end of our relationship, David and I conducted a test of our own. Although Dr. Mountebank was a cardiologist, he was willing to treat his patients and his patients' relatives for problems that had nothing to do with the heart. David went to see him complaining of a sprained finger. The good doctor subjected him to a cardiac stress echo. That was the last test he ran on either one of us.

My mother was lucky. She died while living at home. She died without pain. And, she died with dignity. She died like most people would like to die—drifting away from life surrounded by people they love. She died a good death, but not as a result of her doctors. A bureaucrat in the guise of a Technician had intervened and declared her in need of care on a 24/7 basis, but too fit for end-of-life care. Had we had a chance to move Mom into a nursing home, she is likely to have died in an alien place in the arms of strangers, afraid and alone.

While we had unfortunate experiences with both the Cowboy, Dr. Mountebank, and the bureaucrat, not all Technicians are troublesome. Dr. Kepler, the electrocardiologist who implanted my CRT-D, behaved like a pure Technician when I first met him. He appeared after his assistant had tested my defibrillator. (Another electrocardiologist had implanted the original device.) He proceeded to print out several feet of paper showing my heart's rhythm during the prior six months. He studied the paper inch by inch, stopping only when he saw an aberration. Then he looked at the paper more closely, pursed his lips, closed his eyes for a moment and then continued looking at the remainder of the printout. When he finished, he looked at me, and said, "You had one incident on May 3rd. It lasted only a few seconds. You probably weren't even aware of it. It happened shortly after one o'clock in the morning." That was the beginning and end of the conversation. I had no idea whether my "incident" was serious or not. I assumed it was not since the device hadn't shocked my heart back into rhythm.

During a subsequent visit, while the nurse was testing my battery, my heart began racing until it registered 142 beats per minute. Obviously concerned, she called in Dr. Kepler. This time he was not reserved. On the contrary, he was clearly upset as he arranged for me to have an emergency electrocardiograph. When it was done, he came in and studied the output. "This is not normal," he said more to himself than to me. "Am I having a heart attack?" I asked.

"No," he said, still studying the output.

"What caused this?" I asked.

"We don't know. It happens when it happens," he said as he ushered me into yet another room.

It took almost a half hour for my heart rate to drop. When it reached 114 beats per minutes, Dr. Kepler stood up and left the room.

"Am I free to leave?" I asked the nurse.

She nodded. That was the end of the "incident."

I've often wondered if Dr. Kepler would have been more forthcoming if I had asked more questions. I didn't do so because I saved them for Dr. Caldus, the doctor I regarded as my primary cardiologist. She looked after my heart. Dr. Kepler looked after the device implanted in my chest to make sure my heart kept beating. I suspect my attitude made him even more uncommunicative than he might otherwise have been. It smacked of a chicken and egg dilemma. Did he act like a technician in a white coat because I treated him that way, or did I treat him that way because he was so reticent and detached? I suspect the answer to both questions is "Yes."

During my next two visits with Dr. Kepler, I made it a point to be more forthcoming about how I'd been feeling. I even asked a few questions. "Do the leads in an ICD implant ever have to be replaced? Is it ever advisable to remove an implant? Can cardiomyopathy be reversed?"

While still reserved, he began to talk about his profession. "All we can really do is alleviate the symptoms. Unfortunately, we can't cure a sick heart."

At the next visit, he began talking about resynchronization therapy, and suggested I might be a candidate. The doctor I experienced that day was not simply a technician in a white coat He was genuinely excited about having the opportunity to improve my quality of life. I felt like I was in the hands of a skilled healer. That feeling was reinforced the day of the surgery when he stood over me in his surgical gown and explained what was about to transpire. As I lost consciousness, I was confident that I was in the hands of a skilled and caring artisan.

That occurred two years ago. Last week I went to see Dr. Kepler to "have my battery checked." When he walked into the room, I had no fear. On the contrary, I felt genuinely glad to see him. When his nurse took my blood pressure, it was almost normal. For fifteen years, I have suffered from White Coat Syndrome. If I walk into a doctor's office, my blood pressure skyrockets. That Dr. Kepler had temporarily managed to overcome my irrational fear of doctors is testimony to his healing manner.

The Healer.

Healers are warm, personable, interested and friendly. They use the power of a kind smile and hope as opposed to information to mend patients. Adept at listening, they are responsive in their communications. They ask questions about their patients' lives. Their emphasis is not on themselves, but on those they hope to heal. For this reason, they are most comfortable with patients who want to be nurtured and protected, but do not want too much information. This is the classic definition of the Stargazer. Healers relate to the interpersonal openness of Celebrants, but can be put off by their desire to be part of the conversation.

Dr. Ventus, my first pulmonologist, was a Healer. I first saw him in 2001, shortly after the fall of the Twin Towers. Dr. Hertz, my New York cardiologist, had sent me to see him after detecting a slight wheeze in my chest. From the beginning, Dr. Ventus treated me like a valued friend as well as a patient. During our first appointment, he asked questions about my life, and told me a bit about his daughter who shared my interest in organizational psychology. He behaved as though he had all day to spend with me. Only when I was comfortable with him as a person did he turn to medicine. Telling me what we were doing, but not why we were doing it, he put a plug on my nose and told me to breathe as hard as I could into a tube attached to a big blue machine.

When the test was over, I asked, "So how did I do?" Instead of answering me, he said, "Hmmmm" and looked away. Taking an inhaler out of the cabinet and handing it to me, he said, "I want you to take two puffs. After each puff, breathe in deeply."

Then, Dr. Ventus asked me to sit in his waiting room for twenty minutes. Nineteen minutes later, he called me back into the examining room. We repeated the test. When we finished, he told me to gather my things and meet him in his office.

When I walked into the small, spartan room, he was on the telephone with my cardiologist, Dr. Hertz. As I lowered myself into the chair on the other side of his desk, I heard him say, "Yes, Dr. Hertz, I've seen Pamela Cuming. Her lung function improved forty-two percent with albuterol. I think we should take her off the Coreg. It could be contributing to her asthma. I'll need a scan, but I believe she has COPD as well as asthma."

When he hung up, I said, "I don't have asthma. I've never had an asthma attack in my life. Sometimes I breathe better than at other times, but that's not asthma."

"No, that's COPD."

"COPD?" I asked tentatively.

An Apple A Day

"Chronic Obstructive Pulmonary Disease," Dr. Ventus responded in such a quiet voice that I strained to hear him.

"It's curable, right?" I asked.

Failing to meet my eyes, he shook his head and said, "It is controllable."

I saw Dr. Ventus for five years. Each time, no matter how well or poorly I performed on my lung function tests, he allowed me to believe my lung disease was not a significant problem. He continued to communicate a benign message even when I confronted him. As I prepared to travel to Australia for an extended visit, I asked him for a copy of my most recent lung function test. At the bottom of the computer-generated printout was the diagnosis: Severe Obstructive Airways Dysfunction.

"How can my level be "severe" when I can still walk five miles a day, never get short of breath, and live a full life?" I challenged the kind doctor.

"Well, there are other factors we must consider," he stammered, clearly unnerved by my challenge. "We must also consider your functional lung capacity, not just your lung capacity. You have a lot of lung volume. And, you exercise regularly. That makes a difference. Most patients simply give up. You are unusual."

Like a true Healer, Dr. Ventus allowed me to believe that I was special and could prevail over a disease that renders most others immobile. He was warm and supportive and encouraging, and he volunteered very little information that would have destroyed either my illusions or my will to fight.

Unfortunately, Dr. Ventus did not do me a favor when he failed to explain the seriousness of COPD. Had Dr. Ventus been more forthcoming, I might have smoked fewer cigars or exercised more diligently. I certainly wouldn't have been so traumatized when a subsequent pulmonologist told me the truth. I'll tell you more about that shortly.

Mom's primary care physician, Dr. See, was a true Healer. Always warm and supportive, he often reassured Mom by telling her she had a remarkable immune system and was likely to live to be 115 years old. He never told her anything about her failing heart, for doing so would only upset her. He understood that the Queen of Denial knew little about her body and liked it that way. He allowed the Stargazer to continue to believe that good news was on the horizon.

Unfortunately, his quiet optimism helped steer us in the wrong direction during Mom's final weeks. In suggesting we find a way to pool our resources and get Mom into an appropriate facility, he unintentionally colluded with the bureaucrat and sent us down a path that would be very upsetting to Mom during her last days on earth.

Healers make the patient feel good. They inspire faith that the ultimate outcome will be positive. Healers are wonderful to work with when a positive outcome is not dependent on the total involvement and commitment of the patient, or when the patient and members of the family do not have to be prepared for a sudden worsening of the disease. Those physicians who see patients on a recurrent basis, and who deal with ailments and conditions that are better managed when the patient is willing to talk openly about their symptoms and concerns will probably do a better job if they are Coaches.

The Coach.

Coaches are assertive-responsive. They ask questions, and express interest in the life of the patient. At the same time, they are forceful in their assertions. Their patients are neither coddled nor treated like children. On the contrary, Coaches treat their patients like responsible and competent people who deserve and are capable of handling the truth.

Assertive-responsive Coaches maintain a balance between trying to understand the patient and telling the patient what to do. Such a physician invites the patient to collaborate in finding the best treatment plan. The physician's recommendations reflect not only his or her expertise, but the patient's reality and life experience. Because Coaches spend time listening, they are more likely to understand which of their patients' abilities give their life meaning and are worth preserving, even at the cost of other capacities.

Coaches are personable enough to get their patients to talk, and forthcoming enough to explain a course of therapy in sufficient detail to motivate the patient to adhere to the regime. If the course of therapy requires that the patient change his or her life style, or embrace a rehabilitation regime, then the Coach is likely to be the most effective type of physician.

Coaches tend to like working with Celebrant Warriors who feel empowered enough to actively participate in their own healing. They relate to the perspective of the Sage and can find themselves engaged in conversations that threaten to throw off their appointment schedule. (David does this all the time to his doctors. They inevitably run late after spending time with him.)

Coaches like the courageousness of the Warrior who is determined to beat the disease. They relate to the Celebrant whose optimism helps them tolerate some painful or difficult treatment regimes. And yet, because they are the most flexible of the physician types, they can work with the Stargazer and the Castaway, understanding that neither type feels empowered and modifying their approach accordingly.

The best primary care doctors and internists are probably Coaches. Our current primary care doctor is a great Coach. I call him Dr. Walmunt, which means *mighty protector* in German. He is *mighty* because he is an excellent doctor—a fine diagnostician and effective healer. He is a *protector* who remains loyal to his patients even when continuing to treat them is no longer financially viable. In a recent conversation he had with David, Dr. Walmunt confided, "Because of government imposed caps on fees for medical services and procedures, I can't afford to take on new Medicare patients. Several physicians I know actually stop treating their patients when they become Medicare-eligible. I couldn't sleep at night if I did that."

David and I are fortunate to be among the three thousand patients his practice services. I have seen him only a handful of times in the last six years, and yet when I do see him, I feel like I am visiting someone who knows me well. He remembers enough to ask me about my writing, my grandchildren, my daughters and my travels. He understands that I see so many specialists that coming to see him on a regular basis is not something I want to do. He works with me when I need to have a cyst lanced or when I have slashed my finger on a cheese knife. He reads the reports my specialists send him on a regular basis, and is up-to-date when I see him. When I leave his office, I am usually smiling. His positive attitude is infectious.

I believe the best cardiologists, pulmonologists, and oncologists are also Coaches. Though they are specialists, they see patients on a recurrent basis over a long period of time. Heart disease, lung disease, and cancer all respond to changes in life style (diet, exercise) and require that the patient be sufficiently informed and committed to following a medication regimen. Coaches are better than the other types of doctors at inspiring this kind of commitment.

I am fortunate that my pulmonologist, Dr. Winden, and my cardiologist, Dr. Caldus, are Coaches. Both are strong, forceful, assertive women. While capable of issuing medical dictates and making pronouncements that would make even the strongest Warrior flinch, they know how to listen. Though both are regarded as preeminent in their fields, neither is arrogant. Finally, both Dr. Winden and Dr. Caldus are compassionate.

Dr. Caldus is widely regarded as an exceptionally talented cardiologist, and yet she has not become so enamored of her tests that she has forgotten that having one's heart examined is highly stressful for patients. There was a period of time when I was seeing Dr. Caldus but still going to Dr. Hertz, my New York cardiologist, for my annual tests. When I told her I was flying back east to see Dr. Hertz and to attend daughter Melissa's wedding, she said, "I suggest you schedule your appointment with the doctor after the wedding. Don't see him before since he might upset you, and you don't want to be upset on such a special day."

I followed her suggestion, even though it meant changing not only my appointment with the doctor, but David's and my flights as well. It was worth it. Dr. Caldus was right. Dr. Hertz did upset me.

Dr. Caldus also relies on the numbers generated by diagnostic tests, but she does not assume that the numbers tell the whole story. Unlike Dr. Hertz, she believes that stress affects cardiac function. She believes that, in some people, stress creates adrenalin and that adrenalin, in turn, affects both blood pressure and cardiac function. "It's obvious to me that you create a lot of adrenalin," she said during one of our appointments. The way she said it made me feel like she really understood me as a person. She understood that I was a fighter. I sensed she even admired that in me.

Dr. Caldus treats me like a competent individual. She trusts me to keep accurate readings of my blood pressure, accepting my claim that I suffer from White Coat Syndrome and, thus, my blood pressure is artificially high when I am in her office, or any doctor's office. Dr. Caldus accepts my numbers in lieu of her own. A Director would never do this. We talk about what's happening in my life. She encourages me to talk about things that have no immediate bearing on my cardiac function. That's the behavior of a Coach, not someone who stands aloof and regards himself or herself as a superior being.

An Apple A Day

Dr. Caldus referred me to Dr. Winden. I remember sitting in one of Dr. Winden's examining rooms waiting for her. It was only my third visit and I still hadn't taken her measure. Based on our first two visits when she informed me that my lung disease was both serious and progressive, I was a little afraid of her. The nurse had already taken my blood pressure and measured my oxygen saturation. When she left, she neglected to close the door. I was able to hear Dr. Winden talking with another physician about a hospitalized patient.

"This morning we removed 4000 cc's of fluid from her lungs. An hour later, 500 cc's had returned. That poor dear. She's preoccupied with concerns about her business when what she should be doing is focusing on her body. She needs help, but she has nobody. She and her daughter are estranged. They haven't even spoken for years. I don't understand it. She's such a nice woman. There's got to be something we can do."

My impatience at being kept waiting disappeared. So did my fear. I began to think she would try to work with me, and not impose medical regimens that I couldn't tolerate. I was right. Though Dr. Winden advised me to use supplemental oxygen at night (as well as when I fly or exercise), she understands why I am reluctant to do so. David is a light sleeper and the recurrent beeping sound of the portable oxygen concentrator would keep him awake. Though he'd probably get used to it over time, I'd rather not put him through that. Further, the presence of the medical equipment would serve as a constant reminder that I am not well. I do not define myself nor treat myself as a sick person, and have asked that David not do so either. I am not trying to deny my illness; I am simply trying to avoid having it dominate our lives.

Because she listens, Dr. Winden understands that. For now, she has stopped trying to persuade me to reconsider. Her emphasis during our last few appointments has been on encouraging me to keep exercising and strengthening my breathing. "You've developed your own pulmonary rehab system, and it's working. Keep it up."

The Coach is without a doubt the most sought after type of doctor. The federal government has decided that all doctors should behave like Coaches. It has mandated surveys and other feedback mechanisms to measure how well a doctor communicates with patients, and how the doctor makes patients feel, from both an emotional and physical standpoint. Compensation is, in part, dependent on patient satisfaction scores.

The attempt to improve the physician's bedside manner has been triggered by the need to improve healthcare while driving down costs. "Research shows that when doctors don't listen to patients, they miss important health cues and misdiagnose illness. Meanwhile, patients who don't understand what their doctors say fail to follow their regimens, leading to preventable hospitalizations, complications and poor outcomes."[38]

In spite of the benefits, I don't think all doctors should be expected to behave like Coaches. Physicians who perform colonoscopies, endoscopies or other invasive procedures that are done infrequently and when the patient is drugged do not have to establish a relationship with the patient, and thus can function quite adequately as Technicians. So can radiologists and anesthesiologists. As I have pointed out, physicians whose primary function is to use machines to generate test results can be Technicians. Their discomfort with sharing information and their tendency to remain detached presents no problem. Healers can be very effective when dealing with Stargazers who want to know little about their bodies or their ailments, and are content to follow orders.

In short, there are advantages and disadvantages to dealing with each type of physician. Further, regardless of their communication or interpersonal skills, every doctor has good days and bad days. And, every doctor, like every patient, has a mindset toward aging and mortality that shifts as their personal circumstances change. With these shifts comes a modification in their behavior with patients.

BEHIND THE PROFESSIONAL FAÇADE.

A cardiologist who was usually a Coach behaved like an aggressive Director at a critical juncture in my life. In so doing, he triggered in me the White Coat Syndrome that persists to this day. I'm talking about my New York cardiologist, Dr. Hertz.

Dr. Hertz was my cardiologist from the spring of 2001 until December, 2006. Under his strict but caring guidance, I had gone from a patient who needed to be on a heart transplant list to a patient who walked a strong

---

[38]Laura Landro, "The Talking Cure for Health Care," *The Wall Street Journal*, April 8, 2012.

five miles a day. I was his prize patient, his success story—a story that he proudly told to cardiologists all over the world during his regular international calls. He was my Coach. If he'd asked, I would have tried to climb Mt. Everest. (Fortunately, he was more realistic than that.)

We were both highly stressed when I saw him on December 9, 2006. As I have told you, I had just experienced a very traumatic three months. I'd spread my mother's ashes in Australia and authorized the cremation of Aunt Jill's body in Sacramento. I had learned that Katherine, my best friend in the Pacific Northwest, was near death. I was clinging desperately to my Celebrant Warrior self, but my confidence was rapidly waning.

When I arrived at Dr. Hertz's small waiting room, I could tell his practice was out of control. It was only 10:15 in the morning, and every chair was taken. The receptionist, Jackie, was scowling and trying not to make eye contact with the waiting patients. When I checked in, I tried to engage her. "Good to see you, Jackie," I said, though that was far from the truth. From the beginning, I'd found Jackie to be sullen and uncooperative. "Is Gabby back from maternity leave?"

"She's not coming back," Jackie said without looking up. "Take a seat. The doctor will be with you shortly."

After forty-five minutes, a nurse I didn't recognize finally came to get me. I put on my shorts, tee shirt and sneakers and went into the examining room. The nurse had just about finished attaching the electrodes to my body when Dr. Hertz appeared. I smiled broadly, as we do when greeting a friend we have not seen for more than a year. I thought it odd that he didn't smile at me in return. He was all business. He said almost nothing as I struggled to keep up with him as he steadily increased the speed and incline of the treadmill.

I had only been on the machine for five or six minutes when Dr. Hertz said, "I have all the data I need." I'd had the test often enough to know that his gathering enough data so quickly wasn't good news. Before I could register my concern, he hurried from the room, leaving the technician to complete the ultrasound.

As I emerged from the tiny closet that served as a dressing room, I bumped into an elderly gentlemen wearing only his briefs and sneakers. I apologized and headed down the hall, seeking the sanctity of Dr. Hertz's office. I was upset to find someone else sitting in my chair. Confused and annoyed, I walked back down the hall toward the waiting room. As I passed the room where the old man was getting wired for his test, Dr. Hertz hurried out.

"You've lost a third of your heart function," he announced so loudly that even the patients in the waiting room could hear. "Before you were borderline. Now, you are definitely at risk of Sudden Death Syndrome."

"But that can't be," I argued, my heart racing. "I've been feeling fine."

"The numbers don't lie," he said, turning and walking down the hall.

Not knowing what else to do, I followed him. He led us into an examining room across the hall from his office. "I want you to wait here. Jackie will be in to take blood."

I scarcely noticed Jackie taking my blood. Nor could I focus on the posters showing hearts in various stages of health that lined the walls. All I could think about was Dr. Hertz's pronouncement. "You are at risk of Sudden Death Syndrome."

I could drop dead at any minute, I thought. *Just like Mom did. Any minute. Right here, even. I might not even make it back to Melissa's house tonight. I might never see David again. The fact that I feel fine is irrelevant. I am on the verge of death and I hadn't a clue.*

By the time Dr. Hertz returned and told me to come into his office, the fight had gone out of me. I had no confidence in my body, and no belief in the future. And, I would never again experience doctors in the same way. I had learned that they could be the source of great pain. They could shock me. They could turn my world upside down. They had the power to destroy my confidence in myself and in my body, and there wasn't anything I could do about it. I had developed a bad case of White Coat Syndrome.

I sat down in the leather chair on the other side of Dr. Hertz's desk. I noticed it was more cluttered than usual. Pushing aside a pile of folders, he picked up a piece of paper. "Your ejection fraction has dropped to twenty-three. That, coupled with bundle branch block, means you could die at any moment from ventricular fibrillation. We're going to put an ICD defibrillator and biventricular pacemaker in your chest. And now, if you don't mind, I am running very late..."

In hindsight, I believe there may have been things going on in Dr. Hertz's life that had nothing to do with me that made him seem so callous. I know his practice was in chaos as a result of the loss of his cardiac nurse. Perhaps his personal life was in chaos as well.

I do know that he regretted his outburst. He called me at my daughter's the next day and took an entirely different approach. It sounded to me as though he was trying to make amends. "Let's just regard the ICD as a security blanket that we're putting around your shoulders," he said. "And remember, you are doing all that you can be doing. Keep up the good work. And place that call to Dr. Caldus. It's three hours earlier on the West Coast."

Perhaps Dr. Hertz' earlier aloofness stemmed from the desire to keep me, the patient, at a safe distance so that he could remain objective. Perhaps he was afraid that his emotions would get involved, compromising his ability to do what had to be done or to say what had to be said. Doctors feel, and they can hurt.

I will never forget the afternoon we visited Katherine, the Miracle Girl, in the hospital in Seattle. She had not yet been told that she suffered from incurable progressive multifocal leukoencephalopathy (PML). A deadly virus was eating the myelin sheaths in her brain. She was expected to live only a few months. With each day that passed, she would lose her ability to control another bodily function. Unaware of her dire prognosis, we were talking about traveling together to San Sebastian, Spain when she got better.

Her three neurologists were standing in the doorway. When Katherine clapped her hands at the prospect of our trip, a tear fell from the eye of the young female doctor standing in front of the others. The knowledge that Katherine was never going to make that trip touched her personally. There was no look of personal despair on the faces of the other two neurologists who were older and more seasoned. Instead, they had a look of generals who had been forced to admit defeat, and were furious at the humiliation.

In *Being Mortal*, Dr. Gawande explains what drives many physicians. "You become a doctor for what you imagine to be the satisfaction of the work, and that turns out to be the satisfaction of competence. It is a deep satisfaction very much like the one that a carpenter experiences in restoring a fragile antique chest or that a science teacher experiences in bringing a fifth grader to that sudden, mind-shifting recognition of what atoms are. It comes partly from being helpful to others. But it also comes from being technically skilled and able to solve difficult, intricate problems. Your competence gives you a secure sense of identity. For a clinician, therefore, nothing is more threatening to whom you think you are than a patient with a problem you cannot solve."[39]

Doctors want to heal and they want to win. Many doctors, especially the Directors, regard themselves as Warriors with a mission: When a person is dying, the Warrior has lost. It's not the disease that has been defeated, but the physician. The patient is at risk of becoming simply the battleground upon which the war has been waged.

Sometimes, it's not the patient and his illness that upsets the doctors, but the changing nature of the medical profession itself. I recently read a disturbing article that suggests malaise over their jobs is affecting a lot of American physicians. Cardiologist Sandeep Jauhar's memoir *Doctored* argues that the medical profession is in a midlife crisis. He attributes this to lack of status. "In the past four decades, American doctors have lost the status they used to enjoy. In the mid-20th century, physicians were the pillars of any community. If you were smart and sincere and ambitious, at the top of your class, there was nothing nobler or more rewarding that you could aspire to become. Today medicine is just another profession, and doctors have become like everybody else: insecure, discontented and anxious about the future."[40]

Part of the doctors' discomfort with their profession stems from "pay for performance" contracts. Under these contracts, doctors who follow standard treatment guidelines are rewarded with bonuses from insurers and given high ratings on insurer websites. Physicians who deviate from the insurer-regulated procedures are penalized.

The long arm of the insurer affects even the medications that the doctor prescribes. For example, the private insurer Wellpoint recently outlined how they believed certain types of cancer should be treated, and with what medications. They announced they would pay an incentive of $350 per month per patient to physicians who adhered to their plan. This is of concern since oncologists themselves have not been able to agree on the optimal treatment regime. Under the new paradigm, it is not the doctors, the experts, who have the say. It is the insurers and the

---

[39]Dr. Atul Gawande, *Being Mortal: Medicine and What Matters in the End.* (New York, Henry Holt and Company, 2015), 8.

[40]Sandeep Jauhar, "Why Doctors are Sick of Their Profession," *The Wall Street Journal*, April 29, 2014.

regulators. The doctors have been demoted.[41]

Who wins? Not the doctors who feel over-controlled, under-paid or under-appreciated and certainly not the patients. Both are suffering from the increasing de-humanization of medicine. This is particularly pronounced when a patient is dying.

CONTROLLING THE BEAST.

Hospitals are places where technology is king, and humanity is simply the raw material on which it feeds. Its appetite is endless. Unfortunately, the "good death"—the death whereby we drift slowly out of life surrounded by loved ones in a home we cherish—is becoming increasingly rare.

In an opinion piece written for *The New York Times*, Ira Byock laments: "Less than 45 percent of dying Americans receive hospice care at home, and nearly half of those are referred to hospice within just two weeks of death. Hospice was designed to provide end-of-life care, but this is brink-of-death care."[42]

It's even worse than that. Once in the hospital or the nursing home, patients are not allowed to die. Writing in Mexico City in 1982, Juis Buñul said, "An even more horrible death is one that's kept at bay by the miracles of modern medicine, a death that never ends. In the name of Hippocrates, doctors have invented the most exquisite form of torture ever known to man: survival..."[43]

In the intervening years, the situation has gotten worse. As David's ninety-year-old stepmother lay dying, her weary body aching from bed sores that refused to heal, the doctors put a pacemaker in her chest to keep her heart pumping. She finally died anyway, but after enduring months of mental and physical anguish. Her story is not unique.

---

[41]Pamela Hartzband and Jerome Groopmannov, "How Medical Care is Being Corrupted," *The New York Times*, November. 18, 2014.

[42]Ira Byock, "Dying Shouldn't Be So Brutal," *The New York Times*, January 31, 2015.

[43]Luis Buñuel, "1982:MEXICO CITY...THE MIRACLES OF MODERN MEDICINE", *Lapham's Quarterly*, Volume VI, Number 4, page 42.

Dr. Gawande draws an intriguing analogy between doctors today and General Custer, cavalry commander in the American Civil War and War with the Indians. Custer's determination to win at all costs got him and his troops slaughtered at the Battle of the Little Bighorn, known as Custer's Last Stand. "The simple view is that medicine exists to fight death and disease, and that is, of course, its most basic task. Death is the enemy. But the enemy has superior forces. Eventually, it wins. And in a war that you cannot win, you don't want a general who fights to the point of total annihilation. You don't want Custer. You want Robert E. Lee, someone who knows how to fight for territory that can be won and how to surrender it when it can't, someone who understands that the damage is greatest if all you do is battle to the bitter end."[44]

In spite of physicians' reluctance to have people die on their watch, and hospitals' desire to manage mortality statistics that affect their performance rating, more and more people are dying in hospitals instead of at home. In a heart-rending story of the prolonged death of her father, Katy Butler explains that, because of technological advances, the doctors have shifted the paradigm. Their focus is no longer on saving lives, but rather on prolonging the process of dying. As a result, two-fifths of deaths now take place in a hospital in spite of the fact that three-quarters of elderly people state they want to die at home. A fifth of these deaths occur in the intensive care ward where the dying take their last breaths plugged into machines.[45]

That seniors incur most of their Medicare expenses during the last six months of life illustrates the extent of the problem. "In 2011, Medicare spending reached close to $554 billion, which amounted to 21 percent of the total spent on U.S. health care in that year. Of that $554 billion, Medicare spent 28 percent, or about $170 billion, on patients' last six months of life."[46]

---

[44]Dr. Atul Gawande, *Being Mortal: Medicine and What Matters in the End.* (New York, Henry Holt and Company, 2015), 187.

[45]Katy Butler, *Knocking on Heaven's Door: The Path to a Better Way of Death.* (New York, Scribner, 2013), 5.

[46]"End of Life Care Constitutes Third Rail of U.S. Health Care Policy Debate," *The Medicare Newsgroup*, June 03, 2013.

An Apple A Day

Most of us will die plugged into machines in the bowels of the beast called the modern hospital. Katy Butler's father was lucky. His wife and his daughter fought for him. "With just a little more bad luck, my father might be wheeled into an intensive care unit, where my mother and I— and even my dying father—would become bystanders in a battle, fought over the territory of his body, between the ancient reality of death and the technological imperatives of modern medicine…If my mother and I did not veer from the pathway my father was traveling, he might well draw his last breath in a room stripped of any reminder of home or of the sacred, among doctors and nurses who knew his blood counts and oxygen levels but barely knew his name."[47]

Unfortunately, most family members are incapable of insisting that their loved one be allowed to die. The opposite tends to be the case. David's father was a surgeon. He often said that the biggest problem in dealing with a dying patient were the family members who demanded that the doctors keep their loved ones alive at all costs. We need to recognize this, and do something while we are well enough to protect our right to die on our own terms. We need to file advance medical directives stating what we want or don't want in terms of medical intervention.

Doctors themselves recognize that end of life medical intervention rarely works; it prolongs dying, not living. As a result, the major of doctors have filed directives stating that no extreme or heroic measures are to be applied. A 2003 survey indicated that sixty-four percent of physicians had filed advance directives, as compared with twenty percent of the general population. Many wear bracelets inscribed with the directive: DNR—Do Not Resuscitate. Many more elect to die at home, and not in the hospitals whose bleak corridors they have walked for years.[48]

David and I both have advance medical directives. Mine declares that if I am diagnosed with a terminal condition or in an irreversible coma, I do not want life-sustaining treatment that would only serve to "artificially prolong the process of my dying." It authorizes the medical establishment to give me oxygen and pain medication, and to suction my air passages and transfer me to another facility, if necessary. It precludes them from

---

[47]Katy Butler, *Knocking on Heaven's Door: The Path to a Better Way of Death.* (New York ,Scribner, 2013), 5.

[48]Ken Murray, "Why Doctors Die Differently," *The Wall Street Journal*, February 25,2012.

giving me "artificially provided nutrition and hydration." It states that, if possible, I should be allowed to die at home.

Advance directives enable us to decide how and when to die. They are an important part of taking responsibility for both our own lives and our own deaths. To do so, we need to act as our own general contractors when it comes to health issues.

ACTING AS OUR OWN GENERAL CONTRACTOR.

Recently David met with Dr. Caldus. He told her that he wanted to stop taking a blood thinner that she had put him on when he was experiencing atrial fibrillation. She smiled and said, "I don't recommend that you stop, but it's your decision. This is not a prison."

Although it sometimes feels that we, as patients, have been incarcerated by our doctors, we are not being held captive by the medical care establishment. They are providers, and we are choosing to let them help us. In the end, we have to behave like our own general contractors both with regard to medical decisions, and with regard to the overall quality of our lives as aging mortals.

Sometimes this means telling a doctor we refuse to undergo a procedure that would extend the duration of our life but compromise its quality. Julie was in her late forties when she learned that her cancer had returned. Aware of how awful the chemicals made her feel and how they had compromised her ability to engage with her husband and young son, she denied treatment and instead embraced an alternative. She spent a month at a health spa devoted to helping people find natural ways to rid the body of cancer. She learned how to prepare foods, which had anti-cancer properties. Once home, she completely changed her eating habits. She continued to see her oncologist, but only to get periodic blood draws. To his amazement, the tumors receded. After four years, she remained cancer free. In the fifth year, this year, the cancer once again returned. This time, she has elected to include chemotherapy in her treatment. Her son is older, and able to fend for himself. Her body is stronger and better able to tolerate the toxicity.

My friend Rob was diagnosed with lymphoma ten years ago when he was in his early sixties. He tolerated a toxic chemo regime that, at times, made him wish he were dead. He survived, and the cancer went into remission. Three years ago, he discovered a lump on his neck. His doctor told him it was probably nothing. He was worried, however, and insisted that it be biopsied. He was right. The lymphoma had returned. To force it back into remission, he had to endure a debilitating stem cell transplant. Today, he is cancer free. He says, however, that if the cancer were to return, he would refuse to undergo a second transplant.

Probably the biggest test of our ability to act as our own general contractor comes when the medicine has failed, and we have run out of acceptable alternatives. A year or so after Katy Butler's father died, her eighty-four-year-old mother, Valerie, was told she needed a heart valve replacement. If she didn't have the surgery, she would die within two years. If she had the surgery, she could live into her nineties. The risks, however, were significant. She could have a stroke. She could suffer cognitive decline. Further, the doctors said they would not perform the operation with a Do Not Resuscitate (DNR) order in place. If she suffered a stroke on the table, they would bring her back. Valerie refused the surgery. Her daughter supported her as she "reclaimed her moral authority, defied her doctors, refused a potential life-extending surgery, and faced her own death the old-fashioned way: head on."[49]

Julie, Rob and Katy Butler's mother all had to make life-changing decisions and challenge the medical profession on their own, without the active help of the family doctor. This is the new face of modern medicine. Once upon a time, when we needed a doctor, we saw the family doctor. If he couldn't fix the problem, then he referred us to a specialist. He kept in close touch with the specialist and acted as our liaison. If we had to spend time in the hospital, our family doctor would pay us a visit at least once a day. He (or she) was our general contractor.

Now, things are different. Under Medicare, we don't even need a referral to see a specialist. Our primary care physician becomes aware of our examination only when (or if) his office receives a report. If we are hospitalized, our primary care physician may not have the right to practice medicine in that facility. When we are down for the count, and barely able

---

[49]Katy Butler, *Knocking on Heaven's Door:The Path to a Better Way of Death.* (New York, Scribner, 2013), 5-6.

to function, we will either have to act as our own advocate or put ourselves at the mercy of someone in a white coat who thinks of us as a type of disease or a series of numbers generated by the last series of tests.

In *Being Mortal*, Dr. Gawande asserts that the more specialized the doctor, the less able they are to deal with the cluster of ailments that tend to present themselves when we get old. "We're good at addressing specific, individual problems: colon cancer, high blood pressure, arthritic knees. Give us a disease, and we can do something about it. But give us an elderly woman with high blood pressure, arthritic knees, and various other ailments besides—an elderly woman at risk of losing the life she enjoys—and we hardly know what to do and often only make matters worse."[50]

David has had an experience with a plethora of specialists that illustrates Dr. Gawande's point. Because he is now engaged in creating digital multimedia works of art, his eyesight is extremely important to him. When he learned that he was developing a cataract in one eye, he immediately sought out a surgeon to correct the problem. Expense was not an issue when it came to restoring his vision. The surgeon was easily able to convince him to buy a special lens implant that cost $2500 more than its Medicare-provided substitute.

He had trouble focusing after the surgery, but was told that would improve. It did not. Instead, he began to have intense headaches. The eye surgeons said that had nothing to do with the implant, nor with his vision. Given his prior history of sinus infections, David assumed that must be the source of the problem. He found a sinus specialist who gave him every test in the book, and found nothing other than a slight inflammation. Refusing to operate, the sinus doctor prescribed prednisone.

The headaches continued. David saw a neurologist who found nothing wrong. He then returned to the sinus doctor who prescribed yet another round of prednisone. That, in turn, contributed to his developing atrial fibrillation. Now, he had a whole new problem. The arrhythmia put him squarely in the cardiologists' stable. They cardioverted him twice, using electrical current to restore normal heart rhythm. Both failed in a matter of months. Now, they couldn't agree on whether he should be

---

[50]Dr. Atul Gawande, *Being Mortal: Medicine and What Matters in the End.* (New York, Henry Holt and Company, 2015), 44.

cardioverted again or have a cardiac ablation in which catheters are inserted to destroy those parts of the heart that are causing it to misfire.

Tired of bouncing between specialists who only seemed to make him worse, David took matters into his own hands. He researched cardiac ablation, and decided he wanted no part of a procedure that would destroy parts of his healthy heart. Finally, the doctors agreed with him. They put him on medication and then cardioverted him again. This time, as a result of the continuing medication, it held. Now, he was free to once again address his headaches and continuing problems with his vision.

He made an appointment to see one of the doctors who works in tandem with the eye surgeons and was fortunate to meet with a new member of the team. That doctor told him his vision was out of balance since he hadn't had the special implant put into his other eye, his healthy eye. David was outraged. Had he known, he would have opted for the Medicare-approved lens, and avoided all of the problems that followed. The doctor told him that the only option other than implanting the second lens was to wear glasses to correct the imbalance. David opted for the glasses. A year and several tries later, David now has three pairs of glasses: one for reading, another for working on the computer, and a third for general use. So much for the expensive implant!

If Dr. Walmut, David's primary care physician, had been involved, perhaps he could have warned David of the hazards of the single implant, or of the adverse effects of too much prednisone. Had he done so, David might never have developed atrial fib, and been spared three cardioversions. But he wasn't involved, at least not as general contractor who had a voice in the recommendations made by an ever-expanding list of specialists.

Unfortunately, the need to function as our own spokesman doesn't stop even when we are on our backs. Paul, a friend in his seventies, who is suffering from pancreatic cancer, was taken to the emergency room of our local hospital. His white cell count had fallen drastically as a result of chemotherapy. His immune system was almost nonexistent. Yet the attendants put his gurney right next to that of a patient with pneumonia. Fortunately, Paul is himself a doctor, and understood the danger. When he pointed it out, the attendant was responsive but not apologetic. "You have a good point," she said. "I suppose it would be better to move you."

The attendant who put Paul next to the pneumonia patient may have been sloppy. Or, perhaps she was unaware of his cancer and compromised immune system. In making her aware, he may have saved his own life.

Making people in the medical profession aware of our conditions is our responsibility. To do so, we need to be able to hand over records. Relying on the administrative help in a physician's office to fax records in a timely fashion is not a good idea. Several of my doctors have told me that themselves. It's better to request copies of test results and to bring them with you if you need to see a different doctor for the same ailment.

Record keeping is only one aspect of acting as your own general contractor. Another aspect is monitoring your own health. I invested in a quality blood pressure monitor, a pulse oximeter, and even a portable spirometer to measure my lung's FEV (forced expiry volume). Now, I can monitor my vitals between appointments, and while exercising. The pulse oximeter measures my heart rate and provides useful feedback when I am on the treadmill or riding the stationary bike. I know now that my respiratory performance varies depending on the amount of pollen or pollution in the air, on whether I have a cold, and even on how much stress I am under. The doctor's test results reflect my level of functioning at one moment in time. Those results are sometimes among my better, and at other times, among my worst. In providing more data points, I insure that the doctor can base decisions on a true picture of my performance over time.

Earlier this week I had an appointment with Dr. Winden. Her tests confirmed what I had told her: my oxygen saturation levels had increased as a result of the implant that resynchronized the chambers of my heart. I asked her if that meant I could now fly without oxygen.

"That depends on the impact altitude would have on your saturation levels. We can make an educated guess about that by doing an arterial blood gas test to measure the levels of oxygen and carbon dioxide in your blood. We can then apply a formula to estimate what those levels would look like at eight thousand feet."

Elated, I went directly to the lab. Dr. Winden called me the next day. "Your levels are fine at sea level, but, according to the formula, they would drop markedly as altitude increases."

"Too markedly?" I asked, my disappointment obvious.

"'In my opinion, yes," she said. "But I want to consult with my colleagues."

The next day I sent her an email with an extract from a study done in Norway that suggested people with my numbers could fly safely without oxygen if the flight duration did not exceed four hours.

She responded immediately, sending me another extract and summarizing the authors' conclusions. "If your saturation on room air at rest is >/= 95% AND your exercise saturation after 6 minutes on your treadmill is more than 84%, then it is unlikely you will need oxygen. Though these providers would suggest a test we do not do—which is a high altitude tolerance test for confirmation." She then suggested a next step. "If you confirm this with your own device and/or want us to independently test you (in our PFT lab) and we see these kinds of results, then we would suspend your oxygen altogether (if your SaO2 is >88% with exercise).

Dr. Winden was saying that if I wanted to conduct my own test, she would honor the results. Now, that's a Coach! In closing, she made it clear that, as my own general contractor, the decision is mine to make, and the consequences are mine to bear. "You should know there is some controversy even within our group about how well you could tolerate a prolonged flight. What I am giving you are guidelines, not guarantees." At our next appointment, we discussed the issue again. She closed by saying, "If you board a plane without your oxygen, I am not going to send the police after you."

That was Dr. Winden's way of reminding me that, in the end, it's up to me. The doctors are simply providers whom we hire to help us make our bodies work better or longer. We, alone, are responsible for our own bodies. That begins with managing the impression our physical appearance makes on our doctors.

While doctors try to remain objective, they can be influenced by first impressions. I came across an article that appeared some time ago in *Men's Health* in which the doctors being interviewed said that the appearance of the patient definitely influenced their perception of the patient's health and quality of life. According to the article, doctors do a preliminary assessment of our health the moment they see us in the waiting room.[51] That preliminary assessment colors their interpretation of everything that happens in the examining room and has a subtle yet undeniable effect on the aggressiveness of their therapeutic approach.

Doctors are more likely to let nature take its course with the healthier-looking patient than with the patient who presents himself or herself poorly. This dynamic is undoubtedly even more true when the doctor is a specialist who has no history with the patient and lacks other data points. It behooves you and I, as patients, to manage that impression. That is the subject of our next chapter.

[51]T.E. Holt, M.D., "Survive Your Doctor," *Men's Health*, October 4, 2006.

6: MIRROR, MIRROR: Loving Our Aging Bodies

"Mirror, mirror on the wall, who is fairest of them all?" asked the vain, aging queen. The magic mirror answered, "You, my queen, are fair, so true, but the young princess is a thousand times fairer than you." That news threw the queen into a murderous rage that finally ended with her own death from exhaustion.

Snow White can be read as an allegory. The queen represents all of us who are convinced that we can only be beautiful if we look like we did when we were young. We'll go to extreme lengths to retrieve our youthful beauty. Unfortunately, in the end, we will fail. This madness afflicts men as well as women. Oscar Wilde understood that when he wrote *The Picture of Dorian Gray*. Rather than age, Dorian makes a pact with the devil: his portrait will age in his stead, its visage changing based on time and the behavior of its subject. Because Dorian leads a self-indulgent, decadent, cruel life, the face in the portrait becomes increasingly disfigured as well as aged. Dorian, himself, retains his youthful beauty but at the cost of his soul and a troubled conscience. Finally, caught in the throes of self-loathing, Dorian slashes the portrait with a knife. His servants find his body lying next to the portrait. The portrait is of a beautiful young man; it is as it was the day it was painted. A knife protrudes from the chest of Dorian's twisted body. His face is so ugly and disfigured that he is barely recognizable.

Countess Elizabeth Bathory of Hungary became one of the most prolific female serial killers in history. In 1611, she was convicted of murdering eighty young women, and was suspected of being instrumental in the deaths of hundreds of others. Unlike the queen in Snow White, she wasn't killing these young women because they were rivals. She wanted their blood. She believed that washing her body in the vital fluid of young girls would keep her young.

Self-mutilation is more common than murder. People are turning in increasing numbers to cosmetic surgeons to restore their youth. They pay them to remodel their faces and to take the sag out of their bellies or their breasts. Sometimes things go wrong, and they emerge from the surgery disfigured. Some even die under the knife. Like Dorian Gray and Countess Bathory, people will go to extreme lengths to avoid what David calls "the shipwreck."

The Shipwreck.

One morning when we were having coffee and talking about how it feels to get older, David swiveled his chair around so that he was facing the window. I had the impression that he wasn't really seeing the view.

"I used to like my body, but no longer. Now I want as little to do with it as possible. That's what age does. It makes you feel like spending time, energy and money on it is a big waste. In the end, all your efforts aren't going to make any difference. Your face is going to sag. Your gut is going to protrude. You're going to get square and chunky. The shipwreck is unavoidable."

The irony is that as our aging bodies inspire less of our affection, they claim more of our attention. It takes us longer to get ready to face the day than it once did. We no longer jump in and out of the shower. We spend time applying creams to minimize our wrinkles and to cover up aging spots and the dark circles under our eyes that no longer disappear after a good night's sleep. We smear tightening cream on our necks and arms to offset the loss of elasticity. We move more slowly, so it takes longer to reach our daily exercise goal. Feeding ourselves is more time consuming as we become less tolerant of junk foods and salt-laden preprepared meals.

The way we deal with the shipwreck is largely a function of our MAM. Warriors declare war on aging by having extensive plastic surgery or taking their aging bodies to bootcamp and forcing them to diet and exercise until a more youthful mirage reemerges from the ashes. Or, they simple refuse to cooperate. They stop taking their medications, and put off seeing their doctors. They ignore the pain in their troubled limbs, refusing to use assistive devices and forcing themselves to move. Like David when he's in his Warrior frame of mind, they rage against the indignity of it all.

They resist turning to others for help and, when forced to do so, will often punish the would-be caregiver.

Celebrants value youth and vitality, and will deny signs of aging and illness. When they can no longer ignore that their physical energy is waning, they will make up for it with an excess of enthusiasm. They often create a unique style to help define their aging selves. They will incorporate assistive devices into their lives, even giving them parts in their drama. "I call him Buddy," one Celebrant said of his pacemaker. "This is Felix," said another in reference to her walker. They adjust their exercise goals so that they can continue to regard their workout performance as a success. If they opt for plastic surgery, it is generally minimal and designed to enhance rather than rebuild. They are able to find the beauty in their mature body, and graciously accept when others offer to help them do what they can no longer accomplish on their own.

Stargazers don't like to think about aging. Many, like my mother, don't like being around old people even though they are old themselves. When they look in the mirror, they see their younger selves. When they can no longer do so, they are likely to avoid looking in the mirror at all. This can lead to some funny outcomes, like applying too much rouge on the cheekbones. They don't just accept help from willing others; they expect it.

Sages accept that no matter what they do, the sands of time will keep moving through the hourglass. They tend to pay attention to things that affect their ability to fight disease in the long term. They watch what they eat, and they adopt a moderate exercise program. They don't focus on whether the body is beautiful or not. Instead, they think of it as the "common denominator" that allows their various selves to continue writing their story. As my friend Luna explains, "I am so many selves, and they are all important to me and yet for any of them to survive, my body has to survive; not just survive, but stay strong. My body is the common denominator."

Castaways tend to give up more quickly than people with other mindsets. They surrender and allow the shipwreck to happen. They get fat and go grey. They no longer attempt to be beautiful. They believe that to be old is to be unattractive. They chose clothes that are comfortable rather than stylish. Some disappear into the garden of the "has beens," and the "once was's" and rarely come out. Others use humor to deflect attention from the seriousness of aging, or to pretend that it doesn't trouble them. Consider these often-told "truths" about growing old:

- By the time a man is wise enough to watch his step, he's too old to go anywhere.
- The cardiologist's diet: if it tastes good, spit it out.
- You're getting old when you get the same sensation from a rocking chair that you once got from a roller coaster.
- Old is when your wife or husband says, "Let's go upstairs and make love," and you answer, "Honey, I can't do both!"
- Old is when happy hour is a nap.

We heard a few of these Castaway jokes and met people with each of the other mindsets the evening David and I took Mom to a cocktail party in Connecticut. She was seventy-five at the time. The party was given in her honor by the Manigans, old friends who still lived in a big house in Greenwich. I've already introduced you to Kitty Manigan—an extraordinary Celebrant Sage who is grateful for having the chance to get old.

To Nip and Tuck or Not.

Because I couldn't leave work early, we were among the last to arrive at the party. A roomful of affluent elderly men and women were sipping wine and nibbling hors d'oeuvres as they circulated among old friends. Most of the men had been executives who commuted to New York every day for decades. Most of the women had been professional housewives who spent their time volunteering for worthy causes, playing bridge or golf at the local club, planning the next dinner party, and trying to control their over-indulged children.

I had met most of them years before. Some had been the parents of my childhood friends. Others I had encountered when they came to parties at my parents' home. Since I had lost touch with most of my childhood friends, and my parents had been living in Australia for more than twenty years, it had been some time since I'd seen them. Only a few looked like older versions of their younger selves. Most I didn't recognize, largely because they'd had a great deal of "work" done on their faces.

Mirror, Mirror

In 2010, 684,768 surgical and nonsurgical cosmetic procedures (e.g. botox injections) were done on people over the age of sixty-five. They included facelifts, eyelid operations, liposuctions, breast reductions, forehead lifts, breast lifts and breast augmentations. The number of these procedures is increasing every year as plastic surgery is more widely accepted as a viable weapon in the war against looking old.[52]

Is that good news or bad? For those people whose procedures turn out well and make them want to smile at themselves in the mirror, it's terrific. For those who lose sight of who they are because the surgery was excessive, it's terrible. Look at the before and after images on the Internet of Melanie Griffiths, Marie Osmond, Barry Manilow, Priscilla Presley, and Michael Jackson. The expressions that once gave their faces character have been nipped and tucked away, leaving them unrecognizable or making them look like foolish mimics of their former selves.

It's not just film stars who resort to excessive cosmetic surgery. As I looked around the room, I noticed that one woman's left eyelid drooped so badly that her face looked like it was melting. Another had had so much "work" done that her face looked like a mask. It was expressionless, like that of an aged china doll.

Standing on the far side of the room was a couple I thought I recognized. They had been members of the club where my father played golf, my mother played bridge, and I played tennis. The woman's cheekbones were so prominent, she reminded me of a Sphynx cat. Work on her eyes made her appear to be in a state of perpetual surprise. She was so thin I wondered if she had cancer. Dressed in a beautifully tailored evening suit, and wearing four-inch heels, she had so much trouble navigating that she seldom moved from her chosen spot. Instead, she leaned on her expressionless husband whose granite face had all the markings of major surgery.

Watching my mother talking with Kitty Manigan, I decided they looked better than any of the other women in the room. Both had highly expressive faces. They were well-groomed and nicely dressed. Kitty wore a simple black sleeveless linen dress that set off a magnificent string of amber beads. My mother wore a navy blue suit with white piping.

---

[52] "Plastic Surgery on the Rise among Seniors," *The American Society for Aesthetic Plastic Surgery*, September 9, 2011.

Kitty was several years younger than my mother. In fact, my mother was probably the oldest woman at the party. She certainly did not look it. Her fine white hair still had the sheen of youth. Petite in stature, she had shed the weight of late middle age, and had regained the hourglass figure so coveted by women decades her junior. She had a ready, natural smile. She emanated a sense of innocence and childlike joy which made people look past her lined face and arthritic hands to the beautiful woman who resided inside the older woman's shell.

My mother had never "gone under the knife." Although she frequently threatened to do so, we all knew it was a request for positive feedback. We always obliged. "You don't need cosmetic surgery, Mom. You have a beautiful neck." "Forget it, Mom. You hardly have any wrinkles. You have beautiful skin."

Buoyed by our words, she resorted to a less drastic method to restore her youthful appearance. When she looked in the mirror, she still saw herself as a younger woman.

Kitty Manigan was not a Stargazer. When it came to aging gracefully, she was a Sage who regarded cosmetic surgery as both "silly" and a waste of time and money. Though she celebrated life, she understood that the journey was not intended to be easy; the body was meant to age. Kitty would have agreed with Eleanor Roosevelt when she said, "Beautiful young people are accidents of nature, but beautiful old people are works of art."

A Work of Art.

Beautiful old people are indeed works of art. Their beauty is complex, like an impressionist oil painting with many layers of different colors that reflect the light in different ways. The complexity is the result of the interplay of lines and clear skin, and the streaks of grey that give the once uniformly dark hair a new depth. It's the radiant smile in the sagging face that conveys the message that, in spite of its struggles, "Life is good."

"Age will flatten a man," Tommy Lee Jones says in the film, *No Country for Old Men*. In his case, it rendered his face powerful and intense. It appears almost ravaged, but out of the devastation emerges a look that is so intense it captures the screen and enraptures the viewer. He is not handsome like George Clooney. His face is intriguing, like a work of art.

At seventy-nine, Vanessa Redgrave is stunning. If you look up images of the actress on Google, you will find that her current beauty is very different from the "accidental" beauty of her youth. In the photographs of her older self, she wears her aging proudly. She does not attempt to conceal the lines that life and tragedy have etched on her regal British face. She pulls back her white hair, accentuating her vivid blue eyes, her wide brow, and symmetrical features.

Perhaps she's one of the lucky ones. She's got the kind of face that ages gracefully. My mother certainly had that, too. Do I? I don't know. I look more like my father. When he died at the age of sixty-seven, his face was still taut and handsome. So, I guess I have a chance. That's fortunate since I have a bias against turning to plastic surgery to create an artificially youthful face on an aging body.

David shares that bias. Several years ago he told me, "If you ever have plastic surgery, I'll leave you." Did he mean it? I don't know. I've never pressed the point. I understand why he feels that way. He has a deep appreciation of natural beauty and respect for the laws of evolution and the primal sanity of nature. And, I believe he loves me for who I am.

That, in itself, makes me feel beautiful. The French playwright and novelist, Francois Sagan, once said, "There is a certain age when a woman must be beautiful to be loved, and then there comes a time when she must be loved to be beautiful."

Loving Your Aging Body.

If you were to visit your local bookstore (assuming one remains), and consulted the shelves on psychology and self-improvement, you would undoubtedly find dozens of volumes that suggest that the key to a happy and fulfilled life is loving yourself for who you are. That means forgiving yourself for your shortcomings, and celebrating your positive characteristics. That begins with your body. Since our sense of self is so bound up with our physicality and the way we look, it's almost impossible to love ourselves if we don't feel the same way about our bodies.

That's a lot easier to do when we are young, nimble and physically resilient. When we're old, and forced to inhabit bodies that are fragile, stiff and uncooperative, it's harder to do. When we look in the mirror and see lines and age spots, we may want to look away. If we adored the face and the body we had when we were young, it can be even more difficult to appreciate the aging version.

Sometimes the mind plays a trick on us and lets us continue to believe we are still young. We tell ourselves that aging is for other people. "It won't happen to me," we say as we smile at our reflection, blind to how much our appearance has changed. An old cliché comes to mind: Love is blind. We look in the mirror and notice the wrinkles around our eyes and the greying of our hair, and yet we still fail to see the old person we have become.

There's a poignant scene in the filmed version of Colleen McCullough's *The Thorn Birds*. Mary Carson, a rich old Australian spinster, is in love with the young, handsome, ambitious priest, Father Ralph de Bricassart. As she stares in her mirror, tormented because he has rejected her, she sees herself as a beautiful young, seductive woman. Her refusal or inability to admit that she has aged makes his rejection more surprising and, therefore, harder to bear.

As I sat with my mother as she lay dying, I often thought of that scene. From the hospital bed that we had installed in my mother's sunny bedroom, she could look directly into the mirror that hung over her dresser. She did not look away. On the contrary, she lingered, turning her head this way and that and even smiling at her own image. I wondered what she saw, who she saw. I believe she was actually admiring her younger self.

Inside of every aging person's body is the young person they used to be. We are often upset when others fail to see that hidden person. One of my favorite authors and philosophers, Doris Lessing, said this about aging: "The great secret that all old people share is that you really haven't changed in seventy or eighty years. Your body changes, but you don't change at all. And that, of course, causes great confusion."

A retired Canadian doctor whom we met when we went on safari in Africa explained it well: "The problem of getting older is that other people think you are getting older."

Because we don't share that perception, we can be shocked when we are forced to realize that, when others look at us, they see an old person. I remember one night we had invited some new friends over for dinner. We got talking about our children's weddings. I left the table and went into the next room to retrieve a photograph taken at daughter Monica's wedding twenty-eight years earlier. Melissa, the maid of honor, and I were standing with the bride and groom in the church right after the ceremony.

I handed the photograph to Mary. After looking at it closely, she looked up at me and said, "You've really changed. I'm not even sure I would have recognized you."

Before I could respond, Mary handed the photo to her husband. "Yes, you certainly have changed," he said and then laughed. "But haven't we all?"

I took the photo from him and put it on the table, face down, and changed the subject. The next morning I told David how Mary and Rick's comments had made me feel. He tried to cheer me up. "You are still a very handsome woman. You're not knockdown beautiful like you used to be, but you're still handsome, and that's more than most of us can say."

Redefining Beauty.

One evening not long after that eye-opening dinner party, David went out to a board meeting. I poured a glass of red wine and began paging through photograph albums. I was still searching for photographs of the "knockdown beautiful" me when I came across a photograph of my mother. It was taken when I was visiting Perth, Australia. I had flown over there to help my mother organize her new villa. One evening my brother and his partner, Sue, invited us for dinner. We gathered in his lush and intimate back garden behind his townhouse in East Fremantle.

In the photograph my mother is sitting on a high back wooden chair. She's wearing her traditional black. Around her shoulders is a fuchsia pashmina shawl. Draped around her neck are the African multi-colored glass beads I had sent her several years earlier. Her fine white hair catches the light, forming a kind of halo around her smiling face. At eighty-six years old, she is still beautiful.

Removing the photo from the album, I began looking for photos of her younger self. I found a black and white photograph taken when she was about twenty years old. I could see why people had often told her she looked like Elizabeth Taylor. I took both photographs into the living room and laid them side-by-side on the coffee table.

The older woman was not simply a faded version of her original self. Her hair was white, not auburn, and she now allowed it to become unruly, and to curl freely around her face. Her once flawless skin was lined, but had more character. Her once delicate hands were now gnarled with arthritis, but they were not ugly. Her almond shaped green eyes could not see as well as they once had but they still sparkled.

Looking at these two photographs, I suddenly understood the importance of redefining beauty as we age. Otherwise, our younger selves can act like anchors, holding us back, and forcing us to regard ourselves as unfortunate derivatives of what we once had been.

Part of loving our aging bodies is accepting or even celebrating our appearance as an older person. But that is not enough. It's also important to express that love through paying attention to how we look and taking whatever steps we can to improve the physical self we present to the world.

Killing the Mouse.

One way of improving our appearance is by "killing the mouse." Every seven weeks, I visit Naomi, a spritely, attractive thirty-two-year-old whom I call "the magician." While we talk about her four delightful children, and my four grandchildren, she proceeds to kill the mouse. She first puts in foils to introduce blond highlights into my otherwise drab mane and then covers my grey roots with number six dye. By the time I leave her three or four hours later, I feel ten years younger.

When my Aunt Jill died at the age of eighty-six, the firemen found her body trapped in her bed sheets. Hair curlers were still in her in her dyed dark brown hair. It was her hairdresser who alerted the police when Jill didn't show up for her weekly Friday morning appointment. Neither illness or injury nor bad weather had ever stopped Jill from keeping her appointment to kill the mouse. The hairdresser knew immediately something was terribly wrong when the clock struck ten and the short, sweet old lady with the square face, perfect skin and crooked smile hadn't made her way to the salon.

There is no shame in killing the mouse. It is not a sign of excessive vanity nor a desire to pretend we are someone we are not. It is simply an attempt to look better and, in looking better, to feel better about ourselves and life in general. The only women in my circle of aging friends who do not color their hair are those few who are fortunate enough to have pure white hair.

Hair coloring is not the exclusive province of women. Though women tend to fill colorists' chairs in greater numbers than men, the dyeing of hair was first adopted by men. As early as the Peloponnesian War (41 to 404 B.C.), men who were turning grey dyed their hair. This is not surprising when we consider that the Greeks celebrated youth and despised old age to an even greater degree than we do today. "By far the majority of (Greek) plays glorify youth in lines that suggest the voices of mature men looking back to a lost paradise."[53]

Dressing It Up.

In coloring our hair we are preparing to present our best self to the public. Our bodies also deserve to be presented at their best. Too often older people think only about being comfortable, not about looking good. Men shun their blazers, chinos and loafers and begin showing up in

---

[53] Jacob Burckhardt, *The Greeks and Greek Civilization*. (New York, St. Martin's Press, 1998),107.

fleeces, sweatpants and sneakers. Women shove their skirts and sleek belted trousers and form-fitting sweaters to the back of the closet and begin wearing baggy pants with elastic waistbands and oversized shirts. Shoes with heels are abandoned in favor of more comfortable, though less flattering, footwear. Though Castaways are more prone to doing this than other MAMs, sloppiness can creep into the lives of even the staunchest Warrior.

Don't misunderstand me. I'm in favor of dressing comfortably. I'm just not in favor of dressing sloppily or of ignoring those few occasions when comfort should take a back seat to style. What's at stake is more than impressing others or even feeling better about ourselves. The way we dress affects the way we behave. I know this for a fact.

More than forty years ago, I was working for American Express when the fashion industry introduced pantsuits for women. My boss asked me to research the impact of allowing female employees to wear pants to work. I spent days in the New York Public Library reading studies of how behavior changed when dress codes were altered. There was an overwhelming amount of evidence that when people dressed professionally, they behaved more professionally.

As a result of my research, the company adopted a policy allowing its female employees to wear pantsuits (defined as jackets and slacks made of the same fabric). Blazers and slacks that were different colors or made of different fabrics were permissible if the employee was not going to have client contact. Jeans were absolutely outlawed, as were tops that showed any part of the midriff.

I became a staunch believer that appearance affects behavior. Years later, when I had a consulting practice based in Southern California with clients located primarily in New York, I would wear my "New York suits" (translation—my best and most conservative suits) to the office if I knew I was going to be on a conference call with my clients. I was certain that I projected my voice differently when I was "suited up" than when I was wearing my blue jeans.

Just as people behave more professionally when they dress professionally, so they behave like a younger person when they make an effort to reflect at least a modicum of the latest styles in their apparel. I am not suggesting that older people should dress like younger people. The bodies of older people are shaped differently. Waists thicken. Breasts sag.

Clothes that look great on a twenty-year-old make a seventy-year-old look silly.

My daughter, Monica, works as a personal trainer at a gym in South Florida. She has told me stories about some of her aging clients who appear for their sessions in outfits that make it very hard to take them seriously. One old lady attempts to strut her stuff like an eighteen-year-old bimbo. She always wears a tight sleeveless leopard-skin bodysuit cut high at the thighs and low at the bust. She accentuates the look with a studded silver belt.

While old people should not try to mimic young people in their dress, they can still pay attention to fashion trends. For example, I recently bought two long, flowing sweaters and a pair of slim leg pants. When I add the boots I have owned for twenty years, I will be "in fashion."

Did I need another sweater or another pair of slacks? No, I didn't. My closet is so full, I could easily live the rest of my life without buying another garment. (David reminds me of that fact every time UPS delivers a box with a clothing store label.) Regardless, because I don't want to look like something out of a long-discarded catalogue, I spend a little money now and then to "refresh" my look.

As I do so, I sometimes find myself copying my friend, Fran. Fran dresses with a lot more zing than I do. She wears jewelry that makes a statement. Though I have nice jewelry, I tend to wear the same gold pendant day in and day out. I do so as much out of laziness as fondness for the piece. Fran experiments with color, while I usually wear black slacks and a black tee and then jazz it up with a colorful vest. Unlike me, Fran doesn't always wear straight-legged slacks. She shows up in long skirts, short skirts, palazzo pants. In short, she's both stylish and inventive. She has fun dressing up her body, and that sense of fun broadcasts a positive attitude that enhances any social gathering.

Keeping It Clean.

Fran is always stylish, and her clothes are spotless. That may sound like an "of course," but I assure you, it is not. When people get older, they tend to overlook spots and stains on their garments. When I went through my mother's clothes after her death, I noticed that many of her favorite garments were heavily stained. Given her vanity, she would have been horrified. Jill's clothes were also soiled in spite of her obsessiveness with keeping things clean and in good order. I imagine neither Jill nor my mother were aware of the food stains. I know I've put a garment on my body without noticing that it needs attention until I'm almost out the door.

I'm trying to pay more attention to the state of my clothing. I'm also spending more time and energy making sure my body is presentable. Every few days, I tweeze stubborn hairs from my chin that never appeared when I was younger. I scrub flaking skin from feet that never flaked before. I apply hydrating lotion to aging skin that was once naturally soft and sufficiently moist. I could go on, but not without unnecessarily embarrassing myself.

When I was younger, I showered and washed my hair every day. Sometimes If I'd played tennis or worked in the yard, I'd shower twice in a day. That was no big deal. I'd be in and out in no time. Now, I regard showering, washing my hair and the myriad of other activities that are required as part of my personal hygiene as a significant commitment of time and energy.

During the last months of her life, Katherine, the Miracle Girl, had a caregiver to help her with her daily hygiene. Together they would shower her body, wash and dry her hair, touch up her nails, and whatever else needed to be done to get her ready to greet her visitors. She once told me that every day the process took longer. "At this rate, one day I won't be ready to greet the day until it's time for bed," she joked, attempting to make light of a sad reality.

I remember my Aunt Jill telling me that her doctor told her old bodies tend to smell bad and that she should use a special deodorant soap with antibacterial properties. Apparently Jill followed his advice for she always smelled fresh even though taking a shower was a real challenge for her in her later years. The one bathroom in her small duplex had only a tub with a showerhead. She found it very hard to climb into the tub. Once in, she had to sit down on a bench I had installed and let the water run over her body. Getting out of the tub was even more unnerving than getting in, since the water now rendered its surface slippery. Looking back, I regret that I didn't install a walk-in shower for her. I would have done so if I'd understood then what I understand now.

That too many old people can't or won't make the effort is apparent in the clichés, "He's a dirty old man," and "She's a smelly old woman." If we love our aging bodies and do our best to stay in shape, dress well and keep them clean, then we make it less likely that young immortals will think that old men are dirty or old women are smelly. In putting our best feet, legs, arms, hands, torso and face forward, we make an affirmation about our continuing worth as people.

Working It Out and Shaping It Up.

Older people who stay in shape broadcast the message that they respect themselves. Staying in shape requires that we pay attention to maintaining our muscles, and fighting fat and flab. We can only do that if we watch what we eat and if we keep moving.

I'm not an expert on nutrition, so I'm not going to talk at length about dieting. I will tell you that David and I have had success with the South Beach Diet. Currently, we are following the Paleo Diet which is all about avoiding "white" foods (pasta, bread, rice, etc.) and dairy. It is a protein intensive diet, which suits me fine. Vegetarians would hate it!

We learned about the Paleo Diet from a fine craftsman who has been doing some work on our house. He was once on the Olympic ski team and was destined for greatness before he crashed when he was going downhill at seventy miles an hour. He broke his back. Unable to ski, he became sedentary. Because his athlete's body was used to exercise, he began to gain weight. Before long, he weighed three hundred and fifty pounds and suffered from a myriad of health problems. When his doctor told him he was at risk of developing diabetes, he heard that as a wake-up call. (His mother was a diabetic amputee.) He bought a book entitled *Younger Next Year* by Chris Crowley and Henry S. Lodge, MD, and began to put its teachings into practice. He shed more than one hundred fifty pounds. As I write this, he is climbing around our roof, as agile as a man thirty years younger. He recommended the book to us.

One particular statement in the book has made a tremendous difference in my life. I remind myself of this message every time I try to excuse myself from my daily workout. It is at once simple and profound: Our bodies are in a state of constant renewal as old cells die and new ones grow. "The trick, of course, is to grow more than you throw out, and this is where exercise comes in. It turns out that your muscles control the chemistry of growth throughout your whole body… So exercise is the master signaler, the agent that sets hundred of chemical cascades in motion each time you get on that treadmill and start to sweat."[54]

Six days a week, I force myself to either walk four to five miles on a treadmill or ride the stationary bike in the garage for forty-five minutes. I do it because it keeps my heart pumping, and my muscles toned and, most important, it makes me feel better about myself and allows me to keep believing that I am in control of my life. It even heightens my ability to perceive life through the eyes of a Celebrant. Perhaps this is because exercise releases endorphins, or peptides that activate the body's opiate receptors. Put differently, exercise makes me happier.

Because of the availability of technology, there is really no excuse for not working out even when our bodies are breaking down. After I broke my ankle while we were traveling through Spain, I couldn't use the treadmill. I bought an inexpensive elliptical machine that enabled me to keep working out without putting stress on my injured ankle.

What about people whose mobility is so limited that they cannot use a treadmill or an elliptical? They can still keep moving with the help of a walker. It's unfortunate that so many older people resist using this device. My mother was horrified that people she knew might see her with her new red walker. Rather than take the chance of being spotted, she stopped going outside. My Aunt Jill never gave in to my repeated suggestions that we get her a walker.

I guess I should understand. I use my oxygen when I exercise. I take pains to put it away when friends come over who might want to see the gym. Having to use it on flights has intensified my dislike of flying. Shame on me. In the interest of keeping moving, I have to get over this!

I am not alone. Many older people feel that when their body breaks down and they need to rely on an assistive device, they have failed in some way. Rather than being proud of themselves for finding a way to keep moving, they apologize for not being like the extraordinary ninety-seven-year-old man who runs marathons or the eighty-six-year-old woman who can still maneuver on a balance beam.

In *Being Mortal*, Dr. Gawande explains why this is happening. "The progress of medicine and public health has been an incredible boon—

---

[54]Chris Crowley & Henry S. Lodge, M.D., *Younger Next Year.* (New York, Workman Publishing, 2007), 63-64.

people get to live longer, healthier, more productive lives than ever before. Yet traveling along these altered paths, we regard living in the downhill stretches with a kind of embarrassment. We need help, often for long periods of time, and regard that as a weakness rather than as the new normal and expected state of affairs."[55]

Comparing our own capabilities to those who are exceptional in our age group is destructive. It destroys our will, our discipline, and our ability to feel good about ourselves. Similarly, it's discouraging to compare our workout capability to what we used to be able to do. It's important to redefine our exercise goals as we age. At the end of her life, when she was confined to bed, my mother used cans of soup as weights to maintain her upper body strength. She did arm lifts, counting outloud until she reached her goal of twelve lifts per side. When she finished, she would smile and say, "I did it!"

During the last ten years, as my heart and lungs have gotten weaker, I have had to progressively reduce both the speed and incline of my treadmill. A few years ago, I could sustain a rate of three and a half miles per hour at an incline of three. A year ago, I had to redefine a rate of three miles per hour at an incline of two as an acceptable workout.

When even that reduced speed and incline began to present too much of a challenge, I shared my concern with my cardiologist. Dr. Caldus explained that my ejection fraction, or the rate at which my heart pumps blood, had worsened. It was then that she and Dr. Kepler recommended that they "upgrade" my pacemaker, adding a third lead which would resynchronize the left and right ventricles of my heart. Hoping the additional lead would give me more energy and help me stay mobile, I readily agreed. Afterall, I was already a member of the Bionic Club.

The Bionic Woman.

My membership in the club began when an ICD or Implantable Cardioverter Defibrillator was implanted in my chest to shock my heart back into a normal rhythm if it suddenly started beating too fast. It just sat there quietly monitoring my heart, ready to save my life if the need arose.

---

[55]Dr. Atul Gawande, *Being Mortal: Medicine and What Matters in the End.* (New York, Henry Holt and Company, 2015), 28.

I tried to think of it as a security blanket, and to regard the scar on my chest as a badge of courage. For a long time, I could do neither. I wore clothing that hid the scar, and I resented my dependency on the device.

David tried to change my perspective. He said to me, "We're all dependent on machines. We're dependent on our cars to get food. We're dependent on our furnaces for heat. We're dependent on the Internet and our computers for ordering our medications. We're dependent on smart phones for staying connected with people."

"I get that, but having a machine inside your body is different. It's a more intimate kind of dependency," I argued.

"That's true. But you're far from alone. Your father couldn't hear without his hearing aid. Your college roommate has a titanium ankle. My knee is partially constructed of synthetic materials. Most of us will be bionic to one degree or another by the time we die."

"It makes me think of the movie, *Blade Runner*," I said.

"Yes, that film was prophetic. Unlike the replicant Roy who pleaded with his maker for more life, we do not have fixed expiration dates. For that we should be grateful."

I have come to believe he is right. The resynchronization device has improved my oxygen saturation and restored my energy. I am now able to work out harder, and to enjoy it more. The device is no longer an unwelcome intruder. I don't get as breathless when I have to race upstairs to find my cellphone before it stops ringing. It has helped keep me mobile. In so doing, it has helped me avoid what researchers call the "inactivity cycle" that afflicts many older people. The onset is frequently a fall.

Fear of Falling.

Falls are a life-threatening event for people over the age of sixty-five. They are the leading cause of injury-related death in that age group. In the decade from 2002-2012, more than 200,000 Americans over sixty-five died after falls.[56]

It is not surprising, then, that somewhere between thirty and fifty percent of older people are afraid of falling, and that the fear itself makes it

---

[56]Katie Hafner,"Bracing for the Falls of an Aging Nation," *The New York Times*, Nov. 2, 2014.

more likely that they will fall.[57] That's because their fear makes them increasingly immobile. Once they stop moving, their sense of balance starts to deteriorate. Vision, muscle strength, proprioception (the body's ability to know where it is in space), and attention all erode. That, in turn, makes them even more afraid to move. The inactivity cycle spirals down upon itself.

For some, the fear is pronounced; for others, it is fleeting. Even for them, the anxiety is often apparent in their gait. Their stride becomes more tenuous, no longer as forceful or assertive as it once was. Hesitant to lose touch with the ground, these elders begin to shuffle and to regard stepladders as hazardous objects.

Even people with no conscious fear of falling get more tentative. Once David's knee began giving him trouble, he started mistrusting his balance. He began to think twice before climbing onto the roof to clean out the gutters. Although I don't have a problem with my knees, I notice that I have begun to move more tentatively on slippery or uneven pavement.

For many older people, a fall is the defining event that marks the true beginning of old age. Suddenly, they find themselves unable to get up without assistance. They become terrified that it will happen again, and no one will be around to help. The fear feeds on itself until any activity is regarded as too hazardous.

Joan Didion's awareness that she was aging happened abruptly, as she tells us in *Blue Nights*. She was sitting on a metal folding chair at a rehearsal, and suddenly was consumed with fear that she wouldn't be able to stand up; that her legs would give out when she attempted to stand. Neither she nor her doctors could explain what triggered the onset of her fear. It had no apparent physical basis. And yet, it changed her life. She had begun to perceive of herself as aging, as frail.[58]

The best way to manage a fear of falling is to minimize the likelihood that it will happen. It's important to do what we can to maintain our balance: yoga, tai chi, balance exercises. We need to stay hydrated, so we don't get dizzy. We should try to eat right. We need to stop resisting the use of walkers and other assistive devices. It helps to remove scatter rugs

---

[57]N.R. Kleinfield, "For Elderly, Fear of Falling Is a Risk in Itself," *The New York Times*, March 3, 2003.

[58]Joan Didion, *Blue Nights*. (New York, Alfred A. Knopf, 2011), 105-106.

or make sure they are properly secured and make sure that floors and stairwells are free of objects. When the time comes, we should consider installing grab bars in our showers, raising the height of our toilets, and wearing an emergency pendant so that we can call for help if we do fall.

Above all, we need to avoid the inactivity cycle by fighting the temptation to get timid and, in the process, to stop living. We need to hold onto the wonder of the Stargazer, the enthusiasm of the Celebrant, the courage of the Warrior and the perspective of the Sage. We need to avoid letting the fear of falling make us a victim, a Castaway stuck at the negative pole. We want to be like the old woman who said, "You shouldn't stop going on living because you have a fear of falling. Once you restrict your life, you're finished. Everything goes. I love life too much for that."[59]

Here's to Life.

Alan Gans, the Old Man on a Swing, recently took a trip to Hawaii. Aware of what a fall could do a man in his late eighties, Alan called housekeeping and requested that they cover the floor of his marble-floored bathroom with slip-free bath rugs. Unfortunately, when he left the bathroom, he tripped over a divan. He was lucky. He didn't break any bones, and his bruises will heal. He is already planning his next trip.

As his poem, *The Voice Within*, shows, Alan refuses to let timidity and fear encroach on his ability to live life fully. He will never fall prey to the inactivity cycle.

THE VOICE WITHIN

Thoughts voiced, O so softly, approval implored,
Words shaped to please, candor deplored.
Real truths never ventured,
Why be frank, why be censured?
Soaring dreams mostly tethered,

---

[59]N.R. Kleinfield, "For Elderly, Fear of Falling Is a Risk in Itself," *The New York Times*, March 3, 2003.

Mirror, Mirror

Bold ideas always fettered,
Chance encounters scarcely dared,
Played it safe – who really cared?
Yes, a life, but was it squandered,
With regrets now sadly pondered?
Yet, look 'neath this mask of civility,
Slow decline and debility,
For there dwells a man, ever hopeful,
Even bold, seldom doubtful,
His spirit fresh and aspiring,
Engines primed, all are firing.
So be damned, past timidity,
Hail to thee, bright serendipity!
Worthless mask, put asunder,
Here's to life, so filled with wonder!

Alan Gans, 2000

7: ANTIDOTES TO AGING:
The Four C's

Antidote: something that counteracts or neutralizes an unpleasant feeling or situation; a remedy.

Doctors can prescribe antidotes to a multitude of symptoms that afflict us as we age. They cannot neutralize the aging process itself. Nor can they counteract a troubling condition—the certainty that we will die. They can prescribe Ritalin, Elavil, or hundreds of other antidepressants that help us ignore the ravages of aging and ease the fear most of us feel as we face the final unknown. As they do so, however, they are muting our sensibilities and diminishing our ability to shape our own lives.

Fortunately, there are other antidotes to aging and remedies for the fear of death that don't require a doctor's prescription. They enhance our sensibilities and enrich our final years. They help us transcend the fear of mortality. I call them the Four C's: **Curiosity, Contemplation, Creativity** and **Connectedness**.

Curiosity is an effective antidote against a stultifying and fear-ridden defensiveness that renders so many old people crusty, combative, stubborn, and closed to new ideas. Inquisitiveness makes us resilient even as our bodies begin to fray. Its first cousin, **contemplation**, can enable us to get in touch with the harmony inherent in the universe. These insights can help us keep our own lives and deaths in perspective.

Creativity and its corollary, imagination, are remedies for boredom and stagnation that tend to creep up on us as our energy and mobility wane, and our world begins to shrink. Inventiveness can keep our mental age young even as our physical age advances. As Hermann Hesse said,

"When artists create pictures and thinkers search for laws and formulate thoughts, it is in order to salvage something from the great dance of death, to make something that lasts longer than we do." In short, we can use creativity and contemplation to re-introduce the spell of potential into our lives, and, if we are connected, into the lives of others.

Connectedness protects us from alienation, or the isolation that can happen when our spouse dies, our middle-aged children are consumed by their careers, and our friends no longer have the energy to entertain. It mitigates against the tendency to become totally absorbed by our ailments and concerns about our aging bodies. It helps us get out of ourselves and, in the process, to free ourselves. It even helps us stay healthy. After all, the surest way to make ourselves sick is to have only ourselves to consider.

Curious George.

When I was a child living in my grandmother's house in Denver, my Aunt Jill often read me stories. A favorite was *Curious George*. I'm sure you've met this delightful monkey who can't resist the urge to explore new places and to learn about new things. If the story wasn't read to you as a child, chances are you read it to your children, and perhaps to your grandchildren. He first appeared in 1941 and is still popular with both children and their parents. His stories are read all over the world. Curious George never dies because he never ceases to delight. He never dies because he never ages. He never ages because he stays open to new ideas.

As we age, we need to behave like Curious George. If we remain inquisitive, we can avoid contracting a disease that is as deadly as hardening of the arteries—hardening of the categories. Curiosity defies the maxim that you can't teach an old dog new tricks. The truth is the surest way to become an old dog is to stop learning new tricks.

If we remain open, and continue to explore either with our feet or in our minds, we discover, as the Old Man on a Swing said, "Life holds surprises even after eighty." Alan is now a robust and curious eighty-eight-year-old. He audits classes at his alma mater, Yale University, and often frequents its museums. He continues to pursue a long-standing goal of becoming fluent in Spanish. He spends months at a time in Mexico and Guatemala where he immerses himself in the culture and the language. When he was eighty-two, Alan went on safari in Africa. He has taken the train across Russia, and traveled through the remote villages of Peru. He hasn't let age or waning health clip his wings. The energy he derives from feeding his curiosity compensates and keeps him going. His openness and ability to be surprised and delighted by life is evident in his poems.

AWAKENING

Stay the calming hand of age,
Speed latent feelings to the fore.
And praise the Lord for life reprised.

For blessings past—and even more,
For youthful eyes that now caress,
No burning fires to suppress.

From chrysalis freed, new wings and desire,
A mandate, compelling, to fly ever higher.
So savor this idyll—it cannot last
A coda, too bright, for memories past.

Alan Gans , age 81
June, 2009

Alan forces himself to abandon the safety of habit and routine in order to find out what lies beyond the next corner, or the next hill. Though a bachelor, he rarely ends up traveling alone. Men and women of all ages are drawn to him. People tend to enjoy the company of those who are curious. In part, this is because curious people tend to stay at the positive pole of their respective MAMs.

Castaways who are feeling pessimistic about life are not likely to be able to summon the energy to inquire and explore. The attitude of "What's the use?" will submerge them. Self-absorbed, petulant Stargazers are too focused on the self to be able to learn about others. It's all about me, me, me. That is the opposite of curiosity. Frenzied Celebrants don't stop long enough to embrace the moment. Pollyannas are too reluctant to take off their rose-colored glasses and refuse to open their eyes to what is happening around them. When Warriors are feeling defensive and obsessed with controlling the uncontrollable, they build barricades to keep others out. Rigidity of thought and opinion replaces an open-minded exploration of possibilities. An attempt to defend the status quo consumes their energy as they hunker down in their bunkers. Even Sages who have fallen into a pit of existential angst cease being curious. They temporarily fall in upon themselves, and are so caught up in their intellectual underwear, they can't see beyond their current philosophical quandary.

Curiosity creates its own energy. In the process, it helps people stay at the positive pole even when they are sick or dying. Katherine, the Miracle Girl, was an intensely curious person. She was an avid reader, particularly of nonfiction. Though she had strong opinions, Katherine spent more time inquiring about other people's thoughts than imposing her views. At her private memorial service, one of her young male friends said, "Even as she lay dying, she asked questions about me and my life. At that frightening time when her focus must have been the end of her own life, she remained curious and interested in me."

Curiosity can even alleviate conflicts and misunderstandings that often occur between the young and the old. Older people who are curious are better able to tune into and relate to today's youth than are seniors who are "stuck" in their defense of "the good old days." One night when we were vacationing in Florida, we took our teenage grandsons, Jack and Ryan, out for dinner without their parents. As we were waiting for our coffee and dessert to be served, they paid us a big compliment. "We like doing stuff with you, Grams and David. You're not crusty like other old people. You're funny, Grams. You've got cool ideas, David. You both just sort of get it."

If we "get it," it's because we're curious about what it's like to be them in their world at this time. I think of curiosity as a workout for the brain. People who are curious spend a lot of time absorbing and processing new information. This stimulates the brain. A recent study done by Professor Michael J. Valenzuela, a brain-aging expert at the Brain and Mind Research Institute at the University of Sydney, Australia has shown that an "active cognitive lifestyle" reduces the risk of developing dementia in later years. "Rather than specifically protecting the health of activated circuits, it seems that a more active lifestyle has general effects on brain health reflected in greater neuronal density and preservation of the blood supply to the brain."[60]

Use it or lose it. That's the message. Using the brain can take the form of contemplation. I think of contemplation as a kind of deep but quiet curiosity. Like the curious mind, the contemplative mind is open to new insights, new ideas, new perspectives.

Plato's Cave and The Golden Mean.

The early Greek sage, Plato, believed that contemplation was the soul's path to knowledge of the divine. In his famous Parable of the Cave, he tells the story of prisoners who are bound and forced to stare only at the back wall of a cave. Between them and the entrance is a fire. Figures walk between the fire and the prisoners, carrying objects that cast shadows on the walls. Knowing nothing else, the prisoners assume the shadows are reality. Then, one day one of them is freed and taken to the fire. He sees for the first time the cause of the shadows. His view of reality begins to shift. When he is taken out of the cave and into the sunlight, he is finally able to see the truth.

Plato's message was that it is the task of the philosophers, or the Sages, to take the prisoners (humankind) out of the caves. I suggest maybe it's up to each one of us to free ourselves of our own unchallenged assumptions, fears and insecurities.

Plato was a mathematician turned philosopher. He believed that the secret of truth and beauty lay in the mathematical properties of symmetry, proportion and, therefore, harmony between the parts and the whole. He believed that the number called the golden ratio or divine mean represents the secret to the universe and all that exists within it.

Two objects are in the golden mean if the ratio of the sum of the two objects to the larger object is equal to the ratio of the larger object to the smaller one. Numerically, this is expressed as 1.618, or phi. Even if math isn't your thing, stay with me for a minute. If you do, we might get out of the cave together.

---

[60]Michael J. Valenzuela et al., "Multiple Biological Pathways Link Cognitive Lifestyle to Protection from Dementia," *Biological Psychiatry*, 2012.

Antidotes to Aging

In the twelfth century, a Sage named Leonardo Fibonacci discovered a series of numbers that bear an incredible relationship to the golden ratio. To build what we now call the Fibonacci sequence, you start with a 0 and 1 and take it from there. The next number is the sum of the two that came before it. 0,1,1,2,3,5,8,13,21,34,55,89,144…and so on. Now, think about this—the ratio of each successive pair of numbers approximates phi (1.618). The ratio of 5 to 3 (or 5 divided by 3) equals 1.666. When you get all the way out to the fortieth Fibonacci number, the ratio is accurate to fifteen decimal places (1.618033988749895).

It gets really fascinating when we realize that the golden ratio and the Fibonacci numbers are manifest throughout nature and the universe. The dimensions of Earth and the Moon are in phi relationship, forming a massive golden triangle. Five conjunctions of Earth and Venus occur every eight orbits of the Earth around the Sun, creating a perfectly symmetrical rosette whose harmonious proportions are true to the Fibonacci sequence and the golden mean.

The human body holds true to the universal design principle. Each section of our index fingers, from the tip to the base of the wrist, is larger than the preceding one by about the Fibonacci ratio of 1.618. We have 2 hands, each with 5 digits, and 8 fingers, each with 3 digits. These are Fibonacci numbers. The ratio of the length of our forearms to our hands is 1.618. In fact, the entire human body, including the face, conforms to the golden ratio. People whose faces most closely reflect the golden mean and are, therefore, perfectly symmetrical, are often regarded as strikingly handsome or stunningly beautiful.

Great buildings conform to the golden ratio expressed geometrically as the golden triangle. Great art also conforms, and thus feels at once dynamic and harmonious. The golden mean is apparent in much of Leonardo Da Vinci's work, as well as in the paintings of Vincent Van Gogh, Botticelli and others.

It's also evident in music. A Russian musicologist discovered that the golden mean appears in ninety-seven percent of Beethoven's work. The sound waves of his symphonies approximate the golden ratio when compared in sequence. The first seven numbers of the Fibonacci series (0, 1, 1, 2, 3, 5, 8) are related to key frequencies of musical notes. Fibonacci and phi relationships are evident in the timing of musical compositions. The climax of songs is often found at roughly the phi point (61.8%) of the song, as opposed to the middle or end of the song.

The fastest animal on earth, the peregrine falcon, spirals instead of diving down in a straight line when it's on a kill. The spiral lets the raptor keep its prey in sight without losing speed. Every quarter turn, the spiral gets wider by a changing factor that adheres to the golden ratio.

I'm at once inspired and comforted by the golden mean. It inspires me because it reminds me that, although I am a tiny particle in the vastness of things, I am still part of the universe and subject to its mysteries and its unknowable and yet remarkable magnificence. I am comforted because I can believe there is a single creative force behind the universal order. It's been called any number of things by people through the ages—God, Brahma, Supreme Being, Yahweh, the Vector. I could go on. Although the beliefs surrounding each of these divine beings differ, they are all based on the existence of a single, unifying creative power.

It's possible to find meaning in life in spite of its inevitable end through curiosity about the universe and contemplation of its mysteries. As the French novelist and philosopher André Malraux said, "The greatest mystery is not that we have been flung at random among the profusion of the earth and the galaxy of the stars, but that in this prison we can fashion images of ourselves sufficiently powerful to deny our nothingness."[61]

The Fountain of Youth.

A few years ago, David and I couldn't find a film to watch after dinner. None of the DVD's in our library appealed. We hadn't yet signed up for Netflix, and there was no such thing as "streaming." We had both spent much of the day reading, and wanted a change of venue. As I sat expectantly on the leather sofa sipping a cup of decaf coffee, David continued looking through our media cabinet. "Let's give this a try," he said, pulling out a laser disc. "I haven't played this in years." He had chosen a concert filmed at the Alhambra in Granada, Spain that featured the Montreal Symphony Orchestra and the Spanish pianist, Alicia de Larrocha.

As she began playing, I saw the pianist as an old woman. The flab on

---

[61]Andre Malraux, *The Walnut Trees of Altenberg*. (Chicago, the University of Chicago Press, 1992), 74.

her arms jiggled as the fingers on her spotted, vein-riddled hands danced along the keys. Her lined face was raised and her eyes closed as she lost herself in the rapture of the music. And then, suddenly, she began to change, almost to metamorphose. Alicia de Larrocha turned into a vibrant young woman in front of my eyes. As the pianist played, the old woman melted away. When her performance was over, I turned to David and said, "I forgot that I was watching an old woman play. It's as though she became her music—vital, young and mesmerizing."

"I'm guessing that's because she, too, temporarily forgot she was an old woman," said David. The next day he invited me to sit down with him in his office. He clicked on a YouTube video of the eighty-two-year-old Igor Stravinsky conducting his own *Lullaby Suite* from *The Firebird*. Like the Spanish pianist, the aging conductor was timeless. Here is the url if you want to watch: http://www.youtube.com/watch?v=5tGA6bpscj8.

Or perhaps country music is more to your liking. Check out Willy Nelson singing "Just Breathe": http://www.youtube.com/watch?v=ow-Cx9IX4So. It was released in 2012 when the singer was seventy-nine years old.

As I listened to Willy Nelson, something Sophia Loren once said came to mind. "There is a fountain of youth—it is your mind, your talents, the creativity you bring to your life and the lives of people you love. When you learn to tap this source, you will truly have defeated age."

Images posted on the Internet of this now eighty-one-year-old beauty offer convincing evidence that creativity can serve as a fountain of youth. For many creative people, the fountain continues to spew forth streams of artistic magic until death finally silences the voice and subdues the hand.

Consider the French painter, Henri Matisse. He is remembered for his fluid line and breathtaking experiments with vivid color. In spite of being wheelchair-bound due to a botched colostomy thirteen years earlier, he continued to paint. In his eighties, when confined to his bed, the artist would sketch on the ceiling by attaching brushes and charcoal to a long pole. When even this became too difficult, and he could no longer draw or paint, he turned to making colorful paper cutouts. When he died in 1954 shortly before his eighty-fifth birthday, he was still creating. On his bedroom wall hung the design he was developing for a stained-glass window to be installed at the Union Church of Pocantico Hills near the Rockefeller estate north of New York City.

The process of creating changed the tenor of the last years of the Miracle Girl's life. In the spring of 2006, as Katherine sat in the oncology unit while toxins dripped into her body, she began reevaluating her priorities. She decided to invest less energy in her interior design practice and more in her artwork. She had refined an ancient process used to marble the endpapers of books—the thick, strong paper found on the back of the front cover and first page designed to absorb the strain of opening the book on the remaining pages. Katherine figured out how to create images by soaking special paper in water infused with acrylics. She was excited about the artistic potential of the process and eager to build her portfolio.

By early June, the tumor was gone and Katherine was in remission. Feeling more energetic than she had in months, she threw herself into her artwork. By the middle of summer, she had amassed an extensive portfolio. Suggesting her art reminded him of the expressionist Frankenthaler, David encouraged Katherine to show her work. To help her bring it to the attention of local gallery owners, David offered to photograph her creations and create a slide show.

By the end of August, Katherine had succeeded in booking gallery space for her first show. It was to be held at the end of January. "I've got so much to do between now and then," she said one evening over dinner. "And so many decisions to make. I mean, do I just sell originals, or do I offer prints as well. If I make prints, how many? Is it better to offer a limited edition or make my art broadly available and relatively inexpensive? I haven't had such a good time in years!"

The good time was short-lived. In November, Katherine was diagnosed with progressive multifocal leukoencephalopathy (PML). The doctors said she probably wouldn't live long enough to see her exhibition. She told her husband, Thomas, that she wanted the exhibit to happen anyway, with or without her.

Because of the tireless efforts of several of her friends, and Thomas' generosity, the retrospective of Katherine's art was held four weeks after her death on January 30 - 31, 2007. The exhibit was appropriately entitled, "The Invisible World: Things We Know Exist But Rarely See." It was very well attended, and all of her pieces sold

Katherine's art was the product of a creative imagination. In the process of imagining, she was temporarily freed from the focus on her deteriorating body and inevitable death. She was able to bind time and to become one with the creative act. These "peak experiences" enriched her final months.

Occasionally I have a peak experience when I am writing. I get so involved with crafting dialogue between two characters that I become unaware that my own fingers are punching keys. I forget that it is my mind that is putting words into the characters' mouths. I even forget that they are of my own invention. Instead of dwelling on my aging body, or worrying about my damaged heart and lungs, or fretting about the future when my mobility will be limited, I concentrate on my characters and on building their world.

Spending time with creative people can also serve as a potent antidote to stagnation. Francois Pinault, the seventy-six-year-old entrepreneur turned contemporary art collector, believes his association with artists and his passion for collecting their works has kept him mentally young. "I'm very tormented by the passing of time and by death, because it's something we can't control," says Pinault. "Art and the relationship with artists could be (gives me) a way to stay younger in my mind for as long as possible. There's a disconnection between physical and mental age. Sure, I'm not thirty anymore, but I reason as if I'm thirty."[62]

It is possible to benefit from the creativity of others without actually being in their physical presence. I knew a man who was diagnosed with late stage cancer. Aware that he had a very short time to live, he rented dozens of films that he believed represented great art. As he waited to die, he immersed himself in the lives of the characters depicted in the films. The portrayals acted like morphine, dulling his fears without numbing his sensibilities.

Music helped Bob, our business partner, die well. He was the chief programmer for the expert system we were building to monitor the non-financial health of organizations. Diagnosed with inoperable stomach cancer when he was in his mid-thirties, Bob chose to work until almost the last day of his life. During one marathon work session at our home in San Diego, he was so sick that all he could do was lie on the sofa and listen to the rest of us brainstorm. When he disagreed with where we were going,

[62]Christina Passariello,"Collecting Art with Francois Pinault," *The Wall Street Journal*, May 21, 2013.

he would force himself to sit up and share his thoughts.

In the evening, we played music for our guests. Watching him, David intuited that Vivaldi's music might bring Bob some peace of mind. When he left, David gave him a recording of *The Four Seasons*. A short time later, David visited Bob at his home in New Jersey. Vivaldi was playing in the background. Bob looked at him, smiled and said, "We all die. I'm just doing it a little sooner than the rest of you. But I have loved life, and I have lived life. Life is good. Vivaldi is wonderful."

Aging and even dying are easier when our lives are filled with creativity, and when they are filled with other people. Connectedness is as important as curiosity and creativity to aging well. Only by staying connected can we avoid the sense of creeping isolation and alienation that characterizes the lives of too many older people.

One for All and All for One.

People on the rugged, mountainous Greek Island of Ikaria, thirty miles off the western coast of Turkey, live exceptionally long, healthy lives. As one still vital old Ikarian woman said, "We forget to die." Researchers from the University of Athens discovered, "People on Ikaria were... living about eight to ten years longer (than Americans do) before succumbing to cancers and cardiovascular disease, and they suffered less depression and about a quarter the rate of dementia."[63]

The researchers concluded that a diet in which processed foods are noticeably absent was part of the reason for Ikarian longevity. Exercise also played a role. It's almost impossible to get through the day without walking up a number of steep hills. Socializing is also cited as a critical variable. People on the island start the day sharing cups of tea made from mountain grown herbs and end it sharing several glasses of wine. They spend hours before and after their daily naps talking and playing dominoes, or helping one another in their gardens. Their homes are always open to friends and strangers alike.

The culture emphasizes the importance of community, of one for all and all for one. One of the island's few physicians explained that the

---

[63]Dan Buettner, "The Island Where People Forget to Die," *New York Times Magazine*, October 24, 2012.

emphasis on community that stemmed from the early communist years had not been erased by money and greed and a resultant focus on the self. He said, "For the many religious and cultural holidays, people pool their money and buy food and wine. If there is money left over, they give it to the poor. It's not a 'me' place. It's an 'us' place."[64]

Getting connected and staying connected on the island of Ikaria is easy. In fact, the residents have no choice but to be sociable. It's not as easy to stay connected in other parts of the world. It doesn't happen unless you make an effort. For those of us who tend to be introverted or who need a lot of time alone, that effort can be substantial. The path of least resistance is to remain alone, unconnected.

I know this to be true because I am that way. If I have more than one structured social event a week, I get jittery and feel crowded. I resist "doing lunch." My excuse is that it breaks the rhythm of my writing. I particularly despise large cocktail parties. While I am good at schmoozing, I don't find it much fun. It's work, not play. Fortunately, David is more of a social creature. He often initiates gatherings at our home, and doesn't give me a chance to refuse an invitation to other people's houses. He has learned to ignore my protests. He knows that I generally enjoy myself after I get to the event.

In forcing me to leave my mountaintop, David is doing me a great favor. As Albert Schweitzer expressed, "In everyone's life, at some time, our inner fire goes out. It is then burst into flame by an encounter with another human being. We should all be thankful for those people who rekindle the inner spirit."

After she was forced to retire, Aunt Jill lost her inner fire, and had no one around to help her rekindle it. Feeling like a victim, she began to perceive others as potential persecutors. She trusted only three people in her immediate world—her minister, her neighbor, Frank, and her old friend Mary. Worried about her, Mary urged Jill to go to the senior center where she could make new friends, play cards and have a hot lunch. Jill tried it for a few days, and then quit. She told me she didn't like the people who frequented the center. "They spend all their time gossiping and talking about people who aren't there. Playing cards is a waste of

---

[64]Dan Buettner, "The Island Where People Forget to Die," *New York Times Magazine*, October 24, 2012.

---

time."

Isolated, Jill's attitude soured. She became critical of everything and everyone. I even found it hard to spend time with her, and had to force myself to make the obligatory Sunday call. Her health began to deteriorate because she wasn't eating properly. Her socializing was limited to the few times Mary dropped in, and the coffee after church on Sunday. Then, Mary's daughter took the car away from her mother, and insisted that she move in with her. Because the daughter lived on the other side of town, that effectively ended Mary's impromptu visits with Jill. The only way Jill could spend time with her friend was to go to the senior center where Mary spent her days. She relented, and began going to the center.

In time, Jill made other friends and began to like spending time with other seniors. She mastered canasta and soon began winning hands. As a result of the full course hot lunches, her energy levels began to improve, as did her temperament and her attitude. When Mary died following surgery to replace her mitral valve, Jill turned to their shared friends at the center for solace. The bonds between her and the other seniors strengthened. During the last years of her life, Jill never missed a morning gathering.

Senior centers can be found in most communities and offer a social venue for the aging. Charitable pursuits also offer a way to render a service to the community while getting connected with a group of like-minded people. Activities that were once favorite pastimes or hobbies can also be used to create a new network of friends and associates.

Golf is a pastime that helps many older men and women stay connected. It's not a coincidence that a number of retirement villages are built on the edge of golf courses. I have a continually upbeat and welcoming Australian friend who is now in his late eighties. The last time we got together for dinner, I asked him about the secret of growing old gracefully. He smiled and said, "The secret is playing in a golf foursome every day and having a glass of good whiskey with a good friend every night."

Bridge was a favorite connecting pastime of my mother's. Because she played well, she was often invited to join games hosted by much younger players. In that way, she was able to diversify her friends and, in so doing, enrich her life. My mother always enjoyed having friends around. And, she was good at making them.

So was Katherine, the Miracle Girl. As she lay dying, so many people wanted to come and see her that Thomas had to post a note on the front door saying that the hour of 11:00 AM to noon was reserved for family. During the first of two memorial services, an elderly gentleman took the podium and said, "Katherine always made my wife and me feel like we were her very best friends. Looking around this room, I can tell she made hundreds of others feel the same way."

Katherine died of a terrible illness at the "young" age of sixty-nine. And yet, she still managed to make her final years rich and full in spite of her battles with cancer. She had the antidotes, all four of them.

The Magic of the Four C's.

Creative people, **curious** and **contemplative** people, and people who are **connected** or involved with others age more gracefully than those who are "stuck" in despair (the Castaways) or who suffer from existential angst (the Sages), or get blinded by delusion (the Celebrants) or self-absorption (the Stargazers) or who are preoccupied with maintaining the rigid boundaries of a defensive bunker (the Warriors). They are the ones who are best equipped to avoid falling prey to involutional melancholy, or the depression of old age. They are the ones who can dispense the wisdom of experience for they are able to inspire younger people and make them want to listen. They are the ones who are more likely to summon the energy to explore the world. And they just might be the people who live the longest.

Consider the story of the pianist Alice Herz-Somner. When she died on February 23, 2014, she was 110. Biographers attribute her longevity to the role the four C's played in her life. She was endlessly curious and resilient, able to find beauty and something to live for anywhere. She was manifestly creative, and an amazing piano player even when two of her fingers were severely arthritic. Biographer Caroline Stoessinger explains how it felt to hear her play shortly before her death: "You're riveted when she plays…Not because she's an old woman you don't expect to be able to play, but because the playing is riveting. It's like a laser beam to your heart."[65]

---

[65]Ralph Gardner Jr., "Urban Gardner: Examine a Life Well Lived," *The Wall Street Journal.* Feb. 26, 2014.

Like Katherine, Alice Herz-Somner remained connected until the end. "She rarely used the word *I*," explained her biographer. "She was interested in the other. She'd ask you about you and your family and she wouldn't forget."[66]

In *Being Mortal*, Dr. Gawande draws on the insights of the early twentieth century philosopher Josiah Royce to explain why the four C's matter. Royce believed the key to living a meaningful life and to escaping the horror of one's own mortality was **loyalty** to something beyond the self. In his paradigm, the opposite of loyalty is self-interest. Dr. Gawande explains, "The individualist puts self-interest first, seeing his own pain, pleasure, and existence as his greatest concern...In fact, human beings need loyalty. It does not necessarily produce happiness, and can even be painful, but we all require devotion to something more than ourselves for our lives to be endurable. Without it, we have only our desires to guide us, and they are fleeting, capricious, and insatiable. They provide, ultimately, only torment...The only way death is not meaningless is to see yourself as part of something greater—a family, a community, a society. If you don't, mortality is only a horror. But if you do, it is not."[67]

Being **creative** or attempting to build something that will outlast ourselves, being **contemplative** about the universe that exists outside of our own bodies, being **connected** to and concerned about others, and being **curious** about others' work or how they live helps us enrich our lives and transcend our own mortality. All of these states of being often occur when we travel.

Traveling distracts us from the aches and pains that afflict aging bodies and alleviates the ennui and lethargy that often creeps into our later years. It forces us to take a break from our routines, making it less likely that they will turn into habits and make us rigid. Exploring other parts of the world helps us expand our mental grid, our horizons and in doing so, fires our imaginations and changes our perspective on life. Going on a journey helps us to get out of our own way, and to see the world through the eyes of people who speak a different language and have a different

---

[66]Ralph Gardner Jr., "Urban Gardner: Examine a Life Well Lived," *The Wall Street Journal*. Feb. 26, 2014.

[67]Dr. Atul Gawande, *Being Mortal: Medicine and What Matters in the End.* (New York, Henry Holt and Company, 2015), 126.

culture. Traveling helps us transcend the boundaries of our individual selves, and thus temporarily frees us from a dark obsession with our own mortality. Exploring fuels our curiousity, inspires our creative instincts, and gives us things to contemplate. It encourages us to connect with strangers and even helps us reconnect with our partner.

The Nester and the Nomad.

Before I talk more about the benefits of travel, I have to make a confession. I am not a natural traveler. I like to spend time at home. I am comfortable with my own company, and interested in my own thoughts. I can sit for hours in my office working on my books. I read a lot, often about places I've never been. That's a wonderful way to travel. I don't have to get on an airplane.

Flying these days is a horrible experience for even the healthiest traveler, and it's worse for people like me. Because I have a defibrillator and cardiac re-synchronizer implanted in my chest, I can't go through the body scanners. I have to have a personal pat down. I hate them. They're so intrusive.

I have to use oxygen in flight because my oxygen saturation levels fall at high altitudes. Being in an airplane is the equivalent of trying to breathe at eight thousand feet above sea level. To use my portable oxygen concentrator on board, I have to file forms signed by my doctor before the flight, and every airline has a different form. I can only sit in certain seats reserved for the disabled. I am not disabled, but people look at me like I am when I have a breathing tube crisscrossing my face. Their stares make me very uncomfortable.

Even when a flight is not involved, I resist leaving home for an extended period. Like a true nester, I like my routines. Travel disrupts them. David hates routines. He claims they "smash his spirit down into grim necessity." He loves to travel—the further from home and the longer the trip, the better. If he has to stay home for long periods of time, he gets cranky, even belligerent. I am a nester by nature. David is a nomad.

"So, how did the two of you ever get together?" I imagine you're asking.

When we met, David was convinced I was an avid traveler. He had good reasons to think so. I've already told you about the card I kept for years above the telephone in my kitchen. On it I had printed in big black bold letters a quote by Helen Keller, "Life is an Adventure or Nothing At All." David assumed that "adventure" referred to travel. The rate at which I accumulated frequent flier miles reinforced that impression. When we met, I was living in Southern California and most of my clients were in New York. I had to fly so often on business that, by the age of forty-two, I had earned the right to be an Advantage Gold member for life. What David failed to realize was that, while I had traveled a million miles, I hadn't seen much other than conference rooms. I always came directly home when the business meetings were over. I felt I had no choice; I was a single mother with two young daughters.

David's belief that I was a great traveler was reinforced when I suggested we get married in Perth, Western Australia and that we spend our honeymoon in Bali. It might amuse you to hear what happened there. It turned out that his and my idea of what we should do on that magical island differed dramatically. I intended to lie on the beach all day and drink sweet alcoholic drinks while lounging in the pool in the evening. He intended to rent a four-wheel-drive vehicle and explore the island. His wishes prevailed until he got sick from eating shellfish and had to spend an entire day and night on the toilet. So began the marriage of the Nomad and the Nester.

Speaking of Bali, you may be wondering if David ever made it there. Indeed he did. He spent three glorious weeks in a magnificent villa high above the rice fields. He attended traditional ceremonies and was invited to participate in cremation rituals. Traveling through the interior, he went where few tourists go. Because of his understanding of Hinduism and Balinese customs, coupled with white hair that is so rarely seen on the streets in Bali, he was treated as a very special person. As he has told me often, it was very hard for him to come home.

Life as an Adventure.

As David is well aware, travel wakes up our senses, as the sights and sounds of everyday life that we take for granted are replaced by new views and different notes. Suddenly, we're paying attention again. Travel creates a sense of anticipation, of potential, of expectation, all of which tend to dissipate as we age. When we take a journey, we look at everything anew. Excitement replaces tedium.

Traveling can even free us from the illusion that we are the center of the universe as it reminds us of our place in the larger scheme of human affairs. The fifty, sixty, seventy or eighty years we have lived represents a nanosecond on the timeline of history. Our journeys can remind us that we are simply one small part of the story of evolution and that our individual lives and our concerns make little difference. That happens when we visit natural sites that are majestic in their beauty or raw power.

Shortly after David and I moved to the Pacific Northwest, we took a road trip around Washington. As part of our itinerary, we visited Mount St. Helens and the scene of the devastating volcanic eruption that occurred in 1980. More than twenty years later, hundreds of square miles remained scorched and barren of life. Charred remains of once giant pines still lay on the surface of the dead lake that had once been the site of family parties. As I looked at the devastation, I was awed by the power of nature and felt a keen sense of personal insignificance. Somehow I found that comforting.

In *The Art of Travel*, Alain De Botton explains why I felt that way. "Sublime places gently move us to acknowledge limitations that we might otherwise encounter with anxiety or anger in the ordinary flow of events. It is not just nature that defies us. Human life is overwhelming. But it is the vast spaces of nature that perhaps provide us with the finest, the most respectful reminder of all that exceeds us. If we spend time in them, they may help us to accept more graciously the great, unfathomable events that molest our lives and will inevitably return us to dust."[68]

That traveling can help us begin to accept our own mortality is apparent in the number of older people who chose to endure the rigors of travel even when disease and disability threaten to immobilize them. As of 2009, eighteen percent of Americans who traveled for leisure were sixty-five or older. Many of these people suffered from poor health or immobilizing disabilities. Consider Nancy Berger. Five strokes had left her immobile and with the mental functioning of a three-year-old child. In spite of the difficulties it entailed, her husband Nate decided to help her live out her dream of traveling to the most exotic parts of the world. Ultimately crossing through seven continents, they saw the legendary gorillas in the mist, explored the Amazon Rain Forest, experienced the

---

[68]Alain De Botton, *The Art of Travel*. (New York, Pantheon Books, 2002), 176.

frozen tundra of Antartica, stayed in a bush camp on the Masaai Mara preserve in Kenya, and watched the fairy penguins cross the sand on Phillips Island off the southern coast of Australia. As a result of their travels, Nancy's brain functioning has significantly improved. For more information about their adventures, visit their website: http://www.disabledtravelersguide.com.

Sometimes people suffering from a terminal disease travel in search of a cure or at least a release from both physical and existential pain. When she was wheelchair-bound and in the advanced stages of ALS, Catherine Royce traveled alone to a clinic in Nagpur India. She journeyed there to receive five weeks of ayurvetic treaments, and "…. to contemplate my death and ultimately, I hope, to embrace it with joy."[69]

While the trip did not cure her disease nor forestall her death, it did feed her soul. "In Nagpur, my known world was sensory experience. It was defined by what I saw, felt, smelled, heard and tasted. It was all new, and the newness allowed me sublime access to wonder. The very foreignness of it sustained my delight. All my senses were wide open, all the time. And, although things often felt unfamiliar, I never felt lost."[70]

As the Bergers and Catherine Royce discovered, strangers can be very kind. In fact, it is due to the kindness of strangers that older people and people who are sick or disabled can enjoy the benefits of travel.

The Kindness of Strangers.

From the moment we leave home, we are dependent on strangers. We have no choice but to let the pilot fly the plane. It does us no good to argue with the flight attendant when she insists we sit down and fasten our seat belt. We can only hope that our hotel reservation is on record when we check in. If we don't speak the language, then we have even less control. This becomes especially apparent when we get sick or are injured in a foreign country. While none of us wants a physical mishap to occur while we are traveling, when it does, it can teach us a valuable lesson. At least

---

[69]Catherine Royce, *Wherever I Am, I Am Fine: Letters about Living while Dying.* (Xlibris Corporation, 2009), 56.

[70]Ibid.,78.

that was true in my case. During the last week of our second trip to Spain, I learned to trust the kindness of strangers.

The problem began when we stopped in Trujillo, birthplace of the notorious Francisco Pizarro, conqueror of Peru. We visited the old fort and the church before stopping at an outdoor cafe for lunch. The waiter was pushing the paella, and I was hungry, so I followed his lead. David did not. He suggested that I might reconsider ordering fish when we were not near the sea. I didn't pay attention.

I felt queasy as we drove to Seville, but I tried to ignore it. After all, Seville was to be the crown of our journey. David had spent a great deal of time in that dynamic Andalusian city during his years in Spain, and wanted to show me all of it. We were planning to stay for five days at the Casa Romano, a centrally located boutique hotel.

We arrived early in the day, checked in, and immediately left to explore. We visited the cathedral and the Alcazar palace and its magnificent Moorish gardens. We walked the city streets. I was aware of the unpleasant rumblings in my belly, but I managed to ignore them. In the evening, we stopped at a tapas bar. I ate very little. By the time I went to bed, the rumblings had erupted into a full-scale eruption.

For two days I couldn't keep anything down. I had no choice but to lay in bed while David explored Seville on his own. By the afternoon of the third day, I was determined to see something of the city. After all, we had only one more full day before we had to depart for Grenada and then home. Against David's strong advice, I left the hotel. Willing my feet to move, I accompanied him to a bookstore about seven blocks from the hotel. While he looked for a recently released book on the Spanish Civil War, I leaned against the plate glass window at the front of the store and surveyed the buoyant, scurrying crowd. *The Spanish are a life-loving people*, I thought as I tried to focus on them and not on my lightheadedness.

We walked slowly back to the hotel. By the time we got there, I felt somewhat better. I didn't want to return to the hotel room where I'd been confined most of the week. I suggested we have a glass of wine at the bar across the street. David hesitated, but finally agreed. I had one small glass of white wine and immediately realized I'd made a big mistake. "I need to go back to the hotel," I whimpered to David. He paid for the drinks and then helped me to my feet. I managed to get to the pavement outside the bar before I fainted. As I fell, I wrenched my ankle on the rough cobblestone street.

The Spanish were amazing. As I later learned from David, they encircled me, forming a human shield so the cars and busses that sped down that narrow street wouldn't run over me. A waiter came running out of a nearby restaurant with a glass of water. Within minutes, a roving ambulance arrived and determined that I had not had a heart attack, as one interested passerby had feared, but that I had most likely fractured my ankle. They called for another ambulance, of a different color, whose charter it was to transport the injured to the public hospital.

Even though the emergency room was crowded, the doctors saw me quickly. An old man who could barely stand had suggested I be seen before him because I was a stranger and probably frightened. Hours after the mishap, I was back at the hotel armed with crutches that I didn't know how to use and wearing a temporary cast. I had learned to trust the kindness of strangers.

When I begin to think that my disabilities give me a reason not to travel, I remember my time in Spain. And, I visualize a brave woman I met when David and I were returning from a month-long stay at Blenheim Palace near Oxford in the U.K. We had to stay overnight at an airport hotel because our flight left from Heathrow very early in the morning. As we were checking it, a middle-aged woman strapped in a motorized device entered the hotel. She had no legs and only stubs for arms. Using her breath to activate her device, she wheeled herself up to the front desk.

It was apparent from the clerks welcoming smiles that she was a frequent visitor. Using her stubbed arms like chopsticks, she managed to open the bag that hung from her neck and pull out her passport. "I have a very early flight tomorrow," she said in an authoritative voice that belonged in a strong body. "I'd appreciate it if someone could gather me and my luggage around five and take me to my flight."

In spite of significant disabilities, this woman was exploring the world. Watching her, I made a promise to myself to become a better traveler. After all, if I don't travel, I risk shrinking the circumference of my existence to such an extent that my world becomes tiny and circumscribed. If I don't travel, I give up a wonderful opportunity to access the antidotes to aging. Finally, if I refuse to travel, I will miss out on some wonderful adventures with my nomadic husband. Traveling together is part of the dance of life. To decline to dance is to deprive both of us of some life's richest experiences.

8: TEETER TOTTER: Loving Our Aging Mates

When marrying, ask yourself this question: Do you believe that you will be able to converse well with this person into your old age? Everything else in marriage is transitory. Friedrich Nietzsche

A few years ago, we took a riverboat cruise from Amsterdam to Budapest. Although David dubbed the experience "a dress rehearsal for assisted living," we did enjoy meeting a delightful older couple. Bunny and Ted celebrated their sixtieth anniversary while we were on the river. They were proud of having escaped from their assisted living facility for the event. Every evening they entertained the passengers with tales of their earlier lives. (Bunny had been an internationally acclaimed tennis player. Ted had been an engineer.) Their laughter was contagious. Though Ted had a heart condition and a slight limp, they were the first on the dance floor. When Ted got tired, he would stand in place swaying to the music. Bunny would do the moving and jumping for both of them.

Watching Bunny and Ted, I got the impression that when they looked at each other, they saw their younger selves. Perhaps it was the way they flirted, like young adults on a first date. Or perhaps it was the laughter that emanated from their table when no one but the two of them was present. Or perhaps it was the care each took in their person and dress. He always wore pressed slacks and a blazer. She wore colorful skirts that swirled when she danced and shoes with a slight heel. Their relationship appeared to be ideal.

In an ideal marriage, two aging partners dance together gracefully— two separate organisms move as one. Both bring energy to the dance.

Though their arms are entwined, neither is holding up the other. Their limbs move in tandem and of their own accord. If one wants to boogie, the other is up to it. If one wants to waltz, the other is willing. They move through their advancing years mutually supportive and yet each is capable of standing and twirling on his or her own. She teeters when he totters and he teeters when she totters. I am confident Bunny and Ted will continue dancing "as long as they both shall live."

Marriage Vows.

"Will you have this man(woman) as your lawful wedded partner, to live together in the holy estate of matrimony? Will you love him(her), honor him(her), comfort him(her) and keep him(her) in sickness and in health; forsaking all others, be true to him(her) as long as you both shall live?"

"I will."

These standard wedding vows have a glaring omission. They fail to include a reference to aging. Knowing what I know now, I would change the vows to read... "comfort him (her) and keep him (her) **in age as well as youth**, and in sickness as well as health; forsaking all others..." When we are young and invulnerable, we don't worry about getting sick. We certainly don't dwell on aging or think about how it will affect our lives. If we did, we might pause a moment before we promised to be true "as long as you both shall live."

Eos, the goddess of the dawn, fell in love with a mortal noble named Tithonus. So great was her love that she pleaded with Zeus to grant Tithonus immortality. Zeus agreed. The two lovers cavorted happily through life for years until it became apparent that Tithonus was aging. Eos realized too late that she had neglected to ask Zeus for eternal youth for Tithonus.

The day came when Tithonus could not longer keep up with her, physically or mentally. Instead of a source of passion, he became a drag on the perpetually young immortal. Finally, Eos resorted to putting him in the equivalent of a nursing home. Though he no longer recognized her and bore no resemblance to the mortal she had once loved, Eos felt compelled to visit every Sunday for all eternity.

As Eos learned, it can be very difficult to love an aging mate. As age took its toll on her lover, he lost his energy and his optimism and, finally, his sanity. He became like a child, babbling nonsense. He was stuck forever at the negative pole of the Stargazer. At least he was laughing. Many aging mortals become consumed with fear and dread, and begin to approach life with the mindset of the Castaway caught at the negative pole. They become perpetual victims, caught in despair, passively awaiting the next disaster.

Still others get angry at the loss of youth and all it represents. They lash out, punishing even those they profess to love. David and I were visiting Alan, the Old Man on a Swing, in New Haven hospital after his heart surgery. As we were walking toward his room, we heard a man shouting obscenities. "Fuck you, Amelia. Fuck the doctors. They don't know a damn thing. I've had it with all of you. Fuck. Fuck. Fuck."

We stopped and watched as a well-dressed woman in her late sixties hurried out of the room, clutching her chest and sobbing. She took refuge in a corner where she tried to compose herself. A nurse approached and said, "Mrs. Wilding, this will pass. Your husband is just frightened. He's trying to convince himself he's still in control. Men often react like that after a heart attack."

Wiping her eyes, she said, "You don't know Henry. He's not going to get over it. He's paying the price for too many expensive cigars, too many glasses of fine cognac, and too many late nights carousing. Now he's taking it out on me. Sometimes I really think I hate him." She put her hands to her face, and began to weep again.

I imagined Amelia Wilding going home alone that night, and digging out her wedding album. As she flips through the pages, trying to reconnect with herself as that smiling bride in the arms of her handsome groom, she asks herself over and over, "What happened?" Maybe she also asks, "What can I do? What should I do?"

"Maybe I should divorce him," she says to herself as she takes a sip of wine. She sighs, "I can't do that. He might never get out of the hospital. He might die," she tells herself, aware of her ambivalence. "And if he gets better, what then?" She raises her glass again. "We probably don't have enough money to live two separate lives."

She opens another album filled with photos taken when they took a cruise down the Nile. "And even if we did have the money, I don't have the physical or emotional energy to separate and to then establish a whole new life." I imagine her closing the album, sighing and saying to herself, "I have no choice but to take whatever Henry dishes out."

Fear of Being Alone.

I can imagine Amilia saying that because I once heard the same thing from Shelley Phelps, an older friend of mine who was caught in a marriage with an obstreperous, inconsiderate, punishing old man who drank too much at night and did nothing with his days other than curse her and nurse his hangover. When Brent felt well, he'd spend the day on the cliffs with his younger, hang glider buddies. Like them, he saw himself as a risk-taking Warrior. I think he turned to booze to make himself feel like a big man when his age and physical condition made it impossible for him to glide.

Most nights, Shelley and Brent didn't even eat dinner together. Even when she cooked a nice meal for him, hoping to keep him away from the bars, he'd leave the table after a few bites, claiming that he'd eaten a late lunch. He'd then leave the house, or lock himself in the study with a bottle of scotch.

I was thirty years younger than Shelley, and unable to fathom why she refused to leave him. She could afford to. She still worked in real estate, and made good money. And, she was attractive. At seventy, she looked like a sixty-year-old. Once a month she and I met for dinner. One evening, an admirer sent over a nice bottle of wine. We both assumed the complement was intended for me. The waiter quickly corrected us. "No, it's Mrs. Phelps who caught his attention," he said with a bemused smile.

Shelley was attractive, energetic and competent and yet she insisted on staying with her loser husband. "I can't leave him. He needs me," she'd say. When I persisted, she'd explain, "We've been married for almost fifty years. I wouldn't know what to do without him." When I told her she'd have a better life without him, she'd defend him. "It's not Brent's fault that he never learned how to work. He didn't have to with all that family money. And it's not his fault that he lost it all. That accountant he trusted was a real bad guy. That's why he started to drink."

Sometimes I'd let it go. Other times, I continued challenging her. "Shelley, he's abusing you. You have to see that."

I remember one time when I said this, she put down her glass, looked at me intently and said, "I am too old to start over with another man. I just don't have the emotional energy for that. And, I'd rather be with Brent than live alone. There, I've said it. Now, let's get off the subject and talk about something else."

Though I respected her wishes and said nothing further, I watched with alarm as Brent's health began to deteriorate. That kept him home at night, but made him crusty and impatient. He became an unbridled Warrior, attacking everything and everyone in sight. His attacks pushed Shelley to the extreme pole of the Castaway mindset. She grew timid and risk-averse. Her timidity enraged him even more.

How do I know this? Because I've been there. David and I have hit a few rough patches in our marriage when he was behaving like a Warrior at the extreme and I had adopted the mindset of the defeated Castaway.

The Unbridled Warrior and the Defeated Castaway.

While David's predominant mindset is that of a Sage, his Warrior is also strong. When stressed or threatened, he gets angry. I'm different. When threatened, I become fearful, like a Castaway. As I get older, it takes less to make me fearful and less to frustrate him. As he ages, David seems to me to be increasingly macho—more aggressive, more impatient. His ability to connect with his feminine side, his "anima" as he calls it, has almost entirely disappeared. I think both of us regret that. If his softer side were more available to him, perhaps he wouldn't move to the extreme Warrior mindset so readily.

Twice in our married life David and I suffered through a conflict of mindsets. The first occurred in the fall of 2001 when the loss of my job, a negative medical diagnosis and the collapse of the Twin Towers on 9/11 stripped me of my courage and my optimism. I felt defeated and battered. Despair replaced my earlier resilience.

It took months of tormented soul searching before I emerged from the bog of despair, a little wiser about myself and the world at large. As that happened, David's rage at al-Qeada and impatience with me slowly morphed into an inspired assessment of what was happening on our planet and in my world. His mindset shifted to that of a Sage. The crisis passed. We were once again able to join together in the dance called Life.

The last time events transpired to unleash my Castaway and his Warrior was the traumatic nine month period that began in September 2006 when my mother died and continued until the following May when our dear friend Geoff Fairfax died. In the interim, I lost my Aunt Jill and my best friend, Katherine. And, I was told that I needed to have a defibrillator implanted in my chest lest I drop dead from Sudden Death Syndrome.

Overwhelmed by loss, I felt exposed and vulnerable. I became timid and tenuous. Once again, my Celebrant optimism evaporated, and was replaced by a tendency to expect the worst. My attitude shifted from hope to despair. Even my pace changed. I began shuffling instead of strutting. Frustrated by my timidity, David became irritable and impatient with me. He lost his temper over the slightest inconvenience. He raised his voice, and spoke to me as though I was an idiot or a child, or even an idiotic child.

I took it for a while, and then one day, I'd had enough. "Do not talk to me like that," I shouted after he had berated me for refusing to leave the house. He was angry because I had refused to take a "short, easy hike" with him. I had declined because I didn't want to have to struggle when the trail got steep. I knew from past experience that David's "short, easy hikes" never really turned out that way.

"I have my reasons, and they are good reasons. You shout at me like I am a naughty child. I won't tolerate that! Just who do you think you are?"

"I am simply asserting myself. It's because I love you that I have to defend myself. If I didn't, I would drown in your exhausting preoccupation with the mechanics of everday life, and your endless pools of insecurity."

I gave him a nasty look and was about to turn and march out of the room when he suddenly smiled and opened his arms. "I love it when you fight back," he said. "I love it when you're spunky."

Only later did I understand why his attitude and behavior shifted so suddenly. In defending myself, I was behaving like a Warrior confronting another Warrior. David respected that. He couldn't tolerate the Castaway stuck at the negative pole, defeated and despairing. In that moment, we both learned how to sustain the dance when life and aging conspire against us. I have to stand up for myself, and David needs to periodically take a look at his own behavior.

Fortunately, David is remarkably good at self-correcting. More often than not, he realizes his behavior is inappropriate or unnecessarily hurtful, and forces himself to take another approach. His ability to self-correct taught us a very valuable lesson when the Castaway confronted the Warrior in London.

Exasperation and Exacerbation.

In the spring of 2011, when David was seventy-three and I was sixty-six, we spent a month at Blenheim Palace in Woodstock in the U.K. A friend of ours had leased a suite of rooms in the palace when he spent his sabbatical leave lecturing at nearby Oxford University. When his sabbatical was over and he had to return to the U.S., he chose to renew the lease for another year. Because the rooms were often empty, our friend offered them to us.

Midway through our visit, we decided to spend a long weekend in London. The first day, to get our bearings, we took a hop-on, hop-off, open top bus tour around the city. We decided to get off at the Tower of London. When we started walking from the bus stop to the Tower, I had to struggle to breathe. The distance seemed interminable.

Not wanting our adventure to end, and hoping to avoid triggering either David's concern or impatience, I tried to act as though everything was fine. Every twenty feet or so, I stopped and pretended to admire the monument, or point out an eccentric tourist. Eventually, my breathing eased a bit. I managed to see everything except those places that required climbing a lot of stairs. David ventured there on his own while I sat and waited in the courtyard below.

When we finished exploring the Tower of London, we got back on the bus to tour the rest of the city. As five o'clock approached, the traffic got worse, and so did the pollution. Sitting in the open air on top of the bus, with every breath I took, I was inviting an exacerbation of my lung disease.

We got off the bus at the last stop, about six blocks from our hotel. After taking only a few steps, I knew I was in trouble. Forced to stop every ten feet or so to catch my breath, I began to hate the city that had fascinated me only hours before. I began to resent David for forcing me to leave Blenheim Palace (the nester's most recent nest) and make the journey to this polluted, expensive, crowded metropolis.

Every time I stopped, David tried to hail a taxi to take us to the hotel. I read the expression on his face as one of exasperation, and that made me mad. "I don't want a taxi, and you know as well as I do that you're never going to find one in the heart of rush hour on a Friday afternoon."

Stripped of the ability to do anything to help, David's frustration intensified. "We should never have come," he groused as he finally gave up trying to find a taxi. "I can't take you anywhere." By the time we finally reached the hotel, I was experiencing a bad exacerbation and he, a white-hot exasperation.

We went into the comfortable hotel bar that looked to me like a library in a private men's club. We sat down opposite one another in well-worn, wingback leather chairs. Though we tried, we couldn't get past the animosity that a Warrior feels toward a Castaway who is spoiling the adventure, or the resentment that a Castaway feels toward a Warrior who is trying to push her to do more than she can or wants to do. I couldn't find anything positive to say about our day or the city of London. That made David even madder, and provoked a string of accusations. "You're sure not the girl I married. You've completely lost any spirit of adventure."

I don't know why I didn't fight back and defend myself. Perhaps it was because there were other people in the bar and we had to speak in hushed voices so as not to be overheard. Or, perhaps it was because I was really feeling battered, beaten and discouraged. I sat opposite him sipping my wine, picking at my overpriced dinner and thinking how cruel and unfair he was being.

My negative thoughts intensified the exacerbation, leaving me depleted physically as well as emotionally. I couldn't sleep. The queen-sized bed felt small and confining. I couldn't put any distance between me and David, my tormentor. I rolled over on my side, with my back to him and began to weep. Apparently he wasn't asleep. Hearing me, he turned on the light. I waited for him to berate me for weeping. He didn't do that. Instead, he said in a quiet and somewhat sad tone of voice, "Lying here, I have come to realize something."

I dared to turn over and look at him.

"I realize that the more impatient and frustrated I get, the worse you get. I think I may be part of your problem. We know that anxiety can trigger or intensify an exacerbation. When I come down hard on you, that probably makes you anxious. Yes, I am partially to blame."

"Only partially," I said slowly moving closer to him.

We lay there for a while, feeling the tension between us dissipate. Finally, I said, "Turn off the light. Tomorrow is a new day."

We slept in one another's arms for the rest of the night. By morning I felt much better. We decided to walk down the block and have breakfast at a place the locals frequented. It was a beautiful spring day. Because it was Saturday, the city felt less frenetic and more inviting. I had no trouble walking. We ordered hearty English breakfasts, and pretended we were locals.

Over breakfast, David smiled and said, "So, we've learned something very important. My exasperation worsens your exacerbation, which in turn intensifies my exasperation. Exacerbation and exasperation: the evil twins which in the future we will avoid at all cost."

David has learned that if he's patient, I will heal faster. I have learned not to give in or give up, and to find the Warrior within me when David gets short with me. I recognize the value of pushing myself, and he understands that it's a mistake to ask me to push too far.

Now, when I regress because I'm suffering through an exacerbation, David doesn't make it worse by getting exasperated. He has learned to trust that the exacerbation will pass, and, when it does, I will resume the good fight. He knows he can rely on me to muster the will and self-discipline to keep going in spite of disabilities that sideline most others. When his fuse gets too short and he flares or gets impatient, I tell him I won't have him talking to me like that. He backs down.

Teeter Totter.

Two years ago when I had my semi-annual checkup, my cardiologist Dr. Caldus told me I had no signs of heart failure. "This is as good as it gets," she said. Then she asked, "Is it good enough?"

I understood she was asking about the quality of my life. I responded, "Yes. I am able to do just about everything I want to do. The only problem is sometimes I feel I'm holding David back, and I hate that feeling."

Teeter Totter

"Trust me," she said, smiling. "The balance will change. It always does. It's not that I wish your husband ill; it's just that I've watched it happen so many times. One day, something will happen and your roles will be reversed. You will be the stronger one, at least for a while. Then, the roles will shift again. That is life."

A year later, her prophecy came true. It became my turn to drive David the ninety miles to Seattle to see the doctors when he had a cataract removed. A short time later, he began to suffer from excruciating sinus headaches as a result of the lens implant. Again, I took him to the doctor. A month or so later, his strong heart rebelled, and slipped into atrial fibrillation as a result of too much prednisone. He had little energy and spent most of his days sitting on the couch in his office. I looked after him, and took him to the hospital for his cardioversions as we fought together to push his heart and our lives back into normal rhythm.

We were barely out of that crisis when he scheduled surgery on his left knee. Because of his days on the ski slopes, his meniscus was like shredded crabmeat. The pain had gotten so intense that David's mobility has been severely compromised. Warriors don't respond well to such restrictions.

When he announced to Dr. Caldus that he intended to have knee surgery shortly after his second cardioversion, she insisted that he wait. "You can't live your whole life with your hair on fire," she informed him. "Give your heart a chance to stabilize before you subject it to anesthesia."

Though he groused about it, he did as she recommended and postponed his operation for a month. That turned out to be fortunate since he ended up having to help me recover from surgery to "upgrade" my pacemaker from a defibrillator to a resynchronization device. As the doctor had prophesied, the tables had turned once again. The teeterer became the totterer, and vice versa.

Three weeks later, our roles shifted again. The doctors operated on David's knee. I drove him back and forth from Seattle, did the shopping and the cooking, and kept his cold therapy unit filled with ice. Fortunately, because of the resynchronization device, I had the stamina to do all of this. I became a Warrior determined to keep everything under control.

That created a new set of issues. The medications David was on made him incredibly impatient and irritable, and intensified his need to be in control when in fact he was totally out of control. Even as he made demands on me, he groused over one thing or another. Nothing I did was right. Nothing the doctors had done or were doing was right. Only he was right. His behavior did not inspire me to want to nurture him. It actually made me want to strangle him. Sometimes I would hide away in my office and swear at him or imagine ways I could punish him. "I won't make his dinner. Let him starve." "I won't go buy ice. Let him see how that feels."

We got through it. As he got off the medications, his temper improved. He began to concentrate on healing and on his physical therapy instead of picking on me. Once he could drive again, our lives returned to normal. We began working out together. I clocked a few miles on the treadmill while he rode the stationary bike. Teeter Totter. After our workout, we sat down at the dining room table and he reviewed one of my chapters. Then, we went into his office and talked about a new piece of digital art he was considering having printed on metallic paper. We discussed how big the piece should be, and decided it deserved a big footprint. In the evening, I cooked. He did the dishes. Teeter Totter.

Because the surgery to repair his meniscus didn't improve his mobility, a year ago David had his knee replaced. The recovery was long and arduous, and hard on both of us. This time, however, we managed to keep dancing, metaphorically speaking. I assumed the role of nurturer and chief bottle washer, but left David room to make his own decisions. He was careful not to take the frustrations of a slow recovery out on me. Even when under the influence of crazy-making medications, he tried to behave himself.

We've learned how to compensate for one another's weaknesses and vulnerabilities, and to dance together again. Only occasionally do we step on one another's toes. That happens when we begin to meddle in each other's affairs.

Beware the Meddler.

One of the reasons it's difficult to love our aging mates, or to be loved by them, is the state of almost constant togetherness that often happens during the post retirement years. Before retirement, most of us had our own individual circle of influence whether that was a job outside the home or running the house. After retirement, when both mates are spending a lot of time at home, and most of their time together, we begin to challenge the other's decisions, and to endlessly meddle, expressing an opinion about absolutely everything.

One night not too long ago, David and I were discussing the menu for a dinner party. He said, "I'm going to buy mudslide ice cream for dessert."

I nodded and said, "We have a box of chocolates, too."

He flared, "I told you I was buying mudslide. I happen to like mudslide, and you don't even eat dessert, so don't mess with my plans."

"I was only suggesting we could serve chocolates with the ice cream," I shouted to his retreating back.

I wasn't actually arguing with David about his choice of dessert. I was simply amplifying, and yet he heard it as a threat to his autonomy. Why? Because we had both become constant meddlers. We continuously second-guessed the other's decisions, both trivial and major. If I put croutons on the salad, David would say that I had added too many or too few. If I shopped at the local grocery store instead of the larger store three exits north, David would tell me that I was stupid to pay such high prices when I could have driven only a few more miles and avoided getting ripped off. If David decided to drive all the way to Costco to fill the car with gas, I would point out that the prices at a nearby station were just as good.

We have to constantly remind each other and ourselves that meddling and second-guessing are undesirable and hard on our relationship. Fortunately, we recognized the problem before it reached the terminal stage. When mates start telling each other what they can and cannot eat, the meddling affliction is so advanced that it may be incurable.

A few years ago we spent three weeks traveling around Florida. One Sunday morning when we were in Key West, we went to brunch at one of the hotels on the water. I was standing in the buffet line behind a particularly colorful couple. The husband appeared to be several years older than his wife. Though his back was stooped and he shuffled when he walked, I had the impression that he was wealthy and had once been a very powerful man. He was dressed in lime green pants and a pink, starched shirt. On his wrist was a watch that looked a lot like a Rolex. His face was set in a look of pure determination.

Wearing a dress that featured lime green and pink swirls, his wife stood straight and erect behind him. She appeared to be the taller of the two, but that might have been because of his stoop and the slight heel on her shoes. I watched the man put two sausages on his plate. His wife said, "Lawrence, you know you can't have those. You can't have bacon either. They're too salty." With that, she reached over, took the plate out of his hand, and tipped it until the offending sausages fell back into the pan.

Lawrence turned his head and looked up at her. The expression on his face said everything. "I hate you, bitch, but I'm not going to fight you because you'll only get worse. Maybe you'll die before me, and then I can have as many sausages as I want."

Lawrence didn't defend himself, at least not at that moment. Perhaps he punished her later for depriving him of his sausages, and his autonomy. I imagine that he did, and I doubt the quality of their marriage improved as a result.

Beware the Time Thief.

The meddling affliction can turn into a fatal disease when it threatens to deprive an older person of his or her most precious resource: **time.** David and I have struggled with that malady as well. That's in part because we are both high control individuals who, before retirement, were used to calling the shots. That's also because we are both creative people who want the freedom to spend our time creating. I'm a writer who wants to turn out at least a thousand words a day. David wants to perfect his ability to "paint with light," as he creates multimedia digital paintings.

Even though we are both engaged in creative pursuits, we have a different tolerance for interruption. I get upset when service providers or well-meaning friends and acquaintances want to distract me with what I perceive as meaningless chatter. David's hot button is household maintenance.

As I imagine you know by now, David hates maintenance. He keeps his list of dreaded household projects in a file on his computer named Sisyphus, the protagonist in Camus' story about the king who lied to the gods and was sentenced to spend eternity pushing an immense boulder up a hill, only to have it roll back down again, forcing him to start all over. David's boulder is made up of household maintenance chores.

"Maintenance is never done," he often proclaims. "If you let it, it will fill your days and destroy your life."

David gets no joy out of doing chores. Unfortunately, our home is high maintenance. The mountaintop property has steep slopes and rugged terrain. The forest continually threatens to encroach on the formally planted gardens. The house itself is difficult to maintain. Because of its soaring cathedral ceilings, even changing a lightbulb can be a daunting task.

I made the problem worse. Like a good nester, I like keeping my house in order. When the "to do" list gets too long, I get nervous. I started nagging David to take care of those things on the list that we had decided he's better equipped to handle than me. "You promised me two weeks ago that you'd clean out the barbecue. You haven't done that, and you haven't repaired those broken plates. They've been sitting on the workbench for months."

My nagging only made him less likely to cooperate. "I am not going to allow you to run me over," he said. "I do not intend to spend my day on senseless trivia. Life is too short, and my time too precious to let you fill it up with crap. I am aware of what needs doing, and I will attend to it when I decide to do so, and not a minute earlier."

I tried a different strategy. Instead of presenting him with a list, I began picking out one chore and then building from there. "It would be great if you could find the time to change the burnt out bulbs in the kitchen. While you have the big ladder out, you might as well wipe down the top of the cabinets. They've gotten pretty greasy."

David accused me of "building a train," and again defended his right to spend his time on more meaningful pursuits. I persisted. We fought. Then, one morning when I had tried building a train at breakfast, David told me a story to explain and reinforce his point of view.

"Do you know why there were no female monks in early Buddhism?"

"No, why?" I asked, relieved that the irritated husband had given way to the provocative professor.

"People said there were no female nuns because sexual temptation would make it more difficult for the monks to achieve enlightenment, but they were wrong. That wasn't the reason."

I waited, knowing he would continue.

"For many, many years, the man who was to become Buddha sought the path to enlightenment. He renounced his kingdom and all his worldly possessions, and went in search of the great teachers. Failing to find the answer, he became an ascetic, using pain and self-mortification and near starvation to help him discover the ultimate truth. After six years of self-denial, he realized pain and self-mortification were not the answer. He began to meditate and to journey inward. Finally, he was at the point of pure enlightenment when his concentration was broken by the sound of a lovely, lyrical female voice.

"Hello, Buddha," she said. "I know you are busy doing something very important but I thought you should know that the chicken coop is leaking. While you're tending to that, you might give the chickens some grain. While you're gathering the grain, you might want to check on the fields. I think they need weeding. While you're weeding…"

"You get the point," he said.

I nodded.

"If women had been allowed near Buddha, there would be no enlightenment. There would only be an endless round of Sisyphean chores."

His story woke me up. "In *The Hourglass*, I talk about how, as we get older, we have to be careful not to let our children or our paid caregivers decide how we spend our time. I guess the same thing holds true of our spouses."

"The poet Carl Sandburg put it this way," offered David, looking up a quote on his iPad. "Time is the coin of your life. It is the only coin you have, and only you can determine how it will be spent. Be careful lest you let other people spend it for you."

I have managed to stop nagging and building trains. With David's blessings, I hired a young woman to clean the house every two weeks. We found someone to help with the yard. David started voluntarily attending to several of the items that had lingered on my to-do list. He cleaned the third bay in the garage that we call "the studio." He cleared out the room under the house called "the cave" where we keep the yard equipment.

These days, the house is in good order and we're getting along a lot better. We don't meddle as much in each other's affairs, and we try to help each other make the best use of our time on this earth. I have been helping David get his artwork "out of the box" (e.g. the computer) and onto the walls. He reads my chapters, and makes suggestions I find invaluable.

We are doing a good job of making a life out of leftovers.

Making a Life Out of Leftovers.

I have to credit David and his British friend Peter for this title. Years ago, they and their first wives enjoyed a spectacular meal at a French restaurant. David and Peter decided to see if they could replicate the meal. They bought a cookbook, and quickly discovered that the secret of French cooking is leftovers. It's the leftover bacon fat, or charred onion bits that give the sauce its unique flavor. While they never actually cooked a French meal, they did begin to talk about leftovers and life whenever they got together and shared a bottle of scotch. Knowing them as well as I do, I can imagine one of their conversations.

"When you think about it, life really is all about making something great out of leftovers. Second marriages are made out of leftovers of first marriages. Second careers are often made out of the residuals of the first career," says David.

"And the second is often more satisfying and fulfilling than the first," offers Peter.

"If we learn from the past, and incorporate it into the present, then yesterday's leftovers can only enhance the experience of today," says David.

"Yes, the secret is knowing what to keep and what to discard," suggests Peter.

"Perhaps, like the French woman who knows how to make a franc squeal, we should hold onto everything. Perhaps every memory, good or bad, can enrich the present," says David.

Unable to stop himself from correcting his good friend, Peter smiles and says, "By the way, there aren't any more francs. Today French women make euros squeal." He laughs. "But you're right. Our intent should not be to replicate the past, but rather to let the past enrich and inform the present so that today's meal benefits from the leftovers of yesterday's meal, and yet both are unique."

I agree with them. I think the concept applies to the relationship between two people who have been married a long time. Just as a meal of leftovers can be even better than the original meal, so, too, what is leftover in a marriage or a relationship when age or illness has taken its toll can be as wonderful in its own way as the experience of coming together in the first place. Instead of titillation, there are shared memories. Lust is replaced with understanding. False compliments give way to enduring respect. The delights and apprehensions of courtship succumb to the tranquility inspired by deep trust. Serenity replaces jealousy. Instead of strobe lights, there's candlelight. Mating rituals are transformed into deep friendship.

I have a photograph on my iPhone that I often look at when life's leftovers begin to appear uninviting. I would have posted it here, but that would be against privacy laws. I took the photograph while I was waiting to see my cardiologist, Dr. Caldus. Waiting for another doctor in the practice was an aging couple who sat side by side in complete silence. They were staring out the windows at the street and cemetery beyond. Both of their hands were folded on their laps. I caught them in profile. Their silhouettes are remarkably similar. Both have high foreheads, straight and thin lips. While his hair is thinning, and hers is thick, it is apparent both have recently had haircuts. Both are well-dressed. He is wearing khaki pants, a blue shirt and a black silk bomber jacket. On his feet are black socks and polished black tie shoes. She is wearing a grey skirt and grey-and-white sweater that is either new or recently cleaned. I imagine they helped one another dress.

Although they never exchanged a word, nor even glanced in one another's direction, I had the distinct feeling that they were intensely aware of the other's presence. It appeared as though they had gone beyond the need for words. Each was alone, and yet they were together. I found it hard to picture either sitting alone in that waiting room. I imagined that if she died, he would die soon after. If he died, she wouldn't linger.

When we were staying at Blenheim Palace, we frequently visited the famous bookstore, Blackwell's, in Oxford. I happened upon a memoir written by John Bayley, an eminent literary critic who taught at Oxford. In *Elegy for Iris*, he talks about his love for and his life with his wife, Iris Murdoch, a brilliant English twentieth-century novelist. He portrays their life as Alzheimer's destroyed her world-class brain, rendering her powerless and vulnerable and capable of behaving only as a confused child—a child who vacillated between the joy of the Stargazer and the despair of the Castaway.

Even as John Bayley watched the brilliant love of his life deteriorate into a muddled mess of Alzheimer-induced childlike madness, he retained his love for her. He could still derive comfort from being in her addled and often anxious presence. In his words, "It is wonderfully peaceful to sit in bed with Iris reassuringly asleep and gently snoring. Half asleep again myself, I have a feeling of floating down the river, and watching all the rubbish from the house and from our lives—the good as well as the bad—sinking slowly down through the dark water until it is lost in the depths."[71]

John Bayley is courageous enough, patient enough, compassionate enough, and joyous enough to regard Iris' childlike behavior not as a symptom of a tragic disease, but rather as simply another manifestation of the Stargazer qualities he has always loved about her. When her brain functioning had severely deteriorated, he and Iris would watch the Telletubies on television. He often found himself getting lost in the antics of the cartoon characters, enjoying it as much as Iris. Other times, he would resort to infantile chatter to amuse her, or to prevent her from falling into despair. Until the end, he cherished the marriage and the love that nourished him and kept her safe.

The other night David and I watched a very poignant film. It was a French film entitled *Amour*, or *Love*. It's's about an aging professional couple who have spent their entire married life in this cavernous, well-appointed apartment in Paris. One morning as they are sitting at the small table in their kitchen having breakfast, Anna stops responding to her husband's comments. It's as though her mind has gone elsewhere. Minutes later, she recovers and has no recollection of what occurred.

That is precursor of a major stroke that paralyzes Anna on her right side and puts her in a wheelchair. That stroke is followed by another as she begins her rapid descent. With the occasional help of nurses, her devoted husband, Georges, looks after her. He changes the bedding and her gowns when she wets herself. Later, he changes her diapers. He tells her stories to calm her down when she screams for her mama like she did when she was a child.

Finally, unable to watch her suffer any longer, and knowing that she cannot recover, Georges smothers Anna. He then lays her out in her best

---

[71] John Bayley, *Elegy For Iris*. (New York, St. Martin's Press, 1999), 81.

dress, covers her with flower petals, and seals the door to the bedroom with tape. Days later, Georges follows Anna's ghost out of the apartment and onto the street. They remain united in death as they have been in life.[72]

Like John Bayley and Iris Murdoch, Anna and Georges made a life out of leftovers even as death hovered nearby. I believe they were able to do so because they had learned how to love one another not in spite of the ravages of aging, but because increasing fragility and vulnerability intensified their bonds. As Georges said to his obnoxious and formerly distant daughter when she challenged his ability to look after Anna, "We have been taking care of each other for a long, long time, and we intend to continue doing so. We don't need your intrusion. We have each other." (I'm paraphrasing. I don't remember his exact words, but that was the message.)

David and I are trying to make a life out of leftovers. We are still dancing, though at a slower pace than we danced when we met almost thirty years ago. Sometimes we trip, or step on each other's foot, but we've learned to stop, take a deep breath and start over.

We've learned to love the person who stands before us, rather than dwelling on who that person used to be or once looked like. David makes me feel like I am still an attractive woman. Sometimes he says I am "cute." Other times, he says I am "handsome." He no longer uses the word, "beautiful." That's okay with me. If he said I was beautiful, I would know he was lying, and that would be very upsetting. David is my muse and my literary critic. He couldn't function as either if he weren't honest with me. Similarly, I have become his muse and his critic. He trusts me to be brutally honest when he invites my feedback about his digital art. The way we support each other in our creative endeavors has become a fundamental part of our making a life out of leftovers.

Grow Old Along with Me.

It's not easy to get old, and it's not always easy to love an aging mate who is crusty, impatient or fearful, or who is sick and immobile. And yet, regardless, we need to learn to love both our aging selves and our aging

---

[72]Michael Haneke, Director, *Amour*, 2012.

mates. Then and only then will the last phase of our lives be rich.

Not long ago I watched the film, *Elsa and Fred*, starring Shirley McLain and Christopher Plummer. Although the reviewers panned it, I found it uplifting. Irascible Fred had given up on himself and on life when he met the indomitable, vivacious and determined-to-love-life Elsa. Surrendering to her delightful madness, Fred allows her to teach him how to laugh, to play, and even to love. She manages to do so in spite of the fact that she is slowly dying.

When Fred accidentally learns of her illness, he doesn't tell Elsa he knows. He lets her keep her awful secret lest it become the center of their universe and consume their remaining time together. Instead, he concentrates on making her last months vital and rich. Much to his daughter and son-in-law's dismay, he takes the money he had planned to invest in their business and instead buys tickets for he and Elsa to go to Rome. For sixty years, Elsa has been imagining herself as Anita Ekberg playing the scene at the Trevi Fountain in Fellini's *La Dolce Vita*. Fred makes that imagining come true. Shortly after they return home, Elsa dies. Though he grieves, Fred continues to live life with renewed vigor.

I think the film touched me because it reinforces a famous quote of Robert Browning's that I have always loved. "Grow old along with me! The best is yet to be, the last of life, for which the first was made. Our times are in his hand who saith, 'A whole I planned, youth shows but half; Trust God: See all, nor be afraid!"

9: 'TILL DEATH US DO PART: The Journey through the Shadows

As the stories of Anna and George and Fred and Elsa poignantly illustrate, barring a joint suicide or terrible accident in which both partners are killed, one spouse will die before the other. The survivor is left alone, wandering through a desolate emotional landscape. Luna, whom you met in an earlier chapter, described it well in an email she wrote to thank me for giving her a copy of *Widow's Walk* after her husband died. "We are the walking wounded, wandering lost in a landscape no one talks about; one we never imagined for ourselves. Thank you for shining a light on that rocky terrain so that we can keep on picking our way carefully out of the shadows."

The Journey Through the Shadows.

Widowhood does feel like walking through the land of the shadows. The world is blurry. Normal conversation about mundane subjects is strained and tedious. Time moves slowly. The days are endless and the nights are even longer. You struggle to reach through the shadows and grasp something real, but there is nothing there. The word "widow" is derived from the Indo-European widhwe which means to be empty, separated, vacant. When death claims the life of your mate, it claims a part of you, too. You experience a void within yourself, an emptiness that can never be filled. Though you continue to breathe, and your heart continues to beat, you feel as though the life force that used to flare within you has become a mere flicker that can barely sustain you as you struggle through your days.

It feels the same way for a widower. In *A Grief Observed*, C.S. Lewis wrote about his feelings and sensations right after the death of his wife. "No one ever told me that grief feels so like fear. I am not afraid, but the sensation is like being afraid...At other times it feels like being mildly drunk, or concussed. There is a sort of invisible blanket between the world and me. I find it hard to take in what anyone says. Or perhaps, hard to want to take it in."[73]

C.S. Lewis was sixty-two when his wife died of bone cancer. Luna was in her early sixties when Stavros died. I was only thirty-four when Bill died. It's harder to lose a spouse when we're older than when we are young and the future is still filled with the sense of potential. The resilience of the Celebrant is not as strong when we are older. Fewer paths open themselves to us. Because of the waning of energy that often accompanies aging, we may not have what it takes to walk down a new path. We are less likely to find someone to fill the empty chair. We may not even desire to do so, preferring to content ourselves with the memories we have built over the years with our dead mate. This is particularly true of widows. Widowers are far more likely to remarry. [74]

If the marriage was strong, the surviving spouse may feel a loss not just of their mate, but of their very identity. Joan Didion expressed it beautifully when, at the age of sixty-nine, her seventy-one-year-old husband, John Gregory Dunne, suffered a massive heart attack and dropped dead at the dinner table. "Marriage is not only time: it is also, paradoxically, the denial of time. For forty years I saw myself through John's eyes. I did not age. This year for the first time since I was twenty-nine I realized that my image of myself was of someone significantly younger...We are imperfect mortal beings, aware of that mortality even as we push it away, failed by our very complication, so wired that when we mourn our losses we also mourn, for better or worse, ourselves. As we were. As we are no longer. As we will one day not be at all."[75]

---

[73]C.S. Lewis, *A Grief Observed*. (New York, HarperCollins e-books, 1961), 1.

[74]The Society of Certified Senior Advisors, *The Journey of Aging: Working with Older Adults: Part I*. (Denver, Colorado, 2015), p. 43.

[75]Joan Didion, *The Year of Magical Thinking*. (New York, Knopf, 2005), 197.

Joan Didion was totally blindsided by the sudden death of her mate. It was more than a tragedy; more than a trauma; it created a sustained sense of seismic shock. The impact of this kind of shock is so severe that it intensifies the likelihood that the surviving spouse will also die. Studies have shown that the risk of having a heart attack is twenty-one times higher than normal the day after losing a loved one. The risk decreases to six times normal at the end of the first week, but remains elevated for the first month and probably for months thereafter.[76] The likelihood that the surviving spouse will also die is measurably greater if the death was sudden and unexpected. A study done in the U.K. in 2013 concluded, "Unexpected bereavement has a greater relative mortality impact than bereavement preceded by chronic disease."[77]

Given the risk, I am surprised that my mother didn't die soon after my father was killed. Her heart was not healthy. Her blood pressure was too high. And, his death put her in a state of shock that lasted a long time. Because she was a Stargazer, the loss of her Celebrant Warrior spouse left her disoriented and confused, creating a pervasive sense of insecurity and loss of personal identity.

Upon Impact.

My father, Jack, was sometimes a Sage and always a Celebrant Warrior. When he was forty-nine, he insisted that my mother and my youngest sister, Joy, leave their home in Greenwich, Connecticut and emigrate with him to Australia. He was desperately tired of the family-owned hat-and-dye-mold business he had been running, and wanted to resume work as a mechanical engineer. Australia appealed because it was an English-speaking country, its mining operations created a number of positions appropriate for a mechanical engineer, and it had a warm and dry climate. That was essential given his serious hearing impairment. He

---

[76]Dr. Murray Mittleton, MD, PhD, "Risk of Acute Myocardial Infarction After the Death of a Significant Person in One's Life", *Circulation: Journal of the American Heart Association,* (January 9, 2012)

[77]Sunil M. Shah MBBS, MSc, Iain M. Carey, PhD, Tess Harris, MD, Stephen DeWilde, MD, Christine R. Victor, PhD, Derek G. Cook, PhD, "The Effect of Unexpected Bereavement on Mortality in Older Couples," *American Journal of Public Health,* (June, 2013), Vol 103, No. 6.

had sustained damage to the nerves in his ears during World War II when, as a Lieutenant JG in the Navy, he landed planes on aircraft carriers in the Pacific.

Jack, Rosemary and Joy landed in Sydney, bought an orange VW bug, and began looking for a place to settle. After more than a month on the road, they arrived in Perth, a remote city on the Indian Ocean. They rented a small cottage and my father began applying for jobs. Six months later, he finally got an offer from a mining company in Alice Springs, an outback town in the Northern Territory. Surrounded by hundreds of kilometers of red dust, this home of the aboriginals was fifteen hundred kilometers from the nearest major city.

My father wanted to take the job. My thirteen-year-old sister, Joy, refused to go. She had made a few friends, and had just begun adapting to her new life in Perth. My mother, an urban creature by nature, echoed her sentiments. My father capitulated and, instead, accepted the position of Lecturer in Mechanical Engineering at the University of Western Australia. Given his hearing problems, that job presented an enormous challenge. To communicate with his students, he had to learn to visually interpret the movements of the lips of people who spoke with an Australian or Chinese accent.

My father adapted and spent twenty vital years in his adopted country. He would have spent many more had tragedy not intervened. He and my mother were returning to Perth from a weekend in the Porongorups. It had been raining all weekend. Ignoring the weather, that morning my father had dug an immense hole in preparation for the installation of a water tank. At sixty-seven, he was strong, fit and able to take on a project that would have challenged a much younger man.

They began the five-and-a-half-hour drive back to Perth in the mid-afternoon. They had driven halfway and were approaching Williams, a dusty, fly-ridden small outback town in the wheat belt, when my father decided to ignore their long-standing tradition of stopping for coffee at the roadhouse, and, instead, to continue their journey. Joy, who now lived half a world away in Cape Cod, Massachusetts, was due to give birth and he was eager to get home where they could be reached by telephone.

Tired of the road, my mother disagreed, and asked him to stop so that she could at least stretch her legs. He countered by offering to stop somewhere closer to Perth, assuming they were making good time. As he accelerated in order to climb a hill on the two-lane unpaved highway, my mother returned to her book, *The Handmaid's Tale* by Margaret Atwood. Suddenly she heard my father shout, "Oh, my God!" She looked up just as they crested the hill. A white van was coming directly at them. In a frantic attempt to avoid the collision, seconds before impact, my father turned the wheel sharply to the right.

We learned later from the police that an elderly woman was driving the van. She was bringing her husband home to Albany after a medical appointment in Perth. A young man driving a red sports car had pulled up behind her, and repeatedly honked his horn to get her to speed up or get out of his way. In an attempt to let him pass, she had moved into the other lane, putting herself on a collision course with my parents' car.

My father positioned himself to take the full force of the impact. As a result, he saved my mother's life. The steering wheel crushed his chest. The mangled hood was thrown twenty yards across the road. My mother was taken by ambulance to the Royal Perth Hospital. My father's body was taken to the morgue on the other side of Perth.

The Child Bride.

To my brother, Clyde, fell the painful task of identifying our father's body. When he got back to Royal Perth Hospital, he found my sister, Gay, still waiting to see Mom. When they were finally allowed into her room, they found her awake and lucid. As she twisted the lightweight hospital blanket in her hands, she kept repeating the events of the day. She always ended her sad tale the same way.

"I wasn't looking. I was reading. Suddenly your father shouted, 'Oh my God.' Then there was this awful crash. I've never felt anything like it in my life. It felt like the end of the world. I forced myself to look up. The windshield was broken. I couldn't see the front of the car. All I could see were pieces of mangled metal. I looked over at your father to ask him what happened. He was slumped over the steering wheel. He was making a strange rattling sound."

After a moment's pause, she would begin again. "We didn't stop in Williams for coffee. I told your father I wanted to, but he thought we should get home to find out if Joy had had the baby..."

Gay and Clyde let her talk. Finally, she exhausted herself and closed her eyes. When she opened them, she asked, "How long do you think I'll have to stay in the hospital?"

"Just a few days," said Gay. "Then you'll come and stay with us until your wounds heal."

"That would be nice," said Mom, forcing a smile.

The care and feeding of the sixty-eight-year-old traumatized Stargazer shifted for a time to Gay and her husband, Richard. They bathed her, dressed her, cooked for her and made most of her decisions. She was comfortable with that. She was used to having someone else make the decisions.

For the forty-five years they were married, Jack had been the Decider, and Rosemary, the Child Bride. It was he who decided they would move to Australia. It was he who managed the money and paid the bills once they arrived there. It was he who decided she would go back to school and get her teaching degree. It was he who declared when they would clean the house, and when they would do the shopping.

Rosemary never expected Jack to die before her. She had a weak heart, and had been told when she was an adolescent that she was unlikely to live beyond her late thirties. Jack, on the hand, had the constitution of a bull. There was nothing wrong with him other than his poor hearing.

That Jack was dead was something Rosemary could not fathom. When she told the story of the events leading up to the crash and described the crash itself, it was as though her mouth was speaking words her mind could not understand and her heart would not accept. She even seemed unaware that she was injured. The seat belt had ripped the fat off her stomach, leaving deep lacerations. Fortunately, Richard, who had been a nurse in the Air Force, knew how to cleanse her wounds. She let him do so without protest or complaint. She read, played solitaire, watched television and let the children amuse her.

She left it to Gay, Clyde and Richard to manage the details of Jack's memorial. At the service, she seemed disconnected, as though only part of her was present. She smiled. She looked sorrowful, but she did not weep. People remarked on her strength and her courage in the face of such a tragedy. She enjoyed having the approval of others, but felt neither strong nor courageous.

Deciding that she wasn't ready to live on her own, Gay and Richard kept Mom at their house until I arrived on the first of August, more than two months after Dad's death. It had taken me that long to get my business and household to a point where I could leave them.

During the month I spent with Mom, I witnessed her amazing power to deny that which she could not accept. When she passed Dad's closet, she'd look the other way. The door remained shut. When she spoke about him, it was in the present tense. "The grass really needs cutting. Your father will be upset if we don't take care of that." "Your father likes to have a glass of wine in the evening, and we're running low. We better get some." "Your father likes living way out here, but it worries him that I have to drive so far to get to my bridge games."

Sensing that she wasn't ready to cope with the truth, I said nothing. I focused on helping her establish new routines and relaunch those old ones that would still work for her. Paramount was getting her comfortable behind the wheel. The collision had made her anxious about even riding in cars, much less driving them. We began with short trips to the shopping center about five minutes from her home. She'd sit up straight, and hold onto the wheel so tightly that the blood drained from her hands. Fearing to get in the path of an oncoming car, she hugged the curb, often running over it.

Slowly we got more adventurous. We drove to Gay and Richard's house for dinner. A journey that should have taken about twenty-five minutes took forty-five, as she refused to take a route that would require her to make a right-hand turn and to cross a line of oncoming cars. One day, I suggested we go to the casino to play keno and treat ourselves to a special dinner. Driving there would force her to make a number of right-hand turns. I was betting on the fact that her desire to spend an evening that way would outweigh her fear of oncoming traffic. I was right. We managed to get there in one piece.

Mom's delight at the prospect of our shared indulgence made me think she might have begun to heal. As soon as we sat down for dinner, I realized she had adopted a new tactic in her struggle to learn to accept Jack's death. To our thirty-something, plump, bleached-blond waitress, she said, "My husband was killed in a head-on collision on the Albany Highway. It happened just as we crested the top of a hill. He couldn't see the oncoming van. The old woman who was driving the van was killed too. She..."

The waitress interrupted. Handing my mother a menu, she said, "I'm so sorry to hear that, Ma'am. Would you like a drink, a glass of wine perhaps, while you decide what to order?"

Mom seemed confused. She looked at me. "Yes, we'd each like a glass of Sauvignon Blanc," I said. Mom nodded and began studying the menu.

That began a new pattern. Every time we went into a store, she'd find an opportunity to tell the story of the accident to an unwitting clerk. Some let her go on. Others, like the waitress at the casino, stopped her. Some responded warmly. Others treated her like a mental patient who had escaped from the institution. When she was telling the story, she seemed to be somewhere else, talking to someone other than the stranger in front of her.

The time came to spread Dad's ashes in the Porongorups. Clyde, Mom and I drove down there in Mom's new car. Clyde slowed down when we reached the place where the accident had occurred. There, in the brush on the side of the road, was the white hood. At the sight of it, Mom again began to recite the events of that fateful day. There was little emotion in her tone as she re-told the story. It was clear she still had not internalized the truth. Nor had she begun to view herself as separate and apart, as a widow and a survivor.

In the late afternoon, we gathered outside. Clyde carried the box of ashes, and led us down a path through the dense brush dotted with karris and eucalyptus trees. I walked with Mom behind Clyde. Gay, Richard and their four children followed behind.

Mom's step was tentative. She rarely took her eyes off the ground, concerned that she would trip on a vine or turn her ankle in a rut. Now and then she reached out and touched my shoulder as though to steady herself. Every few minutes Clyde would stop, indicating that he had found an appropriate place for some of Dad's ashes. Sometimes he let the rough grey substance sift through his own fingers onto the ground. Other times, he offered the box to me, or to Gay. He had stopped offering it to Mom. The first time he invited her to take a handful of Dad's ashes, she had stepped back, away from the box, almost tripping.

The next day, we headed back to Perth. We stopped at the roadhouse in Williams for coffee. As we sat around the Formica table, Mom was uncharacteristically quiet. She seemed wrapped in a veil of sorrow that none of us could penetrate. I asked her what she was thinking. She sighed. A tear rolled down her cheek, but she said nothing. Only as we were getting ready to leave did she speak up, "If we had stopped here that day, your father would still be alive."

My belief that she had begun to admit and therefore to deal with the fact that Dad was dead was short-lived. The door to Jack's closet remained firmly shut, and she continued to look the other way when she had to pass it. I was concerned. My departure date was only two weeks away, and Mom was clearly not ready to manage on her own.

One morning a week or so before I was scheduled to depart, I got out of bed and went to look for Mom. Her bed was empty. She wasn't in the bathroom, or in the kitchen. I looked out of the window at the back garden, not expecting to find her there. She had never been fond of gardening. Still dressed in her pink nightgown and light blue robe, she had managed to get herself entangled in the prickly leaves of an overgrown weed. I raced outside.

She smiled as I approached. "I was having my coffee and I looked out and noticed this awful weed. Your father wouldn't have let it get this big. Now that he's gone, I'm going to have to take better care of the garden. I just can't seem to pull this one out of the ground." I didn't know whether to laugh or cry. In tackling the weed, she had indicated to me that she was ready to begin rebuilding her life as a widow.

Two days before I was scheduled to leave, I got back from running errands and found Mom standing in front of Dad's closet. The door was open. Draped over her arm was Dad's tan raincoat. Hearing me approach, she turned and said, "I think your father's coat will look wonderful on Clyde."

After I left, Mom busied herself with an endless stream of social activities. She played bridge several times a week. She went to gallery openings and met friends for lunch. She took her granddaughters to the ballet and her grandsons to the movies. She went to church every Sunday with Gay and Richard, and had dinner with them afterward. She traveled around New Zealand with an old friend. On the surface, she appeared to be engaged with life, but it wasn't real. As we would later learn, she was going through the motions but feeling nothing.

Three years after the accident, Mom and Clyde were enjoying a glass of cold white wine on the verandah of her new duplex. Gay, Richard and Clyde had moved her out of the big house north of the city only weeks before. The anniversary of Dad's death was approaching. Raising his glass, Clyde said, "To Dad. He would have liked your being closer to town. He would have liked this duplex."

Mom raised her glass, and put it down on the table without taking a sip. She looked intently at Clyde. "Only now am I beginning to feel again. I've felt numb since your father died. It's as though I was in a terrible state of shock that has taken years to subside. I feel like part of me has been on a journey, while the other part has remained here. Maybe now I can begin to feel like a whole person again. Maybe the move helped. It forced me to get rid of your father's things. It's forcing me to adapt to a neighborhood we never shared, to create my own routines, and to forge my own memories."

Rosemary lived another twenty years after Jack died. She spoke of his death only infrequently. Most of those mentions were directed at Joy when, for whatever reason, she had moved to the negative pole of her Stargazer mindset and wanted to reign Joy in, or exert control over her. At those times, she would remind Joy that if she hadn't been about to give birth, she and my father would have stopped in Williams for coffee. "If we had done that, your father would still be alive," she would say with just the right amount of bitterness in her tone to make Joy cringe.

Although she continued to control through manipulation and to cajole others to help her through a display of childlike innocence, Mom began to make more of her own decisions. I think she began to enjoy being able to run her household as she wanted. She liked sitting up late at night watching television without having someone else tell her it was time to go to bed. She had finally learned to stand on her own two feet, but it had taken more than three years.

There was a lesson in that for me. I realized how important it is to seize the moment, treasure the present, and be loving toward your mate for this could be your last day together. And I learned something else. Don't let the vulnerability of aging make you so dependent on your spouse that you can't stand on your own two feet. Your mate could die suddenly. Or, worse, get struck down by a final and devastating illness that forces you into the role of caregiver and decision-maker.

Death and Mindsets.

That is the way it happens for most older couples. Death's approach is slow. Pacemakers compensate for a severely damaged heart and minimize the likelihood of sudden cardiac arrest. Bone marrow transplants, radiation and chemotherapy slow down the progression of even the worst types of cancer.

Because of it's slow advance, both the dying and their mates often begin with an awareness that, while death is in the room, it exists behind the veil, at the periphery of their vision. That allows each of them to retain for a while their preferred mindset. It allows Stargazers the luxury of ignoring the dark shadow that hovers in the corner. Celebrants can cling to their optimistic belief that new treatments or even cures are on the horizon. Warriors can continue to believe they can postpone dying indefinitely through force and dint of will. Castaways can convince themselves that they are capable of accepting whatever comes, and that they will never fall into the bog of despair. Sages can contemplate what the philosophers have said about death, and find solace in their words.

As the disease advances, the cancer spreads and the vital organs lose functionality. Death emerges from behind the veil with a force that can no longer be ignored. At that point, the dying often move to the extreme pole of their mindset. The dying Warrior becomes angry and impatient. The Stargazer becomes self-indulgent and demanding. The Celebrant grows frenzied in a frantic attempt to cling to life. The Sage becomes melancholic, and begins to doubt whether there is a meaning to life. The Castaway moves from acceptance to despair, from giving in to giving up, and becomes fearful and despondent.

The lucky ones find their way back from these extreme poles, and manage to adopt the mindset of the acceptant Castaway or the transcendent Sage. They give in, grow quiet, reconciled that their life as they have known it will soon end. Experiencing few regrets, they focus on what life has given them.

The likelihood that the dying will find their way back to a healthy mindset depends, in part, on the mindset of their mate. Caregivers who have moved to the extreme pole of their mindsets can be particularly troublesome. Stargazers assiduously avoid talking about death, depriving their dying mates of the opportunity to do so. Celebrants insist their mates summon the energy to do everything on their bucket list even when that list is no longer of interest to the dying. Afraid of being overwhelmed by emotion, Warriors adopt a business-like attitude to the caregiver role. They get overly efficient and impersonal in an attempt to regain control over the uncontrollable. Caregivers who are themselves at the negative pole of the Castaway or Sage mindset can make it particularly hard. The despair or melancholia they exude can made the dying feel they are mourners at their own funeral.

Caregivers who manage to remain at the positive pole of their mindsets in spite of the stress they are under can help their mates die well. The functional Stargazer will do anything to make sure their mates are comfortable, and surrounded by the people and things they love. The Celebrants who bring love into the room, but have managed to set aside all need to perform a dramatic rescue, help the dying remember that life was good. Sages who are at once transcendent and compassionate enable the dying to understand that death is simply part of life. Caregivers who have adopted the mindset of the acceptant Castaway understand that the sick need time to reflect, and are content to sit quietly and hold the hand of their dying mates. Even Warriors at the positive pole can be helpful as they courageously look death in the face, and, forcibly if necessary, insist that the medical profession and other caregivers treat their mates well.

I'm going to tell you two stories about people who died well in spite of their final struggle with horrific diseases, and how their spouses helped them die. The Miracle Girl is Katherine's story. I call her that because she survived cancer four times before succumbing to a nasty side effect of one of her chemotherapy drugs. *The Shrine* is her husband's story. I call him Thomas the Chaplain because he manifests so many characteristics of the joyous Stargazer and the optimistic Celebrant. He is a trusting, compassionate man who insists that people are basically good and, even at the point of death, life is fair.

Five Card Draw is Stavros' story. Stavros because means victory in Greek and, although he wasn't Greek, he was victorious in life. He enjoyed tremendous professional success, becoming the CEO of a major corporation before retiring at the age of forty-six to focus on his consulting practice and the family he adored. He was a spirited, courageous risk-taker who maintained his love of life even when it became apparent that he had failed to beat the odds. A Celebrant Warrior, his wife, Luna, helped him fight back. When it was clear that the fight was over, she helped him focus on the magical years they had had together instead of the years that multiple myeloma was denying them.

The Miracle Girl.

In the year 2000, when she was sixty-three, Katherine was diagnosed with lymphoma. Her oncologist told her that if she didn't have a blood marrow transplant, she would be dead in a matter of months. Not willing to subject her body to that kind of sustained punishment, she opted instead for a treatment regime that included chemotherapy, radiation and visualization.

To the oncologist's amazement, she sent the cancer into remission. She began praying that she would reach the critical five year mark without a recurrence. After five years, the status of "cancer in remission" would be altered to read, "cancer cured."

Katherine had been remission for three years when I met her at a luncheon for women who lived on our mountain. It was the autumn of 2003. Katherine and Thomas rapidly became our best friends. Whenever they weren't busy with other social engagements, they would call and suggest we get together. "We've been out five nights this week, and really need a break from socializing. How about coming over for a casual dinner?"

In late October 2005, two years after I met Katherine, we were at their house for dinner. Katherine and I were sitting together on one of the bittersweet orange upholstered couches in their living room. A roaring fire kept us cozy. We were sipping chilled white wine and looking at the latest photos of her son, daughter-in-law and grandchildren. Thomas and David were in the kitchen nursing martinis and pretending to prepare dinner. Every few minutes Katherine raised a tissue to her nose. She sounded as though she had a cold. As though reading my thoughts, she said, "It's nothing; just an allergy or a problem with my sinuses. I'll make an appointment with the doctor."

Shortly before Thanksgiving, the doctor told Katherine that she had a tumor in her nasal passage. A biopsy confirmed that it was malignant. The lymphoma had returned. The diagnosis was wrenching. Though she reassured Thomas and her children that she would beat the cancer as she had done before, privately she grieved. She wrote in her journal, "This may be my last Thanksgiving."

David and I knew none of this until the night before Christmas Eve when Katherine and Thomas came to have dinner with us. As we gathered around the fire in our living room, Katherine set aside the stocking I had filled with silly gifts. "I have something to tell you," she said. Thomas was lying on the floor in front of the fireplace stroking the head of Coco, their recently acquired black, rambunctious Havanese. As Katherine spoke, he stopped smiling. His body stiffened. He pulled the dog closer.

Katherine turned her head and looked me straight in the eye. "My cancer has returned." Then, she reached over, smiled and patted my hand. "Don't be upset. It's not like I'm going to die or anything. I'm not going to die. I'm just going to have to fight it again." Smiling broadly, she opened her arms indicating that she wanted Thomas to bring Coco to her. "And I have this marvelous little creature to help me through it. Jake helped me through my first lymphoma and Coco is going to help me through this one. She'll help keep positive energies in our home."

Katherine began chemotherapy shortly after the start of the new year. She tolerated the Rituxan very well, keeping her dark strawberry blonde hair and experiencing a minimum of nausea. That, in itself, is a miracle given the drug was strong enough to wipe out all the bacteria and effectively shut down their septic system. By July, all evidence of the cancer was gone.

In August she, Thomas, David and I enjoyed a picnic outing to San Juan Island. Though Katherine's spirits were high, her body was not behaving well. Her step was tentative and her gait unusually slow and labored. In September, because I had to fly to Australia to attend to my ailing mother, David spent his birthday alone with Katherine and Thomas. Katherine made her traditional coconut cake. A few days later, he flew to Australia to join me. We were so preoccupied with Mom's death and then Jill's sudden demise, we didn't dwell on Katherine's health.

After we got back, Thomas invited us to their home for dinner. It was the first week in November. We gathered in front of the fire in the cozy French country kitchen for cocktails and hors d'oeuvres. Katherine seemed disoriented and said little. She picked up a miniature hotdog, bit off a piece and then put the remainder back on the tray. Thomas took a paper napkin and quickly removed the half-eaten roll. I could tell he was embarrassed. He and Katherine both had a strong sense of propriety. We pretended not to notice that anything was amiss.

Later, when we were seated around the dining table, Katherine said, "I learned today that you can tell how dominant a man is by the pitch of his voice." Then she laughed raucously. "The lower the better, and the bigger the better."

I looked at Thomas. His face was beet red. He was clearly mortified and at a loss as to what to do. Before he could intervene, Katherine continued, "If you have an erection that lasts more than four hours..." Then she guffawed.

Thomas stood up. "Katherine," he said sternly. He didn't have to say more. Katherine grew silent, and concentrated on her food. Thomas sat down again. We ate for a few minutes in silence. David finally broke the tension. "I read in the newspaper this morning that a Jackson Pollock sold for 140 million dollars. I think that's absurd."

"I agree," said Thomas, obviously relieved that the conversation had shifted. "What do you think, Katherine?"

Katherine looked at him with a blank stare. Though the rest of us were not yet finished, Katherine stood up, stared straight ahead like a robot, and force-marched her own plate into the kitchen. Moments later, she came back and sat down, but said nothing. A few minutes later, she said, "Good night," and went to bed.

After she'd gone, we helped Thomas do the dishes and then sat around the table in the kitchen enjoying a last glass of wine. Thomas spoke first. "Katherine asked me not to say anything to you or anybody else, but I simply must. Her behavior has been very strange. Wendy called this morning and told me Katherine's driving has become so erratic that Wendy doesn't feel safe driving with her. This morning, she turned on the water, and then simply walked out of the room. I'm afraid I reacted poorly. I shouted at her."

"That's understandable," said David.

"I don't know what's going on. Katherine knows something is not right. She thought maybe she'd had a stroke. She insisted on having an MRI, but it came back clean. All they found were some white spots on the brain."

"Maybe you need to take her to a neurologist," David said.

"Her son Ron is doing some research and making some calls."

"I'm sure he'll come up with something," I said, happy that Katherine's son was involved. A smart, take-charge kind of person, I knew he wouldn't stop until he found the most qualified physician to examine his mother.

We had to leave for Sacramento a few days later to close up Jill's home, and retrieve her ashes. One evening, after a long day of going through Jill's things, we opened our laptop to check our email. There was a message from Thomas.

Dear Friends,

As you all know, Katherine is a miracle girl. We now badly need another miracle. It was with deep sadness that yesterday we checked her into the University of Washington Medical Center with what we believe to be a rather aggressive viral infection of the brain…Several neurologists believe it to be what they call PML…or progressive multifocal leukoencephalopathy.

This nasty virus can attack the brain tissue of people whose immune systems have been compromised…We understand that this is rather nasty stuff. We will need your love, prayers and support…We do believe in miracles, yet realistically we are told that this can progress rapidly. There is no known cure. Your prayers, love and support are most appreciated.

Thomas

After three days and two spinal taps, the doctor's initial diagnosis was confirmed. Because of her compromised immune system, the JVC virus that resides but remains inactive in our kidneys had been unleashed and broke through the blood-brain barrier, infecting Katherine's brain. It was attacking the cells responsible for producing myelin, a fatty substance that enwraps the nerves of the brain. The loss of myelin was accompanied by the rapid deterioration of brain function.

Her Celebrant Warrior mindset engaged, Katherine agreed to try Cytarabine, an experimental drug. It had stopped the progression of PML in a minority of cases like hers. Sadly, she did not respond to the treatment. The virus continued to eat her brain. As it did, her motor functions deteriorated.

Suggesting that it was time for Katherine to go home and think about her legacy, the doctors released her a few days before Thanksgiving. They recommended that Thomas hire a caregiver. Uncomfortable with dealing with bodily fluids, and anxious to protect Katherine's dignity, Thomas did so.

On Thanksgiving Day, Thomas invited the entire extended family for dinner. He asked us to join them for drinks. When we arrived, Katherine was seated at the end of the sofa. Immaculately groomed, she looked like a china doll. Her eyes had a vacant look. It felt as though only the shell of Katherine was with us. She said nothing, simply watching as others talked. I was surprised when she suddenly sat up straight and asked the attendant to help her move to the couch where I was sitting.

For several minutes, Katherine sat next to me without saying anything. Suddenly, she turned her head and said so quietly that only I could hear, "I always knew I was going to get old, but I never thought it would happen so fast." I looked at her. She was smiling. She knew she was dying, and yet she was smiling. My friend was back, but only briefly. Moments later, Katherine signaled to the caregiver to wheel her back into her bedroom.

On the Sunday after Thanksgiving, it snowed hard. Regardless, Ron picked up his mother and took her for a pedicure and then to dinner at his house. By the time dinner was over, the snow had piled up and the temperatures dropped precipitously, creating sheets of black ice on the roads. Katherine ended up spending the week with Ron, Abby, and their two young children.

The next weekend the temperatures rose, the black ice disappeared and the snow receded. Thomas brought Katherine home. Three days later, he invited us over for drinks and dinner. "The invitation is Katherine's idea. Several months ago she made and froze a lamb stew. She said she was making it for the two of you. It's payback for all the times you've served us lamb. Lamb chops. Rack of lamb. Lamb roast. She wants you to come for dinner, even though she won't be able to join us."

That night is permanently etched on my brain. When we reached the house, we found a note on the door. "Please don't ring the doorbell. Katherine might be sleeping. Just come in. The door is open." We did so and were greeted by Coco, barking wildly. Thomas was right behind her. "Ah, you're early," he said. "That's good. Katherine's been waiting for you. Let's go see her."

"How is she doing?" I asked.

"As well as can be expected, I suppose," said Thomas, sipping the martini he had made before our arrival. "Yesterday we went to see the doctor who created Cytarbarine, the experimental drug we tried on Katherine. She is one of the world's foremost experts on PML and she's based in Seattle. She sees very few patients. We were fortunate to be able to see her. Her news, however…"

Before he could finish, his cell phone rang. (Ron had given Thomas the phone when Katherine was admitted to the hospital, insisting that he use it.) Taking it out of his pocket, he smiled. "It's Katherine." Their conversation lasted only a few seconds. Returning his phone to his pocket, Thomas smiled and said, "She knows you're here. She wants us in her room, pronto."

Katherine was in bed, propped up by oversized brocade pillows in a four-poster brass bed draped with elegant, colorful fabrics. She was wearing a silk, purple-hued garment that made her look regal. A large, ornate antique chest filled the far corner, its massive doors designed to hide the television when it was not in use. Now, they stood open. ABC World News was playing. Charles Gibson was summarizing the events of the day. "In Paris, diplomats from the five UN Security Council member states and Germany have failed to reach an accord on Iran sanctions. Today in Thailand, the last remaining bodies of people who died in the tsunami two years ago were buried."

Katherine reached over, picked up the remote and turned down the sound. She patted the bed, indicating that she wanted me to sit next to her. Thomas pulled up a chair for David and a footstool for himself. Taking my hand in hers, she attempted to smile. Her eyes complied, but her mouth refused. Her brain could no longer tell the left side of her mouth to lift.

"Would you like a drink, dear?" Thomas asked.

Katherine nodded and again attempted to smile. Thomas stood and picked up one of the sticks with a sponge that were in a box on the bedside table. He put it in his vodka martini and stirred it around, and then raised the wet sponge to Katherine's waiting mouth. "Cheers," she said as she struggled to raise herself to a full sitting position. Thomas put another pillow behind her back and then sat down.

"We saw the doctor yesterday," Thomas said, picking up where we had left off in the hallway.

"Two to twenty-four months," Katherine said in a voice that was surprisingly clear and strong.

'No, dear," Thomas said. "The doctor said two to four months, not two to twenty-four months." I could tell from the tension in his voice that it had been difficult for him to correct Katherine. It would have been more in his Stargazer or Celebrant nature to leave it alone, and let her hope. Later he would explain that he thought it was important to help her accept what was happening to her.

"Two to four months," Katherine repeated in a subdued voice.

Katherine had another squeeze of vodka and then closed her eyes. Thinking the effort to talk had tired her out, we left the room. As we walked away, we could hear that Charles Gibson had resumed his monologue on the dire state of world affairs.

Thomas served the lamb stew in the blue and white dishes that Katherine had bought in Paris years earlier. We talked about everything in general and nothing in particular. After we finished dinner, Thomas shared with us a letter he'd received from a friend of Katherine's who was an ardent Buddhist. In the letter, the friend criticized Thomas for refusing to let her bring a Hindu Ayurvedic healer to attend to Katherine. The healer had helped Katherine several times before. In the letter, the friend argued that the healer would give Katherine hope and that she had the right to cling to hope until the very end.

Thomas was struggling. "Isn't false hope worse than no hope at all?" he asked.

I said, "Maybe the healer can help Katherine reframe her hope. She can't hope for a long life, but she can hope to live her remaining days without pain. She can hope to have the people she loves around her as she dies."

Thomas nodded.

Looking thoughtful, David said, "I believe false hope takes us away from the present moment and makes us focus on a future that will never happen. Genuine hope, on the other hand, helps us fully experience life in the present moment."

Thomas finally decided he would invite the healer to visit Katherine. "Maybe he can help her. Regardless, that's what she wants, and maybe that alone is reason enough."

"The dying should have more votes than the rest of us," said David, lightening the mood as we prepared to leave.

I heard from Thomas the next day. He was calling to invite me to a meeting of Katherine's friends who were gathering to plan the exhibition of her artwork that she had scheduled for the last weekend in January. Aware that she would probably not live to see the exhibit, she remained adamant that it take place.

About halfway through the meeting, Katherine herself put in an unexpected appearance. The room went quiet when she appeared, her caregiver pushing her wheelchair. She sat next to me as she listened to us arguing about which of her pieces should hang on the gallery walls. After about fifteen minutes, she signaled for the caregiver to wheel her out of the room. After she was gone, we all looked at each other, waiting for someone to say what was on all of our minds. "She's gotten so thin. She's wasting away. Her skin is translucent. It's like she's disappearing right in front of our eyes." But no one said a word.

Katherine rarely ventured out of her bedroom after that. Within days of our meeting, she could no longer get to the bathroom, even with the assistance of Thomas or her paid attendant, or both. Thomas arranged to have a device installed that would lift Katherine and hoist her into the bathroom. It was a failure.

In spite of her predicament, Katherine always smelled fresh. That was due to the tireless effort of a warm and responsive young Hawaiian woman. With sleight of hand and the deft use of plastic bags, she made all evidence of Katherine's incontinence vanish. And, she made sure Katherine was always well groomed—that her hair was washed and blown dry, and that her linen pajamas were ironed.

On December 12, Katherine decided that it was time for hospice. Because she had lost the ability to sit up, she agreed to have a hospital bed installed in her bedroom. Her four-poster brass bed became the repository for gifts brought by an endless stream of diverse visitors. The number of people wanting to see Katherine grew so large that Thomas was forced to block the hour of eleven to noon for family-only visits.

Knowing that we were going to Boise to spend Christmas with daughter Monica and her family, Thomas invited us to visit with Katherine and then to have dinner with him on December 21, the eve of the winter solstice.

When I walked into the living room, I was astounded. The house was replete with signs of the holiday. A large tree meticulously trimmed with delicate and carefully crafted ornaments stood in the corner, its lights reflecting off sliding-glass doors and mirrors. A Santa hat hung from the corner of a huge piece of coral. Wooden apples, pears and grapes covered the mantelpiece. It felt like the home of people who are embracing life. It did not feel like the house of the dying. Clearly, Thomas had managed to retain his Celebrant mindset.

We sat down next to Katherine's bed. For several minutes, Katherine seemed unaware of our presence. She continued to stare blankly at the flickering images of the Nutcracker Ballet on the muted television set. I reached over and took her right hand. She turned her head, and tried to smile.

"Would you like me to raise the bed a little, Katherine?" Thomas asked.

She nodded. Thomas pushed the button, but nothing happened. "Coco chewed the wires," Thomas explained. "You have to fiddle with it for a while."

As though on cue, Coco bound into the room, and, barking wildly, attempted to jump up onto David's lap. David picked her up and scratched her belly until she settled down. She sat quietly for a minute or two and then jumped onto Katherine's bed. David stood up to retrieve the puppy when Thomas intervened. "It's okay. She's learned not to play rough with Katherine."

Indeed, we watched as Coco sat quietly on the bed next to Katherine's inert body. Katherine mumbled something that I couldn't understand. Then, she raised her right arm and began moving her limp hand in a circle. "Life is change, always changing," she whispered.

In that single statement, Katherine had captured the sense of impermanence and detachment that is at the heart of the Buddhist philosophy. Perhaps the spiritual healer had helped her after all. She seemed able to accept death. She was calm that night, even peaceful in her being. It was as though she had become a pure Sage. When we left that night, we knew we would never see her again. Yet we left with peace as well as sadness in our hearts. In accepting her own death, Katherine had helped us accept it as well.

Katherine miraculously found the strength to join her women's group when they came to sing carols the night before Christmas Eve. A photograph shows her slumped down in her wheelchair, a Santa hat on her head. Her eyes are sunken in her gaunt face, and the left side of her mouth is raised in a twisted smile. On Christmas Eve, Katherine wore her favorite red dress. She sat in her wheelchair in the living room for two hours of toasts, presents, prayer and dinner with her children and her grandchildren.

Before dawn on the morning of December 28, the caregiver woke Thomas and told him that Katherine's breathing had changed. Thomas called the children and urged them to come to the house. Later, on the blog Ron had maintained since his mother entered the hospital, he wrote, "Mom peacefully passed away at home this morning with Thomas, Susan, Abby, me, and her dog, Coco, at her side. The sun brightly shone on all of nature's splendor...a good day to die."

The Shrine.

A special private memorial service was held for Katherine the eve of December 30. Though intended to be for family and close friends only, the funeral home was filled to capacity. Hundreds showed up to pay their respects. As I watched Thomas wander among the well-wishers, I had the sense that he was not grounded. His back was slightly bowed; his walk, tentative; and his smile, wan. He let people embrace him, and he hugged them back, but his clasp was without force. He moved like a Castaway.

I wondered how he would fare on New Years' Eve. That night had always been a special event for Thomas and Katherine. Wearing formal attire, they would gather with several other couples at one of their homes for a lavish dinner. Although Thomas was not feeling up to a formal event, he told me he felt he had to at least put in an appearance.

He stayed at the gathering for two hours and then excused himself. Katherine's absence was palpable. He felt isolated and alone even in the midst of old friends. He went home and opened a bottle of wine that Katherine had blended out of a medley of grapes at a winery in Napa Valley a few years earlier. The bouquet was superb. Suddenly, he felt like he was drowning in memories of his dead wife. He didn't want to be alone. He called us. We urged him to cork the bottle and drive up the mountain.

Huddled together in front of the fire, we sipped the wine and remembered Katherine. Thomas wept openly. I shed more than a few tears. Even David's eyes grew moist now and then. By the time we greeted the New Year, Katherine's spirit was very much with us.

During the following week, family members and friends from afar began to arrive for the late afternoon memorial service at the Episcopal Church. We offered to host a buffet dinner at our home after the service. As we approached the day of the service, the weather got progressively worse. Because we live at the top of a mountain, and have a downward sloping driveway with a ninety-degree turn at the top, getting to our home in bad weather is hazardous.

On the morning of the service, we decided it was too risky to have people to our home. We called the Wilsons, mutual friends who have a beautiful home on the water, to see if they would host the dinner. We offered to provide the food and the wine. They didn't hesitate. David put chains on our tires, and wended his way down the mountain with platters of chicken casserole, bowls of mixed salad, and cases of wine.

After a beautiful service in a full church, more than eighty relatives and out-of-town guests made their way to the Wilsons' home for dinner. Thomas behaved more like an observer than a participant. I could tell he was tired. He was a man who needed his privacy, his space. Now, his house was filled with loving relatives who had made the journey to honor Katherine's memory and to comfort Thomas. While he was glad they had come, he wasn't sorry when they left him alone with Katherine's ghost.

Thomas began to join us for dinner once or twice a week. We often talked about Katherine. One evening, Thomas told us that he had finally received Katherine's ashes. It had taken so long because the scientists had wanted to study her brain to better understand the virus that had killed her. "I've put them in a tooled silver box at the end of her bed," Thomas said. "I like having them there. They comfort me."

The exhibition of Katherine's paintings was rapidly approaching. Planning the venue began to consume Thomas' time and attention. That seemed to give him a focus, a purpose beyond himself. He began to seem more centered and energized. By the evening of the retrospective, he was in his old form, ready to mingle and socialize. His Celebrant mindset was returning.

Most of Katherine's pieces sold that night. Thomas kept two of them as well as the poster-sized photograph of her smiling face that had been created for the retrospective. He hung that on a sideboard at the entrance to the kitchen she had designed.

Thomas changed nothing about Katherine's kitchen. He also left her clothing, and her jewelry in her closet. The myriad of treasures she had collected during her travels were visible throughout the house. His own sense of identity was still clearly bound up with hers.

If Thomas could have waved a magic wand and turned Coco into a stuffed toy that he could place on Katherine's four-poster brass bed, I suspect he would have done so. Failing that, Thomas decided he could not continue to look after the dog. It took him less than a week to find a loving home for that delightful animal.

Thomas slowly began to refocus on his social life. He began inviting people for casual, intimate dinners in his French country kitchen. As his confidence grew, he expanded the list of invitees and began to set a formal table in the dining room. An interior decorator by trade, Katherine had enjoyed setting a memorable table. Thomas continued the tradition, doing the work of two, and maintaining Katherine's high presentation standards.

Summer arrived, bringing with it the high season of social life in a small town. People emerged from their rain-drenched burrows to bask in the sun. The classical music festival was in full swing. Thomas, who was one of the original founders of the event, and served for years as its director, was again in his element. His calendar was filled with concerts, and pre-concert and post-concert gatherings. For a few weeks, he seemed happy. I began to believe he was on the other side of the grieving process.

I realized in the middle of August that wasn't true. On the sixteenth, he hosted a charitable gathering at his home. Because David was away, I offered to serve as hostess along with Katherine's daughter-in-law, Abby. Thomas seemed withdrawn that evening. More than once I noticed him standing on the deck staring into the distance. Only after most of the guests had left did I understand. I had gathered my wrap and was about to leave when he said, "Please stay a little while longer. It's Katherine's birthday. Abby has made the traditional coconut cake. I'd like you to be here to share it with us."

I stayed. Eight of us sat around a candlelit table on the deck and remembered Katherine. Thomas wept openly. No one tried to quiet him. No one seemed uncomfortable or embarrassed by his tears.

Thomas continued to host dinner parties, and to be invited back in return. People began to invite a single woman to the events, thereby equalizing the number of men and women and forcing Thomas to become part of a short-lived couple. Sometimes, they would ask Thomas to pick up the woman and bring her to the party. Each time that happened, Thomas worried that others would believe he was "dating" her. The idea of "dating" seemed to unnerve him. He grieved Katherine's death, but did not seek to replace her. He had no missing piece. He wasn't driven to fill the empty space. Even though she was dead, they were still a couple in his mind.

A year after Katherine's death, Thomas still had not changed the recording on his answering machine... "Hello. You've reached the Dufour residence. Neither Katherine nor I can come to the phone right now, but if you'll leave your name, number and a message, one of us will call you back."

That Christmas Thomas once again decorated the house precisely as Katherine had liked. He followed her ritual to the last detail and taped a big red bow on the poster of her smiling face that still hung at the entrance to the kitchen. We had dinner with Thomas the night after he had finished the decorating. When we sat down, Thomas said, "I'm really glad you two could come over tonight. Yesterday, I had to go into Katherine's closet to get the Christmas decorations. I found her journals. I...well...I thought we might read some of them aloud together."

After dinner, Thomas took a faded newspaper clipping from between two pages. He read the title, "The best marriages are refuges from the world," but could read no further. He passed it to me. I skimmed it and then read aloud the next to last paragraph.

"A resting place is what we need as we grow older. A place not to gaze at each other in mutual fascination, but to look out at the world together from much the same angle of vision. A harbor, a shelter, a refuge, a source of nourishment and support. This is not what creates a marriage, but this is what sustains it."[78]

Thomas nodded and wiped away his tears with his napkin. David busied himself cutting slices of cheese and arranging them on crackers. "I'm guessing she kept that clipping because she found repose in your

---

[78]Sydney J. Harris, *Pieces of Eight*. (New York, Houghton Miflin, 1982), p.159.

marriage," I said.

"I hope so. I like to think so," said Thomas.

As we left that night, I kissed Katherine's image and said, "Good night." That became a ritual that many of his guests followed.

After the holidays, we often saw Thomas at social events. He was always flying solo. The spring passed and summer arrived. We were all invited to a party on a boat in the harbor to celebrate the fourth of July. Much to our surprise, Thomas arrived with a "date." Fran was attractive and stylish in her white jeans, pink shirt and snug fitting jacket. She was talkative and funny, and mingled easily with others.

I got to know her quite well during the ensuing months. She'd confide in me, and ask questions about Thomas. "It's like it's still her house," Fran whispered as we entered the ladies' restroom at the opera in Seattle. "I mean, Katherine is everywhere. He hasn't moved any of her things."

"I guess he's not ready," I said.

Nine years have passed since Katherine died. Fran remains a valued friend and an invited guest in a home that continues to exude Katherine's essence. As I write this, it's once again summer. The sun is shining. The music festival is in full swing. Thomas' calendar is filled with concerts, and pre-concert and post-concert gatherings. He has made new friends, some of whom Katherine never knew. He travels a lot, exploring places that Katherine never saw. He is building his own bank of memories that are separate and apart from hers. A stone sculpture that Katherine never saw now sits proudly in the dining room. A jade cat that Thomas found during a recent trip to China sits on the coffee table. The poster of her image has finally been moved to the bedroom hallway.

Yet, to be in his home is to continue to feel the essence of Katherine. Her ashes still sit in the tooled silver box. When we have dinner, we eat on her dishes. We wipe our mouths with her colorful napkins. We admire woven placemats that she chose in some exotic market. We browse through photo books strewn on the oversized coffee table that are rife with her image.

Luna's home is also filled with photographs of her late husband, Stavros. Unlike Thomas, Luna is changing her home to reflect the new self that she is becoming as she emerges from the shadows. Three years after his death, she is remodeling and putting her own unique imprint on the home they once shared. Ironically, part of the reason she feels free to build her new life in her own way is because of Stavros' legacy—what he stood for and the way he died.

Five Card Draw.

When Stavros was diagnosed with multiple myeloma, he and Luna had been together for thirty-eight years. He was fifty seven. The onset of his disease came as a total shock. Even though she is a medical doctor, Luna had agreed with Thomas' assumption that the soreness on his shoulder was the result of having spread thirty bags of manure around their gardens.

He took a break from heavy lifting, but the soreness got worse. Finally, Luna insisted on examining his shoulder. She discovered a lump the size of a golf ball. It was red and warm to the touch. She thought it might be a cyst, and insisted he see another doctor. That physician ordered a cat scan. A diagnosis of multiple myeloma was rendered soon after. Stavros felt like he'd been "thrown from his horse," to use Luna's words. A man who had known only victory was now afraid. He was afraid for himself and he was afraid for his family.

Ultimately, he conquered his fear. Adopting the mindset of the Warrior, he vowed to beat the disease. He told his children about the struggle ahead, assuring them that he had every intention of emerging victorious. Luna shared his determination. She was certain that if they dotted every *i* and crossed every *t*, accessed the best oncologists and followed their directives to the letter, they would prevail. Stavros would beat the cancer or, at the very least, be among those who survived a decade or longer.

They managed to send the cancer into remission. Anticipating that one day it would return, the doctors harvested some of his stem cells so that they would be ready to do a bone marrow transplant if it became necessary. An uneasy year and a half passed during which every blood test represented a major trauma.

Between tests, they tried to live a normal life. Luna treated the sick. Stavros managed his investments and now and then played a game of poker. Together they maintained their beautiful home and gardens. They celebrated their grown children's birthdays, graduations, and new jobs and promotions. They made a very big deal of Christmas, Stavros' favorite holiday. They spent weeks in their home in the Rocky Mountains of Colorado. After Luna retired, they explored the Far East.

Then one day when they had begun to believe Stavros might remain in remission long enough to be called "cured," the moment they had long dreaded finally arrived. The tests confirmed that the cancer had returned, and in a highly aggressive form. Oncologists agreed that Stavros' survival depended on his undergoing a stem cell transplant.

They moved into an apartment near the hospital. Over a period of four days, six different drugs were infused into Stavros' body to prepare it for the transplant. Then they shot him with a high dose of chemo to knock out his immune system. The next day, they reinfused his own stem cells into his vulnerable body.

In an email sent to family and friends, Luna described the process. "Then we wait for his stem cells to move into the now empty bone marrow, set up house, hang some curtains, maybe paint the walls, then finally start making babies—red blood cells, platelets, white blood cells and the all important immune system."

Luna clung to humor to help her through a time that was frightening to both of them. Her email about the stem cell transplant continues…"Till then, Stavros will live as bubble boy here in the apartment with me as his very adorable and sassy German Nazi jailer. 'Did you wash your hands? Did you take your pills? Did you shower? Did you eat? Can I have a new car? Are you drinking enough?' This is guaranteed to make him want to get well QUICK."

Stavros had a difficult time with the treatment. On the fifth day, his heart "went beserko," to quote Luna. It couldn't function under the load of toxins being released into his body. The doctors had to shock his heart back into normal rhythm. Then, he suffered a complication from the transplant as some of the stem cells started to multiply while others lagged, creating a dangerous imbalance. His heart again went into arrhythmia. Shocking it had no effect. The doctors resorted to catheter ablation to cauterize those parts of his heart muscle that were causing erratic electrical signals and the abnormal rhythm.

Things began to get better. The stems cells reconstituted his bone marrow and his own body began making the full range of blood cells. Luna, ever the Celebrant Warrior, called it a miracle. In an email, she wrote, "Truly the human body's capability for healing and regenerating itself is beyond amazing. I have spent my whole adult life studying the human body and honestly, the more I learn, the more in awe I am. We are miraculous. Stavros is a miracle..."

They returned home at the end of February, feeling optimistic that Stavros would be one of the fifty percent of patients who needed only one transplant to rid the body of cancer and push it into remission. Spring unfortunately brought bad news. Stavros learned that he had to have a second transplant. They returned to the hospital for another ride on what Luna called "the medical roller coaster."

Because his immune system was decimated, Stavros developed an upper respiratory infection that spread to his bronchial tree and then to his lungs, leaving the tissues raw and vulnerable. An opportunistic fungus then invaded his lungs. Exhausted and temporarily defeated, he stopped eating. With the love and support of his family who cajoled him into eating, he survived that crisis.

Six months later, he was strong enough to begin a cycle of chemotherapy which his doctors believed would make his remission last longer. It didn't work out that way. In what Luna described as being like "the innocent victims of a random drive-by shooting," they learned that the chemotherapy had induced an even worse cancer. Stavros began building up fluid around his left lung. When the doctors tested the fluid, they discovered metastatic melanoma.

The fight was over. The Warriors put down their shields. Now Castaways, they accepted that death was imminent. They were both preparing for him to die when the doctors gave them a reprieve. They had discovered that Stavros' tumor had a certain mutation that made him eligible for a brand new drug that shrinks or stops the tumor from growing for six months. Their Celebrant mindsets re-engaged, they embraced the six months as though it were a lifetime.

At the end of March, Luna wrote: "We no longer think too much about the future. We just find the moments to savor as they happen, try to corral the disease behind some firm boundaries while cultivating gratitude for what we have...a life full of years of love, friends, family and good memories enough to completely outnumber any sad moments to come. We have led charmed lives...forty years where everything went our way and hardship and stress were just theoretical possibilities. This past year can't hold a candle to the accumulated points in the 'Goodness' column."

It was around this time that I spent an afternoon with Luna in their home. Eager for some company but unwilling to leave Stavros, she invited me for lunch. She and I sat at her kitchen table. It was beautifully set with a festive centerpiece harkening the advent of the Easter holiday. She had prepared a salad and enchilada soup. We sipped wine and talked about the wonderful life she and Stavros had had together and how hard it had been for her to accept that no amount of effort on her part could save him. She wept as she told me how angry she'd gotten at Stavros when he stopped fighting as she wanted him to fight.

"It was as though he suddenly handed the reigns to me. He gave up control. He surrendered. That frightened me, and it made me angry. I hired a personal trainer and bought a treadmill. He behaved himself when the trainer was here, but he wouldn't exercise on his own in between sessions unless I forced him to do so. He left all medical decisions to me. He liked the first oncologist we consulted, but he didn't resist when I told him I thought we could do better. He stopped insisting. He stopped resisting. He grew passive and dependent. That made me crazy. Only now do I understand he did that for me. He wanted to make it easier on me. He put me in charge because he knew I like feeling in control. He allowed me the illusion of control."

She stood up and moved our lunch dishes to the counter, and poured us a cup of coffee. When she sat down, she continued where she had left off. "I was spastic about making sure he got a chance to do everything he wanted to do before he died. I asked him to write down his bucket list, and told him I would move mountains if need be to find a way to make it happen."

"So, what did he say?" I asked.

"He looked at me, smiled and then opened his arms. As I lay my head on his shoulder, he said he'd had all he wanted. There was no bucket list, no unfinished business. In telling me that, he took away the pressure I was feeling to fill his days with perfect activities. He made it possible for me to relax a little and begin living in the moment."

We then talked about the plans for their eldest daughter's wedding six weeks hence, and their prayers that Stavros would be well enough to attend. Luna explained that because the groom was Hindu, there would be two ceremonies, and two costumes for the bride and the mother and father of the bride.

Stavros was well enough to attend the wedding. Though his fever spiked the night before the ceremonies, indicating that another infection had invaded his body, Luna was able to get the supplies necessary to administer antibiotics through an I.V. By morning, his fever was down.

Stavros wore a dark blue suit and fedora for the American ceremony, and a flowing gold sherwani for the Indian ceremony. Though he looked dapper in his western costume, he appeared wise, or even ethereal, in his sherwani. In every photograph he was smiling and his eyes were dancing. It was apparent that he was experiencing the joy of the moment, and not distracted in the least by his fragile body or thoughts of his own demise.

A few weeks later, he relapsed. The myeloma returned with an invading force many times stronger than before. Regardless, Stavros booked a cruise to Alaska to celebrate their thirty-seventh wedding anniversary. He enjoyed the cruise, even dressing every night for dinner. Luna was encouraged. Stavros appeared to be improving.

That impression faded after they were home for only a few days. His pain increased and his mobility lessened as his cancer-riddled bones began to fracture, increasing his pain and lessening his mobility. In a last desperate attempt to beat back the cancer, Stavros endured more radiation and chemotherapy.

His immune system was now so compromised that he suffered from repeated bouts of pneumonia and other complications. Finally, when his motor function had deteriorated severely and pain became intolerable, he was confined to bed. Pain medication made him confused, but less agitated. As his breathing became irregular and weak, Luna sat beside him, breathing with him, and using the steady rhythm of her flow to ease his pain. That became their final way of communicating.

When he died, Luna sent an email to the friends and loved ones who had supported them throughout their ordeal. She wrote: "I am so sorry to tell you that my sweet Stavros passed away this Sunday, surrounded by the family that he loved...When I asked him if he was afraid of dying, he said, 'No. I don't dwell on it much as I have had the most wonderful ride. I have no regrets. I have done everything that was important to me. If I had to do it all again, I wouldn't change a thing.'"

Sitting on the desk in front of me is a transparent white bag containing two black and white poker chips and a note that reads, "I leave you

Gratitude, Love and Good Fortune. Always, Stavros." I got this treasure at Stavros' funeral. His family chose it as a token of Stavros' life because he was a risk-taker, and because until the end, he placed his bets on life and on the living. In spite of the slow progression of a cruel and undignified disease, Stavros died cherishing the life he'd lived.

The Two-Limbed Tree.

The day after Stavros died, Luna went to the cemetery and chose a burial site. She picked a spot at the far end of the grounds next to a large two-limbed tree. She felt the tree symbolized the way she and Stavros had related to each other and to life. Like the two limbs, they were separate and yet inseparable. Luna had Stavros embalmed to slow the rate at which his body would decay. She plans to leave a directive that she not be embalmed, so her body will decay quickly. Eventually, the sands of time will make their remains intermingle beneath the earth that provides nutrients to the tree.

Family began arriving at Luna's home even before she had returned from the cemetery. A mutual friend arranged for neighbors to bring food so that Luna would not have to be hostess as well as grieving widow and mother. I chose to make the dinner for the night before the memorial service and burial. When I delivered an immense bowl of tuna pasta salad, Luna greeted me. A tall woman, she towered over me as we hugged. After a few moments, I tried to pull away, but she held on. I embraced her again, letting her weep. When I left, the top of my head was damp with her tears.

Luna and I began to get together several times a month. Because I had been widowed, she felt comfortable talking with me about her love for Stavros, their life together, and the depth of her loss. She shared with me her struggle to get out of the shadows and, in her words, "to make peace with death."

During the first few months after his death, she fought hard to find a way to keep him not only part of her past and her present, but of her future as well. She wrote in an email: "I am working on memorizing everything I can about him so that I can summon his presence in my mind and my heart whenever I need him. I sense him around me, in me, beside me and it comforts me. I know what he is thinking, what he is feeling even when he is not there…maybe because we have been two parts of a whole for so long. He took a piece of me with him but I kept a piece of him with me and I think, one day, it will help me heal."

She dreamt of him. In her dreams, his body was no longer ravaged by cancer. His muscles had returned. He was able to get in and out of the shower on his own. He could make his way in the night to the bathroom without falling. He could comfort her and make her feel safe as she lay her head on his chest.

When she awoke, and had to again confront her aloneness, the painful journey began anew. She went to visit Stavros' grave almost everyday, rain or shine. She sat and contemplated the two-limbed tree and remembered their lives together. Struggling to hold onto her Celebrant mindset, she focused on what life had given her, not on its deprivations. She often said to me, "It hurts so much but I still honestly feel that I am the luckiest of women. I got forty-one years of joy upfront. The tears I now cry are such a small price for so much happiness."

She told me she found it difficult to make polite conversation. Social gatherings were exhausting because people tried so hard to avoid talking about Stavros and his death. Those who dared breach the subject said only that he is in a better place, and then moved on to other, more comfortable subjects. "It's as though no one wants to admit there's an elephant in the room," she said to me one afternoon. "That's why I like spending time with you. You're not afraid to talk about death and dying, and you've been there. You understand."

I did understand. So did C.S. Lewis. In *A Grief Observed*, he wrote: "An odd byproduct of my loss is that I'm aware of being an embarrassment to everyone I meet. At work, at the club, in the street, I see people, as they approach me, trying to make up their minds whether they'll 'say something about it' or not. I hate it if they do, and if they don't...Perhaps the bereaved ought to be isolated in special settlements like lepers."[79]

Rather than suffer through social events that simply enhanced her feelings of aloneness, Luna turned her boundless energy to putting her household in order. She was clearing out Stavros' desk when she found two sticky notes on which he had noted his thoughts for her Christmas

---

[79]C.S. Lewis, *A Grief Observed*. (New York, HarperCollins e-books, 1961), 5-6.

presents. He intended to buy her a ring, and a surround sound system so that she could play her music throughout the house. The notes reminded her of how well she had been loved. They made her weep, but they also made her smile.

She turned her attention to clearing out a closet in his office. There, she found a large, sealed box on which was written in Stavros' hand, "Do not open until Christmas." She knew immediately what it was. Each year, Stavros put a joke gift for everyone under the tree. Knowing he wouldn't be there, he had chosen his joke gifts early. Luna took that as a sign that she should carry on with their elaborate Christmas rituals just as they would have if he were still with them.

Summoning every ounce of energy in her Celebrant Warrior body, Luna managed to play the parts of both Mrs. and Mr. Santa. She trimmed the tree, wrapped the gifts, and baked. On Christmas morning, she gathered with her son, her two daughters, her son-in-law and her other daughter's boyfriend, and opened Stavros' box. As he had intended, it cheered them up, and helped them enjoy their first Christmas without him. The dead had begun helping the living heal.

The day after Christmas, Luna arranged to have the surround sound system installed. The day before New Year's, she felt emotionally strong enough to assert what I call the "Widow's Declaration of Independence." My assertion had come in the form of a mink coat. I had told Luna about that extravagance, explaining that, after Bill died, I had wanted to prove to myself that I could do for myself what my friends' husbands were doing for them. (That was when it was still politically correct to wear mink.) Luna took my words to heart. She bought a new car; a soft gold luxury sedan of which the more practically-minded Stavros would not have approved. Luna had begun to redefine herself.

We got together a few times in the spring. Each time, she wept a little less and laughed a little more. She's taking care of herself, and looks wonderful. She's playing the piano again, and has gotten involved with the music festival and other community-based organizations. She spent the summer traveling around Europe with her with her mother, her daughter and her son-in-law. In the fall, she journeyed to Bhutan.

Although their symbol is a two-limbed tree, Stavros' death has not anchored Luna. Her concern now is her own mortality. Although she often visits Stavros' grave, Luna is not eager to join him. A Celebrant

Warrior, she continues to vigorously embrace life. She has learned that grieving the loss of the person you loved is not an end to that love, but a part of the process of loving. As C.S. Lewis wrote: "Bereavement is not the truncation of married love but one of its regular phases—like the honeymoon—what we want is to live our marriage well and faithfully through that phase, too."[80]

The Red Couch.

David and I were sitting out on the deck last night enjoying the sunset when David asked me, "What would you do if I died? Where would you go?" I have no clear answer to those questions. I find it hard to imagine what I would do. I like to think I'd grieve hard and openly like Luna, and then begin to rebuild my life. I would not waste years feeling disconnected and numb like my mother.

Like Thomas, I would try to stay in touch with friends and family members. Unlike Thomas, I would not build a shrine. Because I would probably want to move to a smaller and more manageable place, I could not keep all of David's things. I would cherish his artwork, but probably get rid of three quarters of his books. Like Luna, I would try to focus on the love we shared and on the wonderful experiences we had together rather than on the years we were denied. Most important, I would try to remember all of the conversations David and I had about death being part of life.

I have kept the birthday cards David has given me over the years. On the cover of one of my favorites is a photograph of an aging Einstein. The text reads, "My theory about birthdays is age is relative." Inside, David has written: "If we can run fast enough, live fast enough, faster than the speed of light, we might get younger and actually ride on the red couch."

Instead of trying to answer David questions, I turned to him and said, "If I die before you, I'll wait for you. If you die before me, you wait. We'll build a red couch on which we can travel through eternity together." We know there is no red couch. It's a shared fantasy, and an expression of our

---

[80]C.S. Lewis, *A Grief Observed*. (New York, HarperCollins e-books, 1961), 42.

love for one another. We know that each of us must die, and die alone. The best we can do is make life all that it can be.

With that in mind, we look forward to having Luna and Thomas the Chaplain join us for a dinner tonight. We'll laugh and, in between the laughter, we'll talk about living and about dying. In a way, it will be like having an intimate meeting of the Mortality Club.

10: THE MORTALITY CLUB: Talking about Death over Coffee

Writing about aging and mortality has been a healthy and life-affirming experience for me. I believe talking with others about the experience of being mortal can have a similarly beneficial effect. I agree with the mythologist Joseph Campbell who said, "The conquest of the fear of death is the recovery of life's joy. One can experience unconditional affirmation of life only when one has accepted death, not as contrary to life but as an aspect of life."[81]

Some people are better able to contemplate death than others. My friend Emilia who owned and operated several upscale nursing homes in Western Australia told me the story of one of her residents. Betty was a life-loving ninety-one-year-old who enjoyed a good party and only occasionally got confused. One morning she read in the local newspaper that someone she'd gone to school with seventy years earlier had died, and that the funeral was to be held that afternoon. She asked the nursing home staff to call her a car, and then went to make herself presentable.

When she arrived at the funeral home, she couldn't find anyone she recognized. Overhearing the other guests talk about the deceased, she realized that she couldn't possibly have known her at school. She was attending the funeral service of a complete stranger. Since the car wasn't due to pick her up for two more hours, she decided to make the best of it.

People quickly responded to her heartfelt condolences. No one asked

---

[81] Joseph Campbell with Bill Moyers. *The Power of Myth.* (New York, Anchor Books, 1991), 188.

her how she knew the deceased, or even if she knew the deceased. She didn't have to lie. She only had to nod her head when someone else shared a memory. Soon she felt like part of the extended family. She was even invited to join the family when they gathered at a restaurant across the street for drinks and a late afternoon meal. She accepted and enjoyed herself so much that she kept the hired car waiting an hour. Her experience of helping strangers commemorate the death of a loved one was so positive that she repeated it as often as possible. Every morning she scanned the paper for news of a funeral or memorial service she might attend. The celebration of death became her avocation.

Betty's story is unusual. Most people don't like going to funerals. They don't like getting that close to death. While dying may be normal, part of life and in keeping with the natural order of things, it is still the ultimate adversary.

We can talk about death, but can we ever really accept it? Can we even grasp its significance? Perhaps not. This morning David and I sat at either end of the dining room table having coffee. After finishing *The Wall Street Journal* on his iPad, David turned to the ebook he had been reading. "Let me read you something," he said. "We are mortal and can't possibly be expected to fully grasp death, so we inhabit just enough insanity to keep the absurdity manageable. Pretending to be able to deal with mortality sanely makes room for life."[82]

Inspired by David's comment, after he left the table, I sat and imagined a gathering of people interested in talking about death. I called it a meeting of the Mortality Club. The purpose of the club is to help members deal sanely with the knowledge that we will all die. Meetings include no more than eight to ten participants. It's different from and not a replacement for the increasingly popular Death Cafe. The group is smaller, more intimate. Meetings are run by a facilitator and books are an important part of the discussion.

I'm envisioning one of the meetings. Because I visualize the meeting as part discussion forum and part book club, I post an invitation on the bulletin board at the local bookstore. The invitation reads: "If you are interested in talking with others about death and dying, and the challenge of living as a mortal being, then please join us at our home next Tuesday

---

[82]Jaron Lanier, *Who Owns the Future?* (New York, Simon and Shuster, 2013), 210.

afternoon. Coffee and tea will be served. If you have a quote about living as a mortal being or about death that appeals to you, bring that with you. If you have a book about the subject that has inspired you, please bring that along, too."

I call to invite Luna and Thomas but neither is available. Luna is traveling and Thomas is visiting his sister in Wisconsin. Since three people have already expressed a desire to attend, I decide to hold the meeting anyway. Within the next few days, three more people sign up, bringing the total to eight people, including David and me.

I visualize us sitting around the maple table in the dining area of our long and narrow living room with its soaring ceilings, Tuscan columns, and wall of windows. The view of the water and mountains beyond serve not as distractions but rather as a majestic backdrop to our conversation and a reminder of the power of the universe and the mysteries of our planet. It's a clear day in late fall. There is only a slight chill in the air.

I visualize myself seated at the head of the table. My iPad and three books are placed in front of me. The cover of the one on the top features a stone head of an old bearded man with eyes closed. Under the head is the single word in capital letters, DEATH. It is an issue of *Lapham's Quarterly*, a provocative historical magazine. Second in the stack is *Being Mortal: Medicine and What Matters in the End* by Dr. Atul Gawande. Under that lies my recently released book, *The Hourglass: Life as an Aging Mortal*.

I begin the meeting by explaining the rules. "There should be no proselytizing, or trying to persuade others to share your beliefs. And, no one should ever be subjected to criticism or ridicule for things they say or beliefs they hold. Finally, nothing anyone says during the club meetings should ever be shared outside the room. Can we all agree to those ground rules?"

After getting an indication of agreement, I explain why I issued the invitation. "After spending the last several years contemplating aging and dying, I have concluded that it's better to embrace death as part of life than to deny it, or to pretend that it doesn't exist, or to cling to the unstated belief that it's someone else's problem. I have also realized that the contemplation of my own death makes it less scary. I am not saying that I am no longer afraid of dying. Of course I am afraid. I am just less afraid than I was when I began working on *The Hourglass*. As my fear diminishes, my ability to live intensifies. I've initiated the Mortality Club because I think it's healthy to talk about death."

Nodding at David seated at the other end of the table with his human skull and three books in front of him, I say, "Your co-host is my husband, David, who is sitting at the end of the table, along with a long dead friend of his. I'm going to ask David to introduce himself last because I have a feeling he is going to have a lot to say. He usually does."

The other participants laugh.

Turning to the well-fed man with the closely shorn grey hair on my right, I say, "Bruce, would you tell us a bit about yourself and why you're here today?"

He stands to take command of the table. "My name is Bruce," he says in a deep and penetrating voice that is clearly accustomed to issuing directives. "I'm sixty-seven years old. I trained to be a lawyer, but I never practiced law. I decided it would be a lot more gratifying to arrest the sons of bitches than to spend months in court making the arrest stick. So, I became a cop. I was good at it. Within ten years, I became the Chief of Police. By the time I retired, I had been the Commissioner for several years. I called the shots and I liked it that way.

"Retirement has been hard on me. I miss the action and the fight. At least I did until I got diagnosed with pancreatic cancer. Now, I'm fighting for my life. I intend to win that battle, one way or the other. I even fought my way into a trial for an experimental drug. They said they had no room for another participant. I convinced them they were wrong. So far so good. I am responding. My numbers are good."

He sits down, making me think he is finished. I say, "Thank you, Bruce." Just as I am about to turn the floor over to the next person, he utters in a less forceful voice, "I'm here because I'm scared of dying and I can't let myself express that with my friends and family. They think of me as a strong man, and I want to keep it that way. I thought it might be a relief to be able to talk about it."

Feeling compassion toward the ailing Warrior, I say, "I'm very glad you decided to join us, Bruce." I turn to the attractive woman with the long, wavy auburn hair and big brown eyes seated to Bruce's right. "Rachel, would you go next?"

Rachel remains seated. Pulling her grey cardigan over large breasts that are well defined by her black tank top, she says in a modulated voice, "My name is Rachel. I am fifty-eight years old and I am a midwife. I have been bringing babies into the world and celebrating the gift of life for thirty-three years."

She pauses and looks around the table as though trying to decide whether to continue. I smile at her, hoping that will encourage her. She takes a deep breath. "A year ago, my husband died. Four months before his death, he was diagnosed with inoperable brain cancer. I felt helpless. There was nothing I could do to comfort him. All my skills at enabling an infant to take his or her first breath did me no good when it came to helping the man I loved take his last."

Again, she stops and looks around the table, as though taking the temperature of the room. "I decided to devote my free time to volunteering at hospice. That's really why I'm here. I want to become as good at helping people out of life as I have been welcoming them into it. To do that, I need to get better at enabling others to talk about their own end."

Rachel might be a Sage, I think. She seems at home in her body—poised but relaxed. She radiates a kind of inner peace. I can tell that David senses it too. He keeps looking across the table at her.

David comments, "'Our birth is nothing but our death begun.' I've forgotten who said that, but it seems appropriate."

"Yes, I know deep in my being that is true," states Rachel, looking at David and smiling.

I turn to the tall, thin woman with the curly grey hair and brilliant blue eyes to my left. I already know a little bit about Beth. She came to the meeting early. I observed her through the kitchen window as she struggled to get out of a car driven by an older man. He watched intently as she made her way with her cane across the driveway. I opened the door just in time to see her legs give out from under her. He rushed out of the car but by the time he reached her, Beth had taken my hand and stood up. "It's all right, Michael. I'll call you when the meeting is over."

Although Beth pretended to be all right, I could tell the fall had flustered her. She was a bit breathless as I led her into the living room and brought her a glass of water. She thanked me and explained, "Sometimes my legs just stop cooperating."

"I'm sorry," I said. Just then the doorbell rang. I left Beth alone to gather herself. Now, as I am about to ask her to introduce herself, I wonder how much of this she is going to share with the group.

"My name is Beth," she says in a voice that is surprisingly husky. "I am sixty-four years old. I am a wife and mother of three grown children. I have devoted my professional life to dentistry. I sold my practice and retired four years ago. Since then, I have spent a lot of time in Bangladesh with Doctors Without Borders. During my last trip, I was suddenly afflicted with muscle weakness in my legs. I attributed it to fatigue and too many hours in an airplane. Then I developed cramps and fasciculations in my right foot."

Interrupting her, Alicia asked, "Fasciculations? What are those?"

Beth thought a moment and then responded, "Twiches, dear. They are twitches." And then she continued. "I began to get concerned. At the first opportunity, I returned home. Within weeks, my fears were confirmed. I have ALS, Amyotrophic Lateral Sclerosis, often referred to as Lou Gehrig's Disease. It's a progressive neurodegenerative disease that affects nerve cells in the brain."

She pauses a moment. Her voice trembles as she says, "It is a fatal disease. There is no known cure. The doctors tell me I have two years to live; three, at the most." She brushes away a tear and then places her hands on the table as though seeking support. The room remains silent. Finally, she resumes. Her tone is steady and measured as she says, "I am dying. I am here because I want to explore what that means with people who do not love me and are not threatened by the thought of losing me. I am here because I want to be reminded that I am not alone. We are all mortal. We are all dying. I'm just doing it faster."

I say, "Thank you, Beth, for your honesty and for being here today."

Looking at the slightly overweight young man wearing jeans and a long-sleeved black tee who sits directly to David's right, I say, "It's wonderful younger people have decided to join us today. Would you introduce yourself?"

"My name is Erik," he states in a slightly nasal voice. "Erik with a k. I'm an Assistant Professor of English Literature at Western Washington University. I got my PHD from the University of Washington two years ago. I wrote my thesis on Eros and Thanatos in classical literature."

The young woman sitting with the yoga-trained body sitting opposite Erik and to David's left interrupts. "Eros and Thanatos?"

Erik smiles and answers, "Sorry. Love and Death. Eros was the Greek god of love, and Thanatos was the Greek god of death. My thesis was about the theme of love leading to death in classical literature."

"Like Shakespeare's Romeo and Juliet?" asks Rachel.

"Yes, that's one example."

Sensing we are getting off track, I say, "Erik, it appears you've have a long standing interest in Death, or Thanatos."

"Yes, and in Love, with a capital L, but that seems to elude me. I begin to suspect that's because I'm too afraid of loss to let myself love."

"Do you know why are you so afraid of loss?" asks Rachel. "I lost my husband and it was painful, but I cherish the memory of the years we had together."

"Maybe it's because my mother died when I was seven years old. That destroyed me. My father was always away on business. My mother and I were very close."

I wonder whether David is going to volunteer that he, too, lost his mother when he was a young boy. He does not. The young woman speaks next. "How do you know you're afraid to love? Maybe the right girl just hasn't come along."

"The right girl just moved out on me."

Picking up the thin book in front of him, Erik continues. "She left a note and this book, *The Beast in the Jungle* by Henry James. The protagonist, John Marcher, never allows himself to love or to marry his frequent companion and soul mate, May Bartram. He will not and cannot do so because he lies in wait for the spectacular or devastating event that is to be life-defining. As May lies dying, she tells him, "In waiting, you have deprived yourself of experiencing all that life has to offer. In waiting, you have become an old man who has never nor will ever experience the pleasure of love nor the pain of loss.' He realizes that, in waiting, he has missed the beast itself. It has come and gone and left in its wake nothingness."

Looking around the table, Erik realizes that not everyone is following him. "Anyway, Nancy thinks that I refuse to love because love makes you vulnerable. It puts you in a position where you can get hurt. Your lover can leave you, or she can die. The only way to protect yourself is to avoid getting emotionally involved in the first place. The problem, as Henry James portrays, is that refusing to love leads only to loneliness and a failure to really live life. I'm here because I need to get more comfortable being vulnerable. I thought talking with others about death would help me do that. After all, in the face of death, we are all vulnerable. There is nothing we can do to protect ourselves."

"The only defense is to live as rich a life as our imagination allows us," says David.

I look at the young woman in the figure-hugging teal knitted dress seated to David's left. Wishing I'd worn something more exotic than my Eileen Fisher basic black stretch crepe pants and long-sleeved black tee, I say, "Would you introduce yourself next?"

"My name is Alicia," she says in a high-pitched voice that makes me cringe. "I am thirty-two years old and engaged to be married. I'm a yoga fanatic and I love to work out. I write children's books. I am here because my publisher has asked me to write a book to help children deal with the death of someone they loved, like a grandparent, or maybe even a pet."

Removing the scrunchie and rubber band from her hair, she shakes out her golden mane, smiles and then continues. "I can't figure out how to approach it. While I wouldn't say I am deeply religious, I do believe in Christ, and I want to believe in Heaven and in Life Everlasting. It's easier that way."

Reaching behind her head, she twists her hair and ties it up again. Everyone at the table watches closely as though she is performing a magic trick. "If I could talk about Heaven in the book, I'd have no problem writing it. I would love to describe God and Christ in white robes, with Christ seated at the foot of God waiting for the souls of the newly departed. Unfortunately, my publisher wants the book to be relevant to all children: Christian, Jewish, Muslim and even children who don't believe in much of anything. I have a hard time thinking about death if I can't visualize Heaven at the same time. Dark thoughts make me nervous, so I tend to avoid them. My friends tell me I think like a child. Maybe that's why children like my books. I relate to them."

"Thank you, Alicia," I say, wondering when David will find an excuse to sit next to someone else. She is a classic Stargazer, and Stargazers sometimes drive him crazy. On the other hand, she is quite attractive, and he likes attractive women. I say, "You face an interesting challenge."

"I think she's fortunate," responds the tall, lean man with the thinning grey hair seated between Eric and Beth. "I wish I believed in Heaven and in Life Everlasting. My name is Walker. In a few weeks, I'll be eighty-six years old."

"You look a lot younger," says Alicia.

"Thank you, my dear," responds Walker. Looking at me, he says, "I guess I'm next?" When I nod, he continues, "I like to think of myself as an inventor. Well, I used to be an inventor. Now, I guess you'd call me more of a tinkerer. At least that's what my friend Claire says." He laughs.

"What have you invented?" I ask, thinking he might need a little help staying focused.

Taking a small leather folio that holds 3x5 cards out of the pocket of his light grey velour jacket that matches his sweat pants, he answers, "Probably nothing you'd recognize. Mostly things that were used by industry or the military to make their equipment run better. I'm a chemical engineer by training. I worked at DuPont for a number of years. Among other things, I worked on the use of polytetrafluoroethylene, better known as Teflon. Looking back, I should have been the one to apply Teflon to pots and pans. I missed that opportunity."

I am about to ask him why he decided to join us when he continues. "I think of problems as inherent opportunities. Present me with a problem, and I will turn it into an advantage. Until recently, I treated my physical ailments the same way. When cataracts made my vision blurry, I seized that as an opportunity to have lenses implanted that made it unnecessary for me to wear glasses. When it got to the point where I could hardly walk, I got a hip replacement. That worked so well I was able to start hiking again. When the conductor in my heart started playing the music too fast, and I developed atrial fibrillation, I had the doctors implant a pacemaker with a built-in defibrillator. That not only solved the problem but gave me added protection."

"That's a positive way to look at it," I say.

Walker continues, ignoring my comment. "A year or so ago, things started breaking faster than I could fix them. It got harder to see problems as opportunities. Try hard as I might, I could not find the good news in having bladder cancer and having to lie down and roll back and forth to slush the chemo around my sick organ. Nor could I find the advantage to discovering that my arteries were blocked and I needed stents to keep them open. My last physical revealed that my kidneys are wearing out, and my heart and lung function have both deteriorated."

Walker is a talker. He doesn't have a problem staying focused, but he does have a tendency to go on too long. I interrupt him. "Walker, would you tell us why you chose to join us today?"

"I do have a way of going on," he declares, letting me know he is fully aware of what I am doing. "All of you should feel free to interrupt me. Claire does that all the time."

"Who's Claire?" asks Alicia.

"She's my current lady friend," explains Walker. "I've never been married, but I've had a number of wonderful lady friends. Why…"

I interrupt him again. "Walker, you were about to tell us why you joined us today."

"Ah, yes. I am struggling to hold onto my optimism. I thought this group might be able to help me believe what Leonardo da Vinci, the greatest inventor of all time, once said: 'As a well-spent day brings a happy sleep, so a life well-used brings a happy death.'"

A Celebrant struggling to hold onto that mindset, I think to myself. To Walker I say, "I also have an implanted pacemaker and defibrillator in my chest. I like to think of myself as the bionic woman."

"I like to think of her that way, too," says David looking younger than his seventy-eight years in his pressed khaki paints and navy blue sweater. "I'm David, Pam's husband, and I'm here because she gave me no choice in the matter." He laughs. "Seriously, I'm here because I believe death is a terrible thing. It smells bad, and it's frightening. As Erik has discovered, the fear of death can make us reluctant to engage with life."

Picking up a paperback from the table in front of him, David continues, "I also believe that the denial of death can make us so sick that life itself becomes little more than an endless struggle. This author gets it right. It's called *The Denial of Death* by Ernest Becker."

He opens the book to a page with a red flag sticking out of the top. "In the foreword, Sam Keen who interviewed Becker on his death bed, writes, 'For the exceptional individual there is the ancient philosophical path of wisdom. Becker, like Socrates, advises us to practice dying…Living with the voluntary consciousness of death, the heroic individual can choose to despair or to make a Kierkegaardian leap and trust in the 'sacrosanct vitality of the cosmos,' in the unknown god of life whose mysterious purpose is expressed in the overwhelming drama of cosmic evolution.'"[83]

---

[83]Sam Keen, foreword to *The Denial of Death* by Ernest Becker. (New York, The Free Press, 1973), 20.

Looking around the room at the curious and confused faces, David says, "I chose to attend this gathering as part of my ongoing effort to live with the voluntary consciousness of death and, as a result, to become a more vital part of the cosmic evolution."

"What's that skull all about?" asks Alicia. "It's freaking me out."

"This is a human skull I took from my father's office when I was a teenager. My father was a surgeon. He acquired the skull as part of his life-long effort to master his art." Picking up the desiccated cranium, he adds, "I keep this skull as a constant reminder of death. It reminds me to make the most out of every moment."

"Would you like to tell the group more about your background?" I ask.

"In time," he responds, giving me an impatient look. "For now, let's leave it at this: I am a cultural anthropologist by training. I was a tenured professor until Pam rescued me. But that's another story. I have been interested in mortality, evolution and human consciousness as long as I can remember."

I try to compensate for David's somewhat impersonal introduction. "David has been helping me deal with death almost since the day we met. I had only known David for a few months when my father was killed in a head-on collision on a dirt road in southwest Australia. His death really traumatized me. The afternoon my father died, David sat with me in my kitchen and told me the story of *The Rice Bowl*. David, tell the story, please."

"You tell it," he says.

"Please David," I respond. "You tell it better."

Reluctantly, he does so. "The Buddha and his disciples had congregated in a park high above the village. One day a young woman came to the Buddha with a dead two-year-old child in her arms and asked the enlightened one if he would bring her child back to life. The Buddha gave her an empty wooden bowl and told her to go back down into the village and go house to house, searching for someone who had not suffered the loss of a loved one. When she found someone who had been spared the pain and suffering she now felt, her bowl would be filled. He instructed her to bring him the bowl full of rice. In exchange, he promised to renew the life of her son.

"She took the empty bowl and went down into the village and spent days going from house to house. She talked to the old and to the young, to men and to women, and couldn't find a single person who had not lost someone they loved. She began to understand that her suffering was not unique, but rather part of the experience of living. She accepted that life is impermanence, and death is its only certainty. She thanked the Buddha for enriching her life."

"Thank you, David," I say. Looking around the table at the others, I add, "At the time, I thought that David was trivializing my grief. I was certain that no child other than my own brother and sisters had ever suffered so much due to the death of a parent. My father was different. I was different. His death was tragic, and my suffering unique. It took months and a number of conversations with David about death and mortality before I understood his intent in recounting that story. He was making me aware that death touches everyone. There is no one on earth who has not watched as the sands of time have run out on a loved one. No one can escape the hourglass. No one is immune."

"You can say that again," asserts Bruce. "Until I was diagnosed with cancer, I thought I was bulletproof. Now, I feel like a prisoner on execution row who is waiting for a reprieve from the governor. I hate that feeling. I need to be in control. Even now, when I'm not letting the doctors beat up on my body, I beat up on it myself. I still work out. I lift weights and I walk on the treadmill. Doesn't matter if I don't feel like it. I do it anyway. I'm a disciplined person. In my free time, I'm dictating what I call the 'rules of engagement.' It's all about telling my two sons how to survive in this world. They're grown-up now but that doesn't matter. They'd mess up and become totally self-indulgent if I weren't around to keep them on track. It'll be worse when my wife dies and they inherit our money."

He takes a deep breath, strums his fingers on the table and then continues, "I used to think money was like a shield. I could buy protection. I could buy security. I could buy pretty much whatever I wanted. Then I learned the one thing I couldn't buy was more life."

"Steve Jobs and William Goldsmith learned the same thing," states David. "They both died of pancreatic cancer."

"Thanks for the vote of confidence, Buddy," exclaims Bruce.

David hates to be called "Buddy." Therefore, I'm not surprised when he adds, "Perhaps there's a virus on one-hundred-dollar bills that causes the cancer."

Putting aside the 3x5 card on which he'd been doodling, Walker breaks the tension. "I've been thinking how death is a great leveler. It doesn't discriminate between the Goldsmiths and the Jobs and poor folks. It doesn't favor persons of influence over nobodies. I believe it was Charles de Gaulle who said, 'The graveyards are full of indispensable men.'"

"No one, no matter how rich or how powerful, can outrun death," adds Erik. "A favorite author of mine is W. Somerset Maugham. I teach his pivotal work, *Of Human Bondage*, in one of my courses. He wrote a very short story that is relevant to our discussion. It's called *The Appointment in Samara*. I've read it so often I can retell it from memory."

"Please do," I say.

"There was a merchant in Bagdad who sent his servant to market to buy provisions. In a little while, the servant came back, white and trembling, and said, 'Master, just now when I was in the marketplace I was jostled by a woman in the crowd. When I turned, I saw it was Death that jostled me. She looked at me and made a threatening gesture. Now, lend me your horse, and I will ride away from this city and avoid my fate. I will go to Samara where Death will not find me.'

"The merchant lent him his horse. The servant mounted it, and dug his spurs into its flanks. He went as fast as the horse could gallop. After he was gone, the merchant went down to the marketplace. He saw Death standing in the crowd. He approached her and said, 'Why did you make a threatening gesture to my servant when you saw him this morning?'

"'That was not a threatening gesture,' Death said. 'It was only a start of surprise. I was astonished to see him in Bagdad, for I have an appointment with him tonight in Samara.'"

"Great story. Like the servant, I am at once fascinated and repelled by death," confesses Walker.

"That describes most human beings," I say. "Think about how people rubberneck when there's an accident on the highway. Traffic comes to a standstill because people can't help staring at tragedy. On the other hand, they hate to use the words "dead" or "died" or "death." Instead, they use euphemisms like, 'He bought the farm. She kicked the bucket.'"

"She gave up the ghost," offers Beth.

"He cashed in his chips," says Bruce. "He croaked."

"She's gone off line," adds Erik, laughing.

"He met his maker" offers Alicia. "She's entered a better world."

"He bit the dust," offers Walker.

"He's circling the drain," I say, stealing a line I'd heard on the hospital-based television series, *Grey's Anatomy*.

"It's time to pull the plug," quips Bruce, picking up on my analogy.

"Checkout time has come and gone," says Alicia as she wraps the end of her pony tail around her finger.

"It's natural to deny death," says Beth. "After I was diagnosed, I studied Elizabeth Kubler Ross's model about how people deal with the threat of death. I discovered I was a textbook case. First, I denied it. I convinced myself and my family that the doctor was wrong. To maintain that fiction, for months I refused to get a second opinion. My husband finally persuaded me to do so when I tripped and fell on the way upstairs to the shower. I was doing that a lot. My symptoms were clearly worsening. So, I got a second opinion. That ended my happy stay in the stage of denial and threw me into the stage of anger.

"I raged and raged against the dying light. Why me? It's not fair. I don't deserve this. All my life I've helped other people, and now this? I became impossible to live with. I was angry at everyone and everything, including my own children. I envied them their health and their youth. I got paranoid, thinking that friends and family members were talking about me behind my back."

"I'm with you there," says Bruce.

Beth nodded at him before continuing. "When they started avoiding me when I refused to be pacified, I got really miserable. I started bargaining with them. 'Spend two hours with me, and I promise I won't get mad. Just talk to me. I'll behave.'

"I was able to strike a bargain with family members and friends, but not with God. The disease is progressing. Some of you witnessed my graceful entry. Sometimes using a cane is not enough. My legs just give out on me. It won't be long before I'll be in a wheelchair. I hate it. These days I swing from feeling sorry for myself to feeling really angry. There are moments when I get to Kubler Ross' final stage of acceptance, but then it eludes me again."

Picking up a piece of paper that she has placed in front of her, Beth continues, "When that happens, I try to remind myself of something that the journalist Kenneth Patchen said, 'There are so many little dyings that it doesn't matter which of them is death.'"

"That's very Buddhist," says David.

"Yes, it is," says Rachel, picking up her copy of *The Tibetan Book of Living and Dying* and flipping through the pages. "Ah, here it is. As Sogyal Rinpoche writes, 'There would be no chance at all of getting to know death if it happened only once. But fortunately, life is nothing but a continuing dance of birth and death, a dance of change. Every time I hear the rush of a mountain stream, or the waves crashing on the shore, or my own heartbeat, I hear the sound of impermanence. These changes, these small deaths, are our living links with death. They are death's pulse, death's heartbeat, prompting us to let go of all the things we cling to."[84]

"That's a fine quote," exclaims David, looking at Rachel with obvious respect. "Once we understand that all of life is impermanent, and that all our grasping is for naught, then and only then do we begin to accept death and really live."

Turning to Beth, he adds, "The Buddhists would suggest that your anger stems from your continued insistence on holding onto that which cannot be secured. Nothing in life can be protected, including life itself. Accept that and you might not only accept your own mortality, but actually free yourself to make your remaining time on this earth richer."

"A few years ago, I traveled to Dharamshala, India, with a lady friend," says Walker. "That's been the home of the Dalai Lama since 1959 when he was forced to flee Tibet. We had the opportunity of watching Tibetan Buddhist monks making a mandala out of sand. Six or seven monks had spent many weeks on their knees making the painting. We were there the day it was completed. It was a magnificent piece of art. Shortly after it was finished, the monks destroyed it. When I asked why, one of them explained that the beauty and meaning is in the creation, not in the possessing of that which has been created. I guess what we're saying is that's true of life as well."

I am about to suggest we break for coffee when Bruce speaks. "Maybe the monks destroyed their art so their enemies couldn't take it away from them."

[84]Sogyal Rinpoche, *The Tibetan Book of Living and Dying*, (San Francisco, HarperSanFrancisco, 1994), 33.

Before anyone can disagree with him, he continues, "The important thing is to stay in control. If you have to die, then die when you choose, the way you choose. If I get to the point when I know death is inevitable, then I intend to shoot myself. I'll do it in the hot tub so the mess will be easier to clean up."

"You and me, both," says David. "The hot tub is a great idea."

Unwilling to give up the floor to another Warrior, Bruce looks at me and says, "You suggested we bring our favorite quotation. Well, I didn't have one, but I did an Internet search about death and I found a quote that appeals to me. He pulls a folded sheet of paper out of the back pocket of his jeans. 'One should die proudly when it is no longer possible to live proudly. Friedrich Nietzsche.'"

"That's pronounced Neet-che," asserts David.

"Thanks, Buddy," responds Bruce.

Ignoring the appellation, David notes, "Nietzsche was a great philosopher. *Thus Spoke Zarathustra. The Will to Power. The Apollonian/Dionysian Dichotomy*. His work inspired Kazantzakis who's had a great influence on me."

Picking up a well-worn beige book with a torn spine, David turns to a page marked with a flag. "This is from the prologue of Kazantzakis' *The Saviors of God*. Bear with me, please. 'We come from a dark abyss, we end in a dark abyss, and we call the luminous interval life. As soon as we are born the return begins, at once the setting forth and the coming back; we die in every moment. Because of this many have cried out: The goal of life is death! But as soon as we are born we begin the struggle to create, to compose, to turn matter into life; we are born in every moment. Because of this many have cried out: The goal of ephemeral life is immortality!'"

Scanning the page, he continues, "'Life is itself without beginning, an indestructible force of the universe. Otherwise, from where did that superhuman strength come which hurls us from the unborn to the born.'"[85] Closing the book, he says, "Life, not death, is the indestructible force of the universe. Death is simply a part of life, but it's life which is the force."

The table grows silent. Standing, I say, "I think it's time for a coffee

---

[85]Nikos Kazantzakis,*The Saviors of God: Spiritual Exercises.* (New York, Simon and Schuster, 1960), 43.

break."

Rachel offers to give me a hand. Alicia pipes up, "Just let me run out to the car. I brought us some cookies. They're in the shape of skulls. I didn't know whether to bring them in with me or not, but now I think I will. I mean, all this talk has really made me hungry!"

Walker and Erik follow David into his office. As they cross the room, I hear David say, "*The Beast in the Jungle* is a very important narrative. I think it was Henry James' finest. He has done a masterful job of presenting the four universal themes that preoccupy anyone interested in defining the meaning of life: loneliness, fate, love and death. And, by the way, I understand your discomfort with vulnerability. I lost my mother when I was eight. I know from personal experience that kind of loss can have an effect on one's willingness to trust or get close to others."

I smile, pleased that David has chosen to share something so private. He has become a vital part of the group. He realizes his concern that I might be opening our home to a "group of losers" has been unfounded.

I set up a tray with coffee, tea, sugar, cream and Alicia's cookies and carry it into the living room. After urging everyone to help themselves, I excuse myself to go to the toilet. On the way, I encounter Beth. She is standing in the front hall, looking intently into the mirror. Sensing my presence, she turns and says, "I just can't imagine this world without me in it. How can it be that one day there will be no reflection of me in this or any other mirror? How can it be?"

I stand next to her with my arm around her shoulders. Together, we look into the mirror. "Maybe it's not the reflection in the mirror that matters, but the reflection of our being in the minds of others," I say.

"Maybe so," Beth agrees. "I'm glad I came today. It's helping me, I think."

Letting her go, I say, "Can I get you a cup of tea or coffee?"

"Tea, please, with a little milk and no sugar. Maybe I better sit down at the table so that I don't spill it."

We reconvene around the table a few minutes later. I open the discussion. "We've talked a lot about the human tendency or need to deny death. Let's spend some time talking about the positive aspects of being mortal. Is there anything good about death, or about the fact that each of us must die?"

When it becomes apparent that no one else is going to respond, David breaks the silence. "Accepting that life is change, and nothing is permanent can be liberating. Death gives us a gift in waking us up to that reality, and in inspiring or even enabling us to give up grasping and clinging desperately to those people and things that we falsely believe define us."

"That's true," Rachel says. "Focusing on the fact that someone we love is mortal and could die at any time makes us value their presence all the more. I know that's how I felt when my husband was dying. We love better what we stand to lose. What we believe we will never lose we begin to take for granted. In my mind, that is the single biggest advantage of being mortal."

"I know what you mean," replies Beth. "Now that I have stopped raging and pushing my family away, they are more loving toward me and each other than they have ever been."

"Death can make people more compassionate," says Rachel. "That's true of both the dying and those who are going to be left behind." Picking up her book, and turning to a page marked with a green flag, she reads, '...when we finally know we are dying, and all other sentient beings are dying with us, we start to have a burning, almost heartbreaking sense of the fragility and preciousness of each moment and each being, and from this can grow a deep, clear, limitless compassion for all beings.'[86]

"I guess I'm not dying, then," notes Bruce. "I certainly do not have a limitless compassion for all beings." He laughs.

Rachel looks at Bruce. The expression on her face is one of concern mixed with a touch of pity. "Perhaps one day you will learn to feel compassion," she suggests.

Before Bruce can respond, David replies, "The presence of death reminds us to live richly and fully while we can. Steve Jobs understood that. The day after he died, Pam and I talked about the way he lived his life, and all that he accomplished even after being diagnosed with cancer. I remember Pam read me a passage from his commencement address at Stanford. Pam can you find that passage on your iPad?"

I do as he asks and read the passage aloud. "Remembering that I'll be dead soon is the most important tool I've ever encountered to help me make the big choices in life. Because almost everything—all external

[86]Sogyal Rinpoche, *The Tibetan Book of Living and Dying.* (San Francisco, HarperSanFrancisco, 1994), 191.

expectations, all pride, all fear of embarrassment or failure—these things just fall away in the face of death, leaving only what is truly important. Remembering that you are going to die is the best way I know to avoid the trap of thinking you have something to lose. You are already naked. There is no reason not to follow your heart."[87]

"Yes, I resonate with that," says Walker. "There is no reason not to follow your heart, unless your body won't let you. I guess I believe the advantage of death is that it puts us out of our physical miseries. As the ancient Greek historian Herodotus said, 'Death is a delightful hiding place for weary men.'"

"That brings to mind the story of the Sybil," says Erik. "I teach T.S. Eliot's *The Waste Land* in one of my courses. The epigraph refers to the story of the Sybil. Sybil asked Apollo for eternal life and was granted her wish. Unfortunately, she neglected to ask for eternal youth. She aged and became decrepit. Finally, the townsfolk put her in a basket and hung her from a pole in the town square. I think the basket is a symbol for the nursing home.

"After a thousand years, all that was left of her was her cry. 'Let me die,' she would moan. She wanted to die because she couldn't tolerate the degradation of her body, and the knowledge that it would never get any better.

"I believe Sybil is a metaphor. Her failing body represents our loss of illusion as we learn more about the human condition. We despair and yet we know we are powerless to do anything about it. Death is the only possible release."

"Death can feel like a release," claims David. "I was run over by a car when I was doing field research on Spanish migrants in German industrial settings. The year was 1968. One foggy fall evening, I decided to take a walk. I was walking down a road between the house and the asparagus fields when suddenly I heard the roar of an engine behind me. Before I could turn around, it hit me. The force of the impact was so great that I was literally flung into the night sky. It was a harrowing experience. Even jumping out of an airplane at fourteen thousand feet couldn't compare.

[87] *Stanford News*. Stanford Report, June 14, 2005. Prepared text of the Commencement address delivered by Steve Jobs, CEO of Apple Computer and of Pixar Animation Studios, on June 12, 2005.

When I landed, I automatically let my body roll, like you do when you land with a parachute. My Special Forces training may have saved my life."

"I knew you weren't just a softie professor type," says Bruce. As an afterthought he adds, "Sorry, Erik. I meant no disrespect."

Ignoring Bruce, David continues. "Anyway, I passed out. When I woke up, I was in an ambulance. I hurt like hell. Later I would learn that I had a severe concussion, a broken arm, leg, and collar bone, and I was bleeding profusely both internally and externally. At the time, I only knew I was close to death. I remember thinking how easy it would be to just close my eyes and drift into eternal sleep. It was staying awake that was hard. Death would have been by far the easier path than life at that moment. The only reason I lived was because I decided to live."

"Were you afraid?" Alicia asks, her eyes wide.

"No, I was not afraid. I was only aware of having to fight to stay alive. Like I said, dying is easy. It's living that's hard."

"You can say that again," exclaims Walker.

"Are you no longer afraid of dying because of that experience?" asks Rachel.

"I would like to say that's true. However, I believe everyone is afraid of dying. It's hardwired into the species."

I picked up *Lapham's Quarterly* and turned to a page I had marked. "When John Stuart Mill thought he was dying, he wrote this in his diary, 'In quitting forever any place where one has dwelled as in a home, all the incidents and circumstances, even those which were worse than indifferent to us, appear like old friends that one is reluctant to lose. So it is in taking leave of life: even the tiresome and vexatious parts of it look pleasant and friendly, and one feels how agreeable it would be to remain among them.'"[88]

"People who have accepted that they are dying and that death is not far off seem better able to contemplate their own demise," says Rachel. "The certainty of death somehow makes it less ominous. In the months before he died, my husband and I talked very openly about his death. He was not frightened. He had no regrets about how he had lived his life.

---

[88] John Stuart Mill, "Morbid Diary," *Lapham's Quarterly*, Volume VI, Number 4, Fall, 2013, p.26.

Although he didn't want to die, he was not afraid. I have the impression that as death approaches, it loses its power to terrify."

"David and I have a wonderful friend named Alan who has written some moving poems about aging and mortality." Removing a sheet of paper from underneath the books, I unfold it. I'd like to read you one about finding serenity.

MOVING ON

How, dare I ask, will I face my mortality?
Will I hover, I wonder, like a weightless moth
In the light of a beckoning infinity?
Will I pause, though, as memories betray and intrude,
Demanding, each one, a moment's recognition,
These markers, good or bad,
Of a life in full fruition?
Will I seek to linger,
Assessing tasks still unfulfilled,
And fertile fields as yet untilled?

Will I sigh when I see that it's time to surrender,
Will I say 'that's enough, just give in, old centender,
Strive no more, can't you see that the battle has ended,
And life, as you've lived it, is all but suspended?'
What bliss, then, to thwart that old rogue, my Uncertainty,
And toast, glass on high, a new arrived entity-
The prize, the reward, the new friend called Serenity."

Alan Gans, age 78,
Spring, 2006

"That's beautiful," says Rachel. "I would love to have a copy."
"I'll print one out for you," I respond.
"Children also seem to be able to find serenity in the face of their own death," says Rachel.
"Someone posted on Facebook a link to a YouTube video of an eighteen-year-old boy who was dying of bone cancer," offers Alicia,

playing with her ponytail. I can bring it up on my iPad and pass it around, if you like. It's really inspiring. This kid has clearly accepted that he's dying. In his final months, he celebrates his short life with a song that goes viral."

"We can access it through Apple TV and watch it on our big screen" suggests David. His offer surprises me.

"Let's do it," says Alicia, standing. Others follow her lead. We move the party into the red room. We watch *My Last Days: Meet Zach Sobiech*. I can tell that everyone in the room is touched by the curly blond-haired, broad-faced seventeen-year-old with the wide smile. Even Bruce strums his fingers in time with the music when Zach plays *Clouds*, the song he has written for those he is leaving behind. During the interview that follows, he says, "You don't have to find out you're dying to start living." He died only weeks after his eighteenth birthday.

"It's really sad when someone like Zach dies so young," says Alicia as we gather once again around the dining room table.

Once again, I pick up my copy of *Lapham's Quarterly* and turn to the page I've marked with a sticky. "I'd like to read you something written in 1573 by a philosopher named Michel de Montaigne. He argues that there's little difference between living a long life and a short life."

"Nothing can be grievous that happens only once…Long life and short life are made all one by death. For there is no long or short for things that are no more. Aristotle says that there are little animals by the river Hypanis that live only a day. The one that dies at eight o'clock in the morning dies in its youth; the one that dies at five in the afternoon dies in its decrepitude. Which of us does not laugh to see this moment of duration considered in terms of happiness or unhappiness? The length or shortness of our duration, if we compare it with eternity, or yet with the duration of mountains, rivers, stars, trees, and even of some animals, is no less ridiculous…"[89]

"Maybe so," volunteers Walker. "I would still choose to bear the indignities of old age rather than dying young."

"I think the point is not how long we live, but rather how well we live the life we have," says David. "The boy featured in the YouTube did not

---

[89]Michel de Montaigne, "Auitaine: Living at Life's Expense," *Lapham's Quarterly*. Volume VI, Number 4, Fall 2013, p.47.

live long, but his life was rich—filled with passion and compassion."

"He reminds me of one my first hospice patients," says Rachel. "Rickie was thirteen when she died of leukemia. Like Zach, she had learned to accept her mortality. She spent her last months helping her parents and her older sister prepare for her absence."

"I have a lot to learn from these children," replies Beth. "It seems they are less afraid of death than I am."

"Perhaps it's because children haven't had time for their egos to harden around the artificial props that come with accumulation, status and success," suggests David. "Perhaps they are still at the naturally curious stage where change is embraced rather than resisted."

Walker continues looking down as he doodles on his 3x5 cards. "Sometimes in the dead of night, when I get to thinking about my own death, I console myself with the thoughts of all the less courageous people who have already made the leap into the great unknown." Laying down his pen, he continues. "If my mother could do it, so can I, I tell myself. If Aunt Betty could do it, then I certainly can muster the courage to let go. But these children...not only do they die with courage, but with compassion. Astounding."

"Children die well, but do they take the death of a parent or grandparent well? I am especially close to my granddaughter, Nina," says Beth. "My daughter is very worried about how Nina will react to my death. She didn't tell me that of course. She shared that with my husband. She doesn't know whether to let Nina watch me deteriorate, or to shield her from the truth. My husband doesn't know how to advise her. Neither do I."

"I think you or your daughter should tell the child the truth," advises Rachel. "Help her not be afraid of the physical changes that will happen to you. Let her be able to spend as much time as possible with you. That will benefit you, and give her memories of her grandmother to carry with her throughout her life."

"Her thoughts of you will help speed you on your way," adds David. "I believe it takes several years for our spiritual connectedness to our bodies and to the earth to evaporate. Until then, we are not truly free, and need the help of mortal beings to speed us on our journey."

Bruce laughs. "I tell my sons they better get on with it and give me some grandchildren." Looking at David, he adds, "You said it takes years to completely disconnect from this place. Do you think it's possible to control the behavior of earthlings during that period?"

"You mean you intend to dictate to your sons after your death?" challenges David. In an attempt to break the tension, I tell them about hearing violins when we brought Jill's ashes home. That provokes other stories of communication with the dead.

Rachel says, "I went to visit the family who had lost their daughter to leukemia a few days before. The mother was certain her daughter had visited her as she slept. In the dream, the daughter was sitting on a log by a river dressed in blue jeans and a white billowy shirt. Her feet were bare, and her hands were crossed. She said, 'Mom, don't worry about me. I am fine.'"

"My brother and sister both had a similar dream the night after our father was killed," I say. "Their dreams were identical. Both saw Dad sitting up on a steel table. He was wearing a hospital gown. He opened his arms as though to embrace them and said, 'Don't worry about me. I am fine.' It's a bit eerie that my father and the young girl spoke the same words."

"Pam caught me staring at myself in the mirror in her hall," says Beth. "I can't pass a mirror without looking at my reflection and trying to grasp that one day it will not be there."

"I guess I don't believe the human brain is capable of thinking about its own demise," says David.

"We can't stop worrying about how much time we have left, either," muses Bruce. "I know what the Buddhists say. 'Have compassion.' 'Live in the moment.' As far as I'm concerned, those are just nice words. Life doesn't work like that. You have to fight back. You have to fight to live. You have to fight for more time."

The word "time" resonates with Alicia. Reaching into her oversized red faux leather tote bag, she once again takes out her iPad. "My favorite book is called *The Time Keeper* by Mitch Albom. You know, he's the man who wrote *Tuesdays with Morrie*. I love that book too. It was made into a movie. It's about a man who had your disease, Beth. You might want to watch it."

"Yes, I've seen it," murmurs Beth.

"Anyway, *The Time Keeper* is a wonderful story, a fantasy, but with a message," continues Alicia. "The message is that our focus on time gets in the way of our living our lives. Wait, I'll read a passage to you. 'As mankind grew obsessed with its hours, the sorrow of lost time became a permanent hole in the human heart. People fretted over missed chances, over inefficient days; they worried constantly about how long they would live, because counting life's moments had led, inevitably, to counting them down.'"[90]

"That's why the Buddhists believe it's important to live in the moment," says Rachel.

"That's easier to say than to do," responds David. "I have accepted life's impermanence on an intellectual level, and yet I still cling and grasp, and forget to live in the moment. When my body shows signs of decay, I get angry. I want to cling to my youth."

"In the book, there's this crotchety old man named Victor who's really angry about getting old and dying," says Alicia. "A successful businessman, he is the fourteenth wealthiest person in the world, and yet he is dying of kidney cancer. He arranges to have his body frozen and revived when there is a cure for his disease."

"I've been looking into cryogenics myself," says Bruce. "One of these days that's going to be a real alternative. I'm going to try to stick around long enough to take advantage of it."

"Victor didn't go through with it," explains Alicia. "Father Time intervened and showed him that if he persisted in his attempts to defeat death, he would end up a blob of naked flesh with wires in a tank in the corner of a massive room. People would come from all over to listen to his memories and to tune into his emotions."

"I've read that book," I say. "It's not Albom's best, but it does have a message. The reason people would flock to see the blob that was Victor is that they have no memories or emotions of their own. Deprived of death, they have lost all feeling. They have become like zombies, the living dead."

"When we were a nation of believers, we could envision life in death," says David. "Now that we have lost all belief in anything beyond ourselves, we can only envision death in life. Witness the popularity of the television series, *The Walking Dead*. While I can't stand it, I understand why it was the most popular series in the history of cable television when

---

[90]Mitch Albom, *The Time Keeper.* (New York, Hyperion, 2012), 61.

it aired."

"Or think about the movie, *Death Watch*," I suggest. "I watched it again the other day when I was on the treadmill. A journalist named Roddy has a camera implanted in his brain. He is then hired by a television producer to film a documentary of terminally ill Katherine, without her knowledge. His footage will then be run on the popular TV series, *Death Watch*. Because almost no one dies of illness anymore, and because the old are stuck away out of sight and out of mind, people are fascinated by death."[91]

"I think that we are fascinated by death because we, ourselves, are going to die," argues Beth. "I have to confess I've been reading the obituaries lately. Maybe that's because misery loves company. Or maybe I'm trying to learn how to think about death. I sat down one day to write my own obituary, but I just couldn't do it. Like I said before, I just can't imagine the world without me in it."

David responds. "Beth, before you can think about the world without you in it, you have to first define what it is that is 'you.' If you are only your body, then you will die. If, however, you are the bundle of experiences, feelings and sensations that you have accumulated over a lifetime, then perhaps you won't die. Consciousness is energy. Energy can neither be created nor destroyed."

"What about people who are in the late stages of dementia or Alzheimers ?" I challenge David. "I mean, if they have lost sight of who they are and have no memories, then haven't they already lost their sense of self—their awareness or consciousness of self? Isn't that energy already dead even as their hearts continue to beat and their lungs continue to draw breath?"

David is quick to respond. His voice dominates the room as he explains, "Consciousness is not the same thing as the self, or the sense of self. It's more like an amorphous awareness of being alive. It's a primal force; a life force that exists even in the addled brain of an Alzheimer's patient. It exists in all of us. It is of us, and it is beyond us."

Erik finally breaks the silence that has ensued. "Immortality itself is not an impossibility."

People look at him expectantly. He continues. "Not long ago I read

---

[91]Bertrand Tavernier, Director, *Death Watch*, 1980.

an article about immortal jellyfish. They were discovered more than twenty years ago by a German marine biology student who caught them in his net while snorkeling off the Portofino coast. He put them in petri dishes and watched astounded as they became younger and younger until they reached their infancy and could begin their life again. Later, other scientists described how the hydrozoans transformed themselves back to polyps. The process is akin to a butterfly turning back into a caterpillar and then becoming a butterfly again, or an aging chicken turning itself into an egg so that it can begin again as a chicklet. Because the process can repeat forever, it defies the natural law that all living things must eventually die."[92]

Walker stops doodling on his 3x5 cards. "In human terms, that's like my turning myself back into a fetus in the womb, and then getting born again. What a strange and frightening idea."

Pulling out the scrunchie and letting her hair fall loose, Alicia asks, "Isn't that like reincarnation?"

"More like rebirth," David answers. "Consciousness is continually evolving. It is not like a personality. It is more like a changing stream. When a person is reborn, they do not take with them the same consciousness that they had in a prior life. There is no such thing as a 'self" that remains intact and enters another body, as in reincarnation. At least I don't believe there is."

"I guess then I'd rather be reincarnated than reborn," says Alicia. "I like the idea of myself staying intact."

Bruce stops strumming. "I'm not putting my faith in reincarnation or rebirth. I'm sticking with the miracles of medical science."

"And well you should," says Erik. "Medical science appears to be on the brink of significantly expanding human life expectancy. Tissue engineering, gene therapy, cloning, stem cell research, even printing human organs on 3-D printers are all combining to extend our lives."

"Not in time for me, I'm afraid," says Walker.

"Arrange to get yourself frozen," suggests Bruce.

"I think a better route is virtual immortality," exclaims David. "According to Ray Kurzweil, the futurist and father of optical recognition

---

[92]Nathaniel Rich, "Can a Jellyfish Unlock the Secret of Immortality?" *The New York Times*, (November 28, 2012).

technology and other life-changing devices, we will soon be able to upload the entire contents of our brains: our memories, thoughts, feelings, experiences, sensations, values, beliefs, expertise. Add to that hologram technology and you have an avatar who thinks, talks, feels and acts exactly like you do. The only difference between you and your avatar will be that it doesn't age and it doesn't die."

Rachel laughs. "I guess hospice better expand its IT department."

Removing her wire-rim glasses and rubbing the top of her nose where the nose pads have made an indent, Beth comments. "Although I don't relish the idea of becoming an avatar, I do think I'll begin recording my thoughts and bits of family history that will probably get lost once I'm dead. I want to record certain memories to preserve them."

"Post your stuff on Facebook. It'll be there long after you're gone," said Alicia, smiling.

"I don't do Facebook," responds Beth.

"Well, you should," challenges Alicia. "It's a great way to communicate with your kids and your grandkids."

"She has a point," says Walker. "Claire got me onto Facebook. I don't post much, but every year I get a notification that it's my friend Charles' birthday. He's been dead three years now! Facebook makes me stop and think about Charlie. I look up his Facebook page and remember him and the times we had together."

"I suppose I could ask my daughter to help me get on Facebook," responds Beth more out of a desire to appease the room than a sign of commitment to the social networking site. "What's really important to me is to die in such a way that my family's better memories of me are preserved."

"Sylvia Plath said that dying is an art, like everything else," offers Erik. "She also said that she does it, dying that is, exceptionally well." He laughs, but no one joins him.

"Beth, do you know how you are going to die?" asks Rachel, her compassion obvious.

"I do," says Beth. "Before all of my voluntary muscles are paralyzed and I am unable to speak or even to breathe on my own, I intend to gather my family around me." Picking up a slim paperback book, she continues. "Like Catherine Royce did. She describes how she intends to die in her book, *Wherever I am, I'm Fine*. Her story is inspiring. In spite of having

ALS, she managed to celebrate life right to the moment when she had the oxygen turned off. I hope to be able to do the same thing. I plan to have the attendants slowly turn off the oxygen. I'll have a morphine drip to ease the pain. Like Catherine did, I intend to leave my family with the memory of me smiling."[93]

"You'll be writing your own story right to the end," I said. "That's something we should all aspire to do."

Picking up the book *Being Mortal*, I continue, "Consider what Dr. Gawande says about the importance of retaining our autonomy as we get older. '…Whatever happens, we want to retain the freedom to shape our lives in ways consistent with our character and loyalties. This is why the betrayals of body and mind that threaten to erase our character and memory remain among our most awful tortures. The battle of being mortal is the battle to maintain the integrity of one's life—to avoid becoming so diminished or dissipated or subjugated that who you are becomes disconnected from who you were or who you want to be."[94]

"That's why Alzheimer's is such a horrific disease," says Walker. "God, please give me anything but that."

"I agree," says Beth. "I would rather die of ALS than Alzheimer's. I'm told that my mind will continue to function after everything else has shut down. Though I hate the idea of being awake and entombed in my own body, unable to speak or even to breath on my own, I would rather that than lose my mind. As long as I can think, I can decide how and when I will die."

"Even visualizing the way we will die helps us write our own stories," I suggest. "At night, when I can't sleep, I often pretend that I'm lying on a white raft in the middle of a blue lake. Gentle waves are slowly taking me away from the shore. I am at peace, and content to lie on that raft for all eternity."

"A ship is often a metaphor for death," notes Rachel. "I'd like to share with you a description of death that I often use with my hospice patients and their families. 'I am standing upon the seashore. A ship in front of me

---

[93]Catherine Royce, *Wherever I Am, I'm Fine: Letters about Living while Dying.* (Xlibris Corporation, 2009).

[94]Dr. Atul Gawande, *Being Mortal:Medicine and What Matters in the End.* (New York, Henry Holt and Company, 2015), 141.

spreads her white sails to the morning breeze and starts forth on the blue ocean. She is an object of beauty and strength. I stand and watch her until at length she hangs like a speck of white cloud just where the sea and sky come to mingle with each other. Then someone at my side says: 'There, she is gone!'"

"But she has not gone. She has only gone from my sight. That is all. She is just as large in mast and hull and spar as she was when she left me and she is just as able to bear her load of living freight to her destined port. Her diminished size is in me, not in her. Just at the moment when someone at my side says, 'There, she is gone!' there are other eyes watching her coming and other voices ready to take up the glad shout: 'Here she comes!' That is dying."

"Do you think we know we're dead?" asks Walker. "I mean, isn't it possible that just like Rachel's ship, we just experience ourselves as landing on a different shore?"

"Or maybe we don't experience ourselves at all," says Erik. "If that's true, then we can't know we're dead."

"When I was a teenager, I suffered from school phobia," I say. "My psychiatrist taught me to manage my fears by envisioning worst possible scenarios. Sometimes when I lie in bed, I do that with death. 'What's the worst possible thing that could happen to you after you die?' I ask myself. 'I wouldn't exist,' I answer myself. 'And if you didn't exist, you wouldn't be frightened,' I conclude. Try it some time. It helps."

Alicia looks confused. Turning to Rachel, she says, "I really like your ship, Rachel. Would you mind if I used that in my children's book? I'm beginning to think I can write it after all."

"Of course," says Rachel, smiling.

"I like it too," says Beth.

"And I," adds Walker.

"I think it's bullshit," states Bruce, but with less force than before.

David smiles. "The future just isn't what it used to be, isn't that right Bruce?"

Bruce grumbles but says nothing.

"Should we plan to meet again in a month?" I ask, looking around the table.

"I'm in," says Walker, raising his hand.

"Me, too," says Rachel.

"And me," echoes Beth. "This meeting made me feel better about myself."

"Wouldn't miss it," says Erik. "I've learned a lot today."

"So have I," echoes Alicia. "I'll be here."

Everyone turns to look at Bruce. He grumbles something under his breath.

"Will you be joining us?" I ask.

He shrugs his shoulders. "Maybe so. I don't know."

"If you're not going to come, we'll offer your seat to someone else," I say.

"Okay, okay. I'll be here."

"David, will you join us? " I ask.

"You're going to meet here, I assume." Trying to repress a smile, he adds, "What choice do I have?"

"If you want, we can meet at my house next time," offers Rachel.

"Thank you, Rachel. That would be nice."

"Will you still attend, David?" asks Rachel with a twinkle in her eyes. David doesn't respond.

"I'd like to invite two others to join us," I say, thinking of Luna and Thomas.

"No problem," says Erik.

"The more the merrier," says Alica.

The others nod in agreement.

"Would anyone like to suggest a book about aging or dying that we can all read before we meet so that we can incorporate it into our discussion?" I ask.

Before anyone else can offer a suggestion, David says, "I'd like to recommend Pam's new book, *The Hourglass*. Copies are available at the bookstore, or you can get the Kindle version on Amazon. I've read it a few times, and can attest that it's a good book. Show it to them, Pam."

Grateful to David for doing that which I would have hesitated doing for myself, I pull the book out from the bottom of the stack and hold it up.

"Wow!" exclaimed Alicia. "That's a powerful cover! My publisher says covers sell books."

"I agree with David," says Rachael. "Our first book should be *The Hourglass*. Afterall, how many clubs have an author in their group?"

"I'm an author, too," Alicia said, frowning at the oversight.

The Mortality Club

"And when your book is finished, we'll read it, too," says Walker.

"It's going to be an astounding sunset," exclaims David as he stands and goes to look out the window. "Would any of you care to join me for a glass of wine as we watch the sun go down?"

"I will," answers Walker. "Five o'clock is a very respectable time to begin drinking."

"Thank you, I'd love a glass of wine," says Rachel. "Red, if you have it."

"I'll call my husband and tell him the meeting is over," says Beth. "It'll take him ten or fifteen minutes to get here. I can't have wine, but I'd love a glass of water, or juice if you have it."

"Tell him the front door is open and to join us on the deck," says David.

"I've got to run," declares Erik. "I have a class tonight and I've got some preparation to do. Maybe next time."

"I gave up drinking ten years ago," announces Bruce. "Haven't had a drop since. I'll be on my way."

"I can't stay, either," says Alicia, "I would love to, but I'm meeting my fiancé at six and I have to change into something more conservative. We're taking his parents to dinner."

Glasses in hand, five of us gather at the railing at the edge of the deck. Only Beth is seated. The sky, variegated with streaks of purple, pink and orange, is so astounding as to make us forget the chill in the air. The sun, a blazing ball of fire, hovers just above the horizon.

David says, "As mere mortals, we are not equipped to fathom the scale and scope of the universe. It is infinite, and we can understand only that which is finite."

"The magnificence of the universe gives me great comfort," says Rachel. "It makes me certain there is a god, or a higher power. That we cannot prove the existence of God does not mean there is no god. Perhaps our salvation lies in our unknowing."

"I find great comfort in nature," says Beth. "Lately, when I can't sleep at night, I watch *The Private Life of Plants* by David Attenborough. He reminds me that life is mysterious and magical and that it all makes sense even if we can't make sense of it."

"It's the sky itself that gives me solace," I say. "Sometimes when I look up into the sky, I imagine I can see or at least feel the energy of those who have died. For a while after his death, when I was thinking intensely about my father and wondering what he wanted me to do for my aging mother, I would go outside and almost invariably find a circle of clouds in the sky. The circle was so perfect it looked almost like skywriting. Somehow, that circle helped me put things into perspective. I'd go back inside calmer and knowing what to do."

"The universe itself has fascinated me since childhood," says David. "I'm talking about the universe as a whole, and not just our solar system. Our Sun is more than a hundred times the size of Earth. That's nothing compared to what's way out there. The star Arcturus makes the Sun look like it's a tiny bee. Then there's Antares, the fifteenth brightest star in the sky. It is so big that even the Sun is scarcely visible in a drawing depicting their relative scale. Antares is more than a thousand light years away. Can you conceive of that distance? A single light year is about six trillion miles."

"It's unfathomable," says Walker.

"Like death," says Beth, softly, as though speaking only to herself.

"To the end of another day of life on this planet," I say, raising my glass as the sun begins to dip beneath the horizon.

"To the sun, without which there would be no life," says David, raising his glass. "And to the gods and goddesses," he adds as leans over and pours a bit of his wine onto the plants below.

We linger for a few minutes after the sun has set, each lost in private thought. Beth's husband arrives and breaks our shared reverie. It is time to go. We have reached the end.

THE HOURGLASS PROFILE: MAPPING YOUR MINDSET

INSTRUCTIONS: Place a checkmark next to TWO responses under each of the following statements that most closely describe how you would react or feel if the situation were to occur today.

1. If some part of my body began to hurt, I would....
   a) ____ assume it's nothing and trust that it will heal on its own
   b) ____ see the doctor to get what is wrong fixed
   c) ____ take an aspirin and force my body into action, refusing to let the pain control my life
   d) ____ try to determine if my body is sending me a message about the way I am living my life
   e) ____ worry about myself
   f) ____ endure it, figuring occasional pain is part of getting older
   g) ____ contemplate the fact that no matter what we do, our bodies will deteriorate
   h) ____ think of all the bad medical conditions the symptom could portend
   i) ____ pamper myself until I feel better
   j) ____ tell my family and friends about it

2. If I were to look at photographs of my much younger self and compare them to the way I look today, I would ....
   a) ____ get motivated to get my act together and work on my appearance
   b) ____ focus on how great I used to look, refusing to dwell on how much I've changed
   c) ____ figure, "Why bother? I'll never look that good again."

d) _____ tell myself that my aging face has more character than my younger face

e) _____ accept that time must take a toll on our appearance

f) _____ feel sad that time has had such an impact on the way I look

g) _____ get concerned that, as my looks fade, so will my ability to make things happen

h) _____ try to remember who that younger person was

i) _____ think about how youth wanes so quickly and life is so short

j) _____ try to convince myself I haven't changed that much

3. If a good friend's spouse or lover died and (s)he was overwhelmed by grief, I would...

a) _____ talk to him (her) about life's essential impermanence; while we can't hold onto people we love, we can hold onto cherished memories.

b) _____ be uncomfortable spending a lot of time with him (her)

c) _____ question the meaning of life or the existence of God or Allah when there is such suffering

d) _____ urge him (her) to focus on dealing with the business of death (filing the estate tax, getting rid of clothes, etc.)

e) _____ begin to grieve along with him (her)

f) _____ tell him (her) when I have grown tired of his(her) grieving and insist (s)he get on with life

g) _____ urge him (her) to remember the good times and reassure him (her) that the pain will pass

h) _____ urge him (her) to cry and cry and cry until (s)he has no more tears to shed

i) _____ try to think of things to do to cheer him (her) up and distract him (her) from grieving

j) _____ keep him (her) so busy socially that (s)he won't have the time or space to grieve

4. If my relatives or caregivers told me that the time had come to surrender the keys to my car, I would....

   a) _____ manipulate them into letting me keep the keys for a little while longer

   b) _____ refuse to voluntarily hand over the keys

   c) _____ think about the benefits of not having to maintain a car and drive myself everywhere

   d) _____ reflect on the fact that life is change and try to adapt

   e) _____ despair that as we age, we become once again like children

   f) _____ feel sorry for myself

   g) _____ be shocked or taken by surprise and uncertain how to respond

   h) _____ accept that the good times are over

   i) _____ get revenge by creating such a long list of errands for them to do they would wish they had never taken away my keys

   j) _____ throw a tantrum

5. If I was diagnosed with a serious disease, I would ....

   a) _____ expect the worst

   b) _____ rage about the unfairness of it all

   c) _____ distract myself and try to deny or ignore the bad news

   d) _____ hope that a cure would be discovered in time

   e) _____ believe in my body and its ability to beat the odds

   f) _____ remind myself that everyone dies; that death is part of the human condition

   g) _____ spend a lot of time thinking about the meaning of life

   h) _____ put my trust in God or Allah and in my doctors

   i) _____ accept that my turn to die may have come

   j) _____ vow to fight back; it's not over until it's over

6. Having to spend time with frail, old people would make me ....

   a) _____ curious about the life experiences they have had

b) _____ question the meaning of life

c) _____ restless and jittery and eager to get out of there

d) _____ depressed

e) _____ want to show off or make them laugh

f) _____ vow to exercise or to do whatever it takes to stay strong

g) _____ feel compassion for them

h) _____ try to find something beautiful in each one of them

i) _____ reflect on the human condition

j) _____ frustrated and impatient

7. If I couldn't remember the name of the movie I'd watched the night before, I would...

a) _____ worry that I'm getting Alzheimer's

b) _____ assume it happened because I have so many other more important things on my mind

c) _____ tell myself it's not so important in the larger scheme of things

d) _____ not beat myself up about it and instead be glad I could remember the film itself

e) _____ tell myself it isn't my fault; it was probably a stupid title

f) _____ recite twenty important historical dates to prove to myself that my memory is working just fine

g) _____ start doing brain strengthening exercises such as crossword puzzles

h) _____ start taking herbal supplements that stimulate brain functioning

i) _____ accept that some short-term memory loss is an inevitable part of aging

j) _____ think about the importance of memory to our sense of self; to our identity as human beings

8. If I had to hire a caregiver, I would look for someone who...

a) _____ is cheerful and upbeat and has only nice things to say about people and life

b) ____ is efficient and task focused, showing little emotion as (s)he does what needs to be done

c) ____ pushes me to do even more for myself than I think I can

d) ____ exudes a quiet confidence; is serene and unflappable

e) ____ acts like an old friend or member of the family

f) ____ helps me focus on what I can still do as opposed to what I can't do

g) ____ tells me jokes about getting old and makes me laugh at myself

h) ____ reminds me it could be worse; I could be an old person in Bangladesh or the Sudan.

i) ____ keeps me so busy having visitors and playing games that I don't have time to dwell on my condition

j) ____ feels sorry for me and makes it okay for me to feel sorry for myself

9. If my doctor told me I had to have a test or undergo a diagnostic procedure, I would…

a) ____ assume it was going to turn out badly

b) ____ put it off as long as I could

c) ____ do everything I can in advance to "fool" the test or increase the likelihood that it will turn out fine

d) ____ just do what the doctor tells me to do, assuming (s)he knows best

e) ____ assume it is just a way for the doctor to make more money

f) ____ assume it will turn out fine

g) ____ tell myself not to worry until I have a reason to worry

h) ____ remind myself that what will be will be

i) ____ remember that it's not too much information but too little that is dangerous

j) ____ bemoan the fact that, because of the technology at their disposal, doctors will inevitably find something wrong

10. If I started having trouble seeing while driving at night, I would...

    a) ____ make excuses so that others offer to drive

    b) ____ start researching the transportation services available in my community

    c) ____ just tell myself to concentrate harder and, if necessary, go slower

    d) ____ think about relocating or moving closer to town to minimize my need to drive without restricting my ability to get around

    e) ____ avoid those circumstances where the problem is the worst (e.g. driving on highways, driving in the rain)

    f) ____ get depressed at having succumbed to yet another sign of aging

    g) ____ get my eyes examined, hoping that a new pair of glasses will fix the problem

    h) ____ dwell on how immobility infantilizes the old by making them dependent

    i) ____ figure out ways to entertain my friends at my house so that I don't have to go out at night

    j) ____ convince myself that it will be nice to spend more of my evenings reading or watching films rather than exhausting myself by going out

To score your profile, simply transpose your checkmarks to the appropriate place on the table on the following page. Then, count the number of checkmarks that appear in each column, and record that number in the bottom row. The largest number reflects your primary MAM. The second largest number reflects your backup MAM.

Mapping Your Mindset

Stargazer	Celebrant	Warrior	Castaway	Sage
1i	1a	1b	1e	1d
1j	1f	1c	1h	1g
2b	2d	2a	2c	2e
2j	2h	2g	2f	2i
3b	3g	3d	3e	3a
3j	3i	3f	3h	3c
4a	4c	4b	4f	4d
4j	4g	4i	4h	4e
5c	5d	5b	5a	5f
5h	5e	5j	5i	5g
6c	6a	6f	6d	6b
6e	6h	6j	6g	6i
7d	7b	7f	7a	7c
7e	7h	7g	7i	7j
8e	8a	8b	8g	8d
8i	8f	8c	8j	8h
9b	9c	9e	9a	9g
9d	9f	9i	9j	9h
10a	10i	10c	10f	10b
10e	10j	10g	10h	10d

Selected References:

Albom, Mitch. *The Time Keeper*. New York: Hyperion, 2012.

Bayley, John. *Elegy For Iris*. New York: St. Martin's Press, 1999.

Becker, Ernest. *The Denial of Death*. New York: The Free Press, 1973.

Bernstein, Elizabeth. (Feb. 23, 2015). "Researchers Study Awe and Find it is Good for Relationships,"*The Wall Street Journal*.

Bhiksu. *Bakti Yoga*. Chicago: The Yogi Publication Society, 1930.

Buettner, Dan. (October 24, 2012). "The Island Where People Forget to Die," *New York Times Magazine*.

Burckhardt, Jacob. *The Greeks and Greek Civilization*. New York: St. Martin's Press, 1998.

Burkeman, Oliver. *The Antidote: Happiness for People Who Can't Stand Positive Thinking*. New York: Faber and Faber, Inc, 2012.

Butler, Katy. *Knocking on Heaven's Door:The Path to a Better Way of Death*. New York: Scribner, 2013.

Campbell, Joseph. *The Masks of God, Volume II, Oriental Mythology*. San Anselmo, CA: Joseph Campbell Foundation, Digital Edition, 2014.

Cohen, Ted. Jokes: *Philosophical Thoughts on Joking Matters*. Chicago: The University of Chicago Press, 1999.

Crowley, Chris & Henry S. Lodge, Henry S. M.D., *Younger Next Year*. New York: Workman Publishing, 2007.

Cuming, Pamela. *Widow's Walk*. New York: Crown Publishers, Inc., 1981.

De Botton, Alain. *The Art of Travel*. New York: Pantheon Books, 2002.

Didion, Joan. *Blue Nights*. New York: Alfred A. Knopf, 2011.

Selected References

Didion, Joan. *The Year of Magical Thinking*. New York: Knopf, 2005.

Eliott, T.S. *The Wasteland*. New York: W.W. Norton & Co., Norton Critical Editions, 1ˢᵗ Editon, December, 2000.

Eberstadt, Nicholas. (Feb 21, 2015). "The Global Flight From the Family," *The Wall Street Journal*.

Flach, Frederic M.D. *The Secret Strength of Depression, Fourth Revised Edition*. Hobart, New York: Hatherleigh Press, 2009.

Ralph Gardner Jr., Ralph. (Feb. 26, 2014). "Urban Gardner: Examine a Life Well Lived," *The Wall Street Journal*.

Gawande, Atul, M.D. *Being Mortal: Medicine and What Matters in the End*. New York: Metropolitan Books, Henry Holt and Company, 2015.

Gilbert, Sandra M. *Death's Door: Modern Dying and the Ways We Grieve*. New York: W.W. Norton & Company, 2006.

Goffman, Erving. *Asylums: Essays on the Social Situation of Mental Patients and Other Inmates*. New York: Anchor Books, 1961.

Grierson, Bruce. (Oct. 22, 2014). "What if Age is Nohing but a Mind-Set?" *The New York Times Magazine*.

Gross, Jane, *A Bittersweet Season: Caring for Our Aging Parents - and Ourselves*. New York: Alfred A. Knopf, 2011.

Hafner, Katie. (Nov. 2, 2014). "Bracing for the Falls of an Aging Nation," *The New York Times*.

Harris, Sydney J. *Pieces of Eight*. New York: Houghton Miflin, 1982.

Harrison, Patricia L., Pope, James E., Coberley, Carer R., Rula, Elizabeth Y. (April 16, 2012). "Evaluation of the Relationship Between Individual Well-Being and Future Health Care Ultilization and Cost," *The Wall Street Journal*.

Hartzband, Pamela and Groopmannov, Jerome. (November. 18, 2014). "How Medical Care is Being Corrupted," *The New York Times*.

Heard, Gerald. *The Five Ages of Man*. New York: The Julian Press, Inc., 1963.

Holt, T.E. M.D., (October 4, 2006). "Survive Your Doctor,"*Men's Health*.

Jauhar, Sandeep. (April 29, 2014). "Why Doctors are Sick of Their Profession," *The Wall Street Journal*.

Kazantzakis, Nikos. *The Saviors of God: Spiritual Exercises*. New York: Simon and Schuster, 1960.

Kleinfield, N.R. (March 3, 2003). "For Elderly, Fear of Falling Is a Risk in Itself," *The New York Times*.

Laura Landro, Laura. (April 8, 2012). "The Talking Cure for Health Care," *The Wall Street Journal*.

Lanier, Jaron. Who Owns the Future? New York: Simon and Shuster, 2013. Lapham, Lewis H. (Fall, 2013). "Death". *Laham's Quarterly*, Volume VI, Number 4.

Lewis, C.S. *A Grief Observed*. New York,:HarperCollins e-books, 1961.

Malraux, Andre. *The Walnut Trees of Altenberg*. Chicago: the University of Chicago Press, 1992.

Mittleton, Murray MD, PhD, (January 9, 2012). "Risk of Acute Myocardial Infarction After the Death of a Significant Person in One's Life," *Circulation: Journal of the American Heart Association*.

Murray, Ken. (February 25,2012). "Why Doctors Die Differently," *The Wall Street Journal*.

Oettingen, Gabriele. (October 14, 2014). "The Problem with Positive Thinking," *The New York Times Sunday Review*.

Passariello, Christina. (May 21, 2013). "Collecting Art with Francois Pinault," *The Wall Street Journal*.

Pattanail, Devdutt. *Sita: an Illustrated Retelling of the Ramayana*. London: Penguin Books, 2013.

Pausch, Randy. *The Last Lecture*. New York: Hyperion, 2008.

Pausch, Randy. *Carnegie Mellon Commencement Speech*, 2007.

Peck, M. Scott. *The Road Less Traveled*. New York: Simon and Schuster, 1978.

Rich, Nathaniel. (November 28, 2012). "Can a Jellyfish Unlock the Secret of Immortality?" *The New York Times*.

Rinpoche, Sogyal. *The Tibetan Book of Living and Dying*. San Francisco: HarperSanFrancisco, 1994.

Royce, Catherine. *Wherever I Am, I Am Fine: Letters about Living while Dying*. Xlibris Corporation, 2009.

Seligman, Martin E.P. ,Ph.D. *Learned Optimism*. New York: Alfred A. Knopf, 1991.

Shah, Sunil M. MBBS, MSc, Carey, Iain M. PhD, Harris, Tess MD, DeWilde, Stephen MD, Victor, Christine R. PhD, Cook, Derek G. PhD. (June, 2013), "The Effect of Unexpected Bereavement on Mortality in Older Couples," *American Journal of Public Health*, Vol 103, No. 6.

Shiflett, Dave. (June 27, 2014). "Life Lessons from Dad: Caring for an Elderly Parent," *The Wall Street Journal*.

Spam, Paula. *When the Time Comes*. New York: Springboard Press, 2009.

Stanford News. Stanford Report, June 14, 2005. *Prepared text of the Commencement address delivered by Steve Jobs*, CEO of Apple Computer and of Pixar Animation Studios, on June 12, 2005.

The Society of Certified Senior Advisors, *The Journey of Aging: Working with Older Adults: Part I.* Denver, Colorado: 2015.

Valenzuela, Michael J. et al., (2012). "Multiple Biological Pathways Link Cognitive Lifestyle to Protection from Dementia," *Biological Psychiatry*.

ABOUT THE AUTHOR

Cuming is a Scottish name that means "courage." Throughout her life, Pamela Cuming has eagerly seized new opportunities and bravely confronted the obstacles that life has put in her way. She embraces Helen Keller's belief,"Life is an adventure or nothing at all."

After graduating from Smith College, she embarked on what would become a multifaceted career during which she would advise CEO's of American corporations, Wall Street financiers, directors of non-profits and medical practitioners on the human and organizational dynamics affecting the health of their enterprises. She published two books on leadership and the use and abuse of power.

While her life has been filled with opportunities, she has known heartbreak. When she was thirty-four, her husband died suddenly. She lost not only her mate and her friend but also her business partner. Pam wrote about the tumultuous journey that ensued in *Widow's Walk*, a candid story of bereavement and healing.

Now, along with her peers, she is facing a new set of challenges as she learns to deal with emerging health problems and other demands presented by an aging body. Contemplating the human condition and confronting her own mortality, Pam believes the last part of life can still be a great adventure.

Pam lives with her husband on a mountaintop in the Pacific Northwest. She has two daughters and four grandsons. For more information about the author or her books, visit her website: **www.pamcuming.com**.

Pam is a Certified Senior Advisor (CSA)® .

31431069R10170

Made in the USA
Middletown, DE
06 May 2016